THE SOVIET UNION
AND CUBA

STUDIES OF INFLUENCE IN
INTERNATIONAL RELATIONS

Alvin Z. Rubinstein, General Editor

THE SOVIET UNION
AND CUBA
Interests and Influence

W. Raymond Duncan

PRAEGER SPECIAL STUDIES • PRAEGER SCIENTIFIC

New York • Philadelphia • Eastbourne, UK
Toronto • Hong Kong • Tokyo • Sydney

Library of Congress Cataloging in Publication Data

Duncan, W. Raymond (Walter Raymond), 1936–
   The Soviet Union and Cuba.

   (Studies of influence in international relations)
   Bibliography: p.
   Includes index.
   1. Soviet Union—Relations—Cuba. 2. Cuba—
Relations—Soviet Union. 3. Soviet Union—Foreign
relations—1945–   . I. Title. II. Series.
DK69.3.C9D86 1985   327.4707291   84-26296
ISBN 0-03-064111-X
ISBN 0-03-064109-8 (pbk.)

Published in 1985 by Praeger Publishers
CBS Educational and Professional Publishing, a Division of CBS Inc.
521 Fifth Avenue, New York, NY 10175 USA

© 1985 by Praeger Publishers

56789 052 987654321

Printed in the United States of America on acid-free paper

INTERNATIONAL OFFICES

Orders from outside the United States should be sent to the appropriate address listed below. Orders from areas not listed below should be placed through CBS International Publishing, 383 Madison Ave., New York, NY 10175 USA

Australia, New Zealand
Holt Saunders, Pty, Ltd., 9 Waltham St., Artarmon, N.S.W. 2064, Sydney, Australia

Canada
Holt, Rinehart & Winston of Canada, 55 Horner Ave., Toronto, Ontario, Canada M8Z 4X6

Europe, the Middle East, & Africa
Holt Saunders, Ltd., 1 St. Anne's Road, Eastbourne, East Sussex, England BN21 3UN

Japan
Holt Saunders, Ltd., Ichibancho Central Building, 22-1 Ichibancho, 3rd Floor, Chiyodaku, Tokyo, Japan

Hong Kong, Southeast Asia
Holt Saunders Asia, Ltd., 10 Fl, Intercontinental Plaza, 94 Granville Road, Tsim Sha Tsui East, Kowloon, Hong Kong

Manuscript submissions should be sent to the Editorial Director, Praeger Publishers, 521 Fifth Avenue, New York, NY 10175 USA

Published and Distributed by the
Praeger Publishers Division
(ISBN Prefix 0-275)
of Greenwood Press, Inc.,
Westport, Connecticut

EDITOR'S FOREWORD

Of all the Soviet Union's relationships with Third World countries, the one with Cuba has had the most strategic significance and persistent regional resonance. It functions with varying degrees of intensity and collaboration in Africa, the Middle East, Latin America, and, of course, the Caribbean region, and underscores Moscow's relentless quest for regional and global advantage over the United States. Ever the irritating mote in Washington's eye, it frequently disrupts efforts to foster detente between the two superpowers.

A great deal has been written on the general subject of Soviet-Cuban relations, but there have been relatively few attempts to analyze the Soviet-Cuban influence relationship with a view toward answering a crucial policy-relevant question: Who influences whom on the specific issues that engage cooperation or cause conflict between them? Cuba is a small country, but it plays a disproportionately important international role, in large measure because of Soviet subsidies that now approximate five billion dollars a year. Fidel Castro is no one's puppet, but so heavy has his dependence on the Soviet Union become for economic and military support that the presumption of essential subservience to the Kremlin's wishes runs strongly through many analyses. Even those who are uncomfortable with such a decisive assessment seem not to come to grips with the elusive reasons for the anomaly of a dependent Castro nonetheless pursuing an often independent line of foreign policy or a policy that advances his ambitions far more than it results in discernible benefits for the Soviet Union.

The issues dominating the Soviet-Cuban relationship have varied greatly during the past few decades. In the early 1960s a highly vulnerable Castro enticed the support of an admiring but uncertain Kremlin, attracted by his anti-imperialist (anti-American) position and readiness to permit the implanting of Soviet missiles in Cuba. The post-Cuban missile crisis period was a time of testing, as Castro demonstrated his dissatisfaction with the terms of the Khrushchev-Kennedy settlement. On the one hand, Moscow and Havana drew closer, as the Soviet Union extended aid and implicit security guarantees against a U.S. attack; but on the other hand, their differences over strategy and aims spawned tensions on the questions of relations with China, revolutions in Latin America, radicalizing the Third World, and detente with the United States. Despite their serious disagreements in the late 1960s, Moscow staked Havana to larger and larger amounts of military and economic assistance. Aid seemed unrelated to acquiescence to Soviet preferences. The collapse of the Portuguese empire in Africa triggered a major Soviet-Cuban military collaboration in Angola, and a couple of years later a massive military involvement in Ethiopia. More recently, their activities extended to Nicaragua, Grenada, and El Salvador. In these and many other instances, the nature of the influence relationship—whether concerted or autonomous, competitive or collusive—remains the subject of considerable debate.

Professor W. Raymond Duncan has written a comprehensive and sophisticated analysis that sheds new light on the Soviet-Cuban influence relationship. His fresh, informative study succeeds brilliantly in illumining the multiple dimensions of influence as it emerges on the key issues, in subtly developing the perceptions, policies, and preferred options of each of the parties, and in assessing the costs and the benefits in this asymmetrical and dynamic relationship. He subjects the issues to dispassionate examination, placing them in their proper historical-political context and probing for the underlying domestic and external considerations that shape the Soviet and Cuban positions. An indispensable source for everyone interested in Soviet or Cuban foreign policy and in the dilemmas of U.S. leaders seeking to cope with the challenges of Castro and the Kremlin in the Caribbean region and in Africa, Professor Duncan's book is a distinguished addition to the Praeger series, *Studies of Influence in International Relations.*

Alvin Z. Rubinstein
Series Editor

PREFACE

Soviet-Cuban relations occupy a key place on the chessboard of world politics. This is so because the United States determined a long time ago that Cuba is a proxy of the Soviet Union, located only ninety miles off U.S. shores. So unique a view about the nature of the Soviet-Cuban relationship became a constant factor in U.S. decision making since the early 1960s. It transmitted, even better than state of the art television, the image of a constant Marxist-Leninist threat, a perceived enemy that will not go away. It stalks other countries in the hemisphere and conditions the United States to weight Marxism-Leninism more than other forces, like nationalism, in international affairs. The consequences of this selective perception attributes more power to the Soviets and Cubans than is probable, creates less flexibility in U.S. policy than possible, and intensifies Soviet-U.S. adversarial relations.

Is the Cuban "surrogate" image accurate? One way to find out is to assume that the relationship is more complex than at first appears. If so, a number of intriguing questions arise. Does the Soviet presence in Cuba translate into automatic control over Cuban decision-making? Is Cuban foreign policy strictly a product of Soviet power exerted on a small and dependent Third World country? What kinds of returns have the Soviets actually received for their huge economic and military investments? Are all the Soviet "successes" in Cuba attributable to direct Soviet efforts to shape favorable Cuban behavior—or to other reasons? In what ways are Soviet and Cuban interests coincidental? In what ways are they not? To arrive at the answers to these questions, we can develop a concept of influence, the subject of this book, and apply it to the Soviet-Cuban case.

Many individuals have been helpful in developing this project. Although the list is long, I would like to thank especially John Tritak, my trusty research assistant who struggled with me to think through the concept of influence, along with Robert Legvold, Barbara Jancar, and, naturally, Alvin Z. Rubinstein. Conversations with Cuban foreign policymakers in Bonn, West Germany, in May 1983, helped clarify Cuban perceptions of their Soviet relationship, as did talks with a number of people in Cuba, in January 1983. Several of my undergraduate research students spent many hours in the library hunting evidence, including Julie

Dombrowski and Ronald Nilon. Vicky Willis of the SUNY-Brockport Document Preparation Center spent endless hours typing and retyping the manuscript, for which I am most grateful. I would also like to thank the staffs of the SUNY-Brockport Drake Memorial Library, especially Margaret Rich, Carolyn McBride, Peter Olevnik and George Cornell, and the staff of the Fletcher School of Law and Diplomacy's Edwin Ginn Library for their always kind assistance.

This book is dedicated to my wife, Ute, and my two children, Erik and Christopher, whose patience and sense of humor made the work enjoyable.

CONTENTS

INTRODUCTION: THE STUDY OF SOVIET–CUBAN RELATIONS

How do we know influence between two countries when we see it? Influence occurs when country A or country B changes or modifies its behavior in response to pressure from the other. Outside of changed behavior owing to more violent forms of influence, such as a military threat or an economic blockade, examples of influence are difficult to document even under the best of research conditions. "Influence" happens less frequently than imagined, and what passes as influence is often a case of two countries simply pursuing compatible objectives. Influence in the Soviet-Cuban case is especially elusive, owing to inaccessible information about Soviet and Cuban decision making. That seems to leave us with surface events: Moscow's power, Marxist-Leninist ties, Cuba's economic dependence and its willingness to fight for other Soviet clients—all pointing to an open and shut case of Soviet dominance.

Yet all is not lost. The search for more subtle and specific examples of influence in relations between the Soviet and Cubans is possible. By developing a conceptual model of influence and applying it to the historical record, we can follow the lead established by other researchers on this subject, like Alvin Rubinstein, to examine systematically a broad range of available data.[1] These data include joint communiqués issued at the conclusion of high-level meetings between the leaders of the two countries, editorials in key newspapers and journals of both countries, official speeches and statements, and radio broadcasts. Research materials also include the evaluation of economic aid, trade, and cultural, ideological and military relations. Two additional types of data are the assessments of specialists in Soviet-Cuban relations and the analyses of leading journalists, such as those who write for major U.S. and foreign newspapers. These sources provide insight into perceptual or attitudinal change as a result of interactions between two countries, as well as the impact of third and fourth states, such as the United States and mainland China.

We use this type of data to structure the argument chronologically, with a focus on the major isues at work in the Soviet-Cuban relationship. Chapter one identifies the parameters of "influence" in terms of types of pressures exerted by one country over another and the range of issues at stake in the influence setting. It provides a conceptual model of issues involved in influence relative to their significance in the perceptions of

xiii

a country's foreign policy-making elite. Chapter one sets the scene for a chronological and systematic investigation of the complexities of influence at work in the experiences of Soviet-Cuban affairs since the early 1960s.

Chapter two explores the historical setting of Soviet-Cuban ties, with emphasis on the early years of the budding relationship. It examines Soviet interest in Latin America before the Cuban Revolution, the significance of the Cuban Revolution in Soviet perspectives, and how the Soviets and Cubans perceived each other at the outset of the relationship. It studies the effects of the U.S. Bay of Pigs invasion of April 1961 and the missile crisis of October 1962. The latter is especially important in early Soviet-Cuban relations. Other issues explored are the armed struggle approach to change advocated by Cuba versus the Soviet emphasis on peaceful politics and "united fronts," Soviet-Cuban approaches to mainland China, and the relations of each country with the Third World. Our overall attempt here is to identify Soviet and Cuban foreign policy goals, capabilities, and any attempts of one country to influence the other.

Chapter three concentrates on the watershed years of 1968-70, when the Soviet-Cuban ties entered a period of converged interests on a number of issues. This period stands in contrast to the 1966-68 era, when Soviet-Cuban relations were severely strained, especially over the question of armed struggle versus peaceful change. From 1968 onward, the Soviets and Cubans began to work out their difficulties, particularly in light of Cuba's need for Soviet economic and military aid, the failure of armed struggle to ignite in Latin America, and Cuba's increasing isolation among the Latin American states. The failure of Cuba's planned ten million ton sugar harvest in 1970 added to Cuba's need to place its policies more in line with the Soviet Union, in order to pursue its own goals more effectively. Did the Soviets influence Cuba on any issues during this period, or did Cuba make its own adjustments because of its changing evaluation of options?

Chapter four examines Soviet-Cuban relations as the two countries entered the 1970s. The period is marked by strikingly high Soviet penetration of the Cuban economy, readjustments of the Cuban political system along formal Marxist lines, and increased Soviet military aid. One is tempted to define this era as a matter of growing Cuban economic dependency on the Soviet Union, but whether the dependency is accompanied by direct Soviet influence over the entire spectrum of Cuban decision making in domestic and foreign policy needs to be probed. This chapter demonstrates growing Soviet-Cuban cooperative interaction on a number of issues and thereby sets the scene for joint Soviet and Cuban military activities in Angola during 1975.

Chapter five looks at the Soviets and Cubans in Africa. It uses available data to discover the nature of Soviet and Cuban foreign policy goals, where and under what circumstances the Soviets may have influenced Cuba to act, or vice versa, and how the two countries' interests may have converged in Africa. Within this analysis it is important to delineate Soviet and Cuban ties in Africa, dating back to the 1960s.

Chapter six explores the Caribbean Basin, with special attention to Soviet and Cuban policy shifts since the late 1970s. As in the case of Soviet and Cuban policy in Africa from late 1975 onward, we attempt to probe why Soviet and Cuban efforts turned to support of armed struggle, abandoning the peaceful approach previously advocated. Explanations for Soviet and Cuban policy turn on regional politics, including the growing strength of the *Sandinistas* in Nicaragua and of other revolutionary groups in El Salvador, as well as the roles played by different administrations in Washington. This chapter highlights not only the opportunities for Moscow and Havana to expand their presence, but also the limits to their power. In this chapter we explore the question of how, and under what circumstances, the Soviets may or may not have influenced the Cubans to back regional revolutionary movements.

Chapter seven examines the benefits, costs, and future strains in the Soviet-Cuban relationship. One of these limits is U.S. foreign policy. Others include the nature of regional politics and Soviet-Cuban economic weaknesses. In the context of the benefit-cost dimensions of the relationship, potential strains exist between the Soviets and Cubans. And this possibility holds interesting implications for U.S.-Soviet and U.S.-Cuban diplomacy in the future.

A number of primary sources have been especially helpful in preparing this study. They include the official communiqués of the Soviet and Cuban governments, official declarations and statements, and the statements and speeches of political leaders in each country. These were gleaned essentially from Soviet and Cuban sources. On the Soviet side, we utilized the weekly *New Times* and the monthly *International Affairs,* as well as the *Current Digest of the Soviet Press* and other publications translated by the *Joint Publications Research Service* (JPRS) and the *Federal Broadcast Information Service* (FBIS). Cuban sources include the *Granma Weekly Review,* FBIS, JPRS, and the *Latin American Weekly Report.*

NOTES

1. See Alvin Z. Rubinstein, ed., *Soviet and Chinese Influence in the Third World* (New York: Praeger, 1975), chap. 1.

ON THE CONCEPT OF INFLUENCE

Who influences whom in Soviet-Cuban relations? This question merits our attention, if for no other reason than its impact on U.S. foreign policy in Latin American and on U.S.-Soviet relations. But other aspects of international relations are illuminated by a study of the Soviet-Cuban case. Can a dependent small country exert influence on a superpower donor? If so, how, and under what conditions? In what ways does the presence of a superpower in a small client state translate into influence and in what ways does it not? What types of conditions trigger an influence action? How is influence managed between A and B? At first glance it appears that Cuba is little other than a Soviet pawn, created by Havana's enormous economic and military dependence on the Soviet Union. Compared to other Soviet aid recipients outside the Soviet Eurasian arena, including the past favorite Soviet clients of Egypt and India, Cuba has received substantially more aid.[1] By 1982 Soviet aid to Cuba ran at about $11 million per day and by then Cuba had an accumulated debt to the Soviets of approximately $9 billion. As one student of Soviet aid to Cuba argues, "there has never been anything quite like it, not in the experience of developing countries in the Third World, nor of the socialist countries, most particularly the USSR."[2] Cuba's leaders laud the Soviets for their help, for as Castro stated at the first congress of the Communist Party of Cuba in December 1975, "Without the decisive, steady, and generous aid of the Soviet people, our country could not have survived the confrontation with imperialism."[3]

These facts lead many observers to agree with the view argued by one scholar in congressional testimony in 1980: Cuba simply "cannot be presented as a sovereign government capable of making independent decisions...the reality of Cuba's economic dependence on the Soviet Union has produced political dependence."[4] This characterization of the Soviet-Cuban relationship, where Cuba is perceived as essentially dominated by its superpower communist patron, is the predominant leitmotiv in U.S. policy toward Cuba since the early 1960s and one popularly held.[5]

Yet it would be difficult to understate Moscow's attraction to Havana. At first skeptical about the meaning and direction of Fidel Castro's movement in the late 1950s, the Soviets were blessed by Castro's unexpected shift to Marxism-Leninism in December 1961 following his assumption of power in January 1959. Subsequent Soviet links with Cuba opened the way for Moscow to project its power into the Caribbean Basin and Latin America. Because the Soviets had enjoyed little success in these areas prior to the Cuban Revolution, at a time when their ties were expanding in other Third World regions, Soviet links with Cuba became especially significant. They made it possible for the Soviets to enter the Latin American arena through a country only 90 miles from U.S. shores and, to use Soviet terminology, lying directly within the U.S. "strategic backyard."[6] Through Cuba the Soviets could pursue opportunities to encourage the development of the socialist system in Latin America, to play the game of superpower politics, and to reduce, hopefully, world capitalism and imperialism, headed by the U.S.[7]

From this perspective it could be argued that instead of the Soviets influencing the Cubans, influence flowed in precisely the opposite direction. Beginning around the mid-1970s, this view became attractive to a number of scholars. They centered less around the notion of Cuba as strictly a Soviet satellite and more on the assumption that Cuba was a unique actor in the relationship. Departing from the theory of Cuba as a Soviet pawn, the second school of thought emerged that perceived Cuba as an autonomous actor where Castro used the Soviets in quest of his own independent foreign policy goals. Key Cuban foreign policy objectives included the island's physical security, its economic development, and its "proletarian internationalism," that is, support for other Third World revolutionary movements.[8] This approach suggested that Soviet control is far less than it seems, that in fact Soviet and Cuban interests frequently converge rather than Cuba acting in response to Soviet dictates.[9]

A third interpretation of the Soviet-Cuban relationship quite logically evolved which viewed Soviet-Cuban diplomacy as something between the first two polar positions. It argues that the Moscow-Havana axis is a more complex interaction, one of mutual interests, costs and benefits for both sides, and with limits to the complete control by either party over the other.[10] Within the Soviet-Cuban arrangement, the Soviets nevertheless remain a predominant factor because they force the Cubans, in the words of one analyst, to "operate within the parameters set by the Kremlin."[11] Our present study is most akin to the third school of thought, for it seeks to explore the complexity of Soviet-Cuban relations as opposed to viewing the relationship as totally Soviet or Cuban controlled. Yet it is different from the third approach insofar as it attempts to look at influence systematically in the Soviet-Cuban case through a conceptualization of influence that provides a framework for analysis of a wide range of issues in their diplomacy.

The thesis here is that a systematic examination of influence, as applied to Soviet-Cuban relations since the early 1960s, reveals a complex and diversified pattern of interaction between the two countries, some of which can be classified as influence. A careful analysis of influence suggests that it operates on a continuum of degrees of pressure and affects multiple kinds of interests at stake in the relationship through diverse issues affecting their ties. Influence is not a zero-sum game with either the Soviets or Cubans in total control, or in which one country's gain is an automatic loss for the other. The Soviet-Cuban relationship is much richer in its interactions than explained by the Cuba-as-a-pawn model or the Cuba-as-an-autonomous-actor depiction.

By *influence* is meant how, and in what ways, country A (the Soviet Union) tries to shape the behavior of country B (Cuba). Influence occurs when A causes B to act in a manner that promotes A's interests under circumstances where B might not have so acted had A's action not inclined B to do so. Here we must avoid the pitfall of assuming that B acts only in response to A's pressure, as through a large foreign aid program, because B may be acting in behalf of its own interests and for reasons other than strictly A's pressure. Indeed, a substantial portion of B's foreign policy may have less to do with A's actions than at first appears. For influence to have occurred in Soviet-Cuban relations, we must identify those instances when Cuba modified or sustained its policies to promote Soviet interests as a result of Soviet behavior.

CONCEPTUALIZING TYPES OF INFLUENCE

Influence is not a single-intensity kind of pressure exerted by A over B where A "influences" B to do x. A close examination of relations between countries suggests that various degrees and types of pressures can be applied by A over B, depending upon numerous elements of the relationship, such as A's leadership's perceptions of the situation, their capabilities in exerting pressure on B and the value B's leaders attach to whatever it is A wishes B do to. Influence comes in different intensities, and the hallmark of effective diplomacy is when A selected a type of pressure appropriate for the value both A and B assign to B's modification of behavior in a specific situation.

A major form of influence is *power*. Power is increased influence, distinguished by the introduction of positive or negative sanctions by A to get B to do x.[12] Sanctions, by which are meant actions or communications that involve threats (negative) or rewards (positive), intensify the pressure of influence.[13] Sanctions come in different forms, as in a threatened or actual decrease of cheap oil supplies by A to B or the promise of more military aid by A to B. Sanctions involve the use of valued resources, as discussed more in detail below.[14] Valued resources include a variety of objective and subjective factors that can be used to reward or punish, provide or deny. They range from money and resources to a country's international prestige and leadership within a specific region or grouping of other states. We need to show how A orchestrates different sanctions to apply varying degrees and types of power to affect B's behavior.

The task of focusing on diverse types of sanctions used by A and B is made all the more imperative due to the variety of relationships at work between two countries within the international community of sovereign states. Various kinds of relationships include, among others, adversarial (the Soviet Union and mainland China), dominant-submissive (the Soviet Union and Poland), allied (the United States and Great Britain), or interventionist (the Soviet Union and Afghanistan). Given the many types of interstate relations, one expects to find different types of influence at work, as in attempted coercion where the relationship is interventionist, or more cooperative in an alliance.

With this understanding of influence in mind, we can conceptualize different types of influence, which suggest distinct kinds of influence patterns between A and B, depending upon the type of pressure exerted. In the present study, we adopt the following types of influence: (1) *indirect-influence*, (2) *cooperative-influence*, (3) *assertive-power*, and (4) *coercive-power*.

Indirect-influence occurs when A does not initiate an influence action toward B, yet B modifies its behavior as a result of its perception and expectations relative to A's actions. One aspect of indirect influence is the anticipated reaction. By this is meant that B may change or sustain its behavior, not because of any special "signal" from A, but because of anticipated results (rewards or punishments) from A. Hypothetically, Cuba may have reverted to the path of armed struggle in Nicaragua in 1979, not because the Soviets urged them to do so, but in part because the Cubans anticipated Soviet support. Country B also may act to avoid an anticipated negative response from A on a relevant issue, or B may read into A's actions some intent or meaning that affects a changed or sustained pattern in B's behavior.

Cooperative-influence occurs when A induces, persuades, cajoles, or bargains with B to encourage it to cooperate with A on an issue of mutual benefit to both A and B. If B accedes to these endeavors, A affected B's behavior. Yet, if the result of the action clearly benefitted B, which motivated its leaders to agree with A, then B was not coerced or otherwise forced to comply with A's demands. Country B perceived benefits from its decision, and it had alternative actions which it could have pursued. Cooperative influence of A over B is a form of pressure that does not utilize positive or negative sanctions.[15] As a case in point, members of the Organization of Eastern Caribbean States (OECS) persuaded the United States to join with them in a cooperative action against Grenada in October 1983.

An *assertive*-power relationship is influence with the introduction of sanctions. It is likely to occur when one country wishes to modify the behavior of the other on a specific interest(s). In applying assertive power, A typically does not intend the action to lead to a break in relations with B, although this is a possibility. Nor does A, in pursuit of assertive power, demand total obedience from B on a wide range of issues. Assertive-power happens when A stresses a prescribed pattern of behavior for B on a specific issue, when A affirms the necessity of its position, and when it emphasizes this insistence through firm but relatively moderate sanctions— compared to the available pressure that A could muster should it be prepared to risk a break in relations with B. Assertive power occurs when B modifies its actions, despite its reluctance, because it calculates that the benefits outweigh the costs in doing so. State B may of course concede to A's insistence because it calculates a trade-off. By bowing to A on one issue, it stands to gain on others.

Country A is successful in getting B to do x, in part because its sactions produced short-term deprivations or rewards for B. It should be noted that the application of assertive-power may produce new conditions for more cooperative interaction between the two countries. The use of an assertive form of influence suggests that A continues to value highly its association with B, that it is not willing to risk a break in relations, and that it anticipates getting back to a more cooperative setting that will sustain the relationship over time. The Soviets used assertive power against

Cuba in 1967-68 when they cut back on their oil supplies to Havana in an effort to encourage Fidel Castro to drop his insistence on armed struggle as the path to change in Latin America, when the Soviets were stressing peaceful state-to-state relations.

Coercive-power characterizes a situation of high power politics, associated with the capacity to affect strongly, to control, or to compel obedience to one's orders through the use of strong positive or negative sanctions.[16] Under coercive power conditions, B is compelled to do x, while recognizing the heavy costs involved, the severely limited alternatives, and the grievous deprivations endured. The application of coercive power may risk breaking the relationship, if it is not already broken, as in the application of a trade embargo, military threat or direct military intervention. U.S. actions against Cuba in the 1960s, for example the U.S.-backed Bay of Pigs invasion, missile crisis diplomacy and trade embargo, or U.S. support of those guerrilla forces seeking to overthrow the *Sandinista* regime in Nicaragua after they came to power in July 1979, are examples of coercive power.

It is important to distinguish coercive power from cooperative influence or assertive power in our study of Soviet-Cuban relations because each suggests different interpretations of behavior and the overall effect of the Soviet presence. The Cuban surrogate model, for example, suggests constantly applied assertive power, or something just short of coercive power, by the Soviet Union over Cuba, where Cuba acts obediently to the Soviet Union because they depend so much on Soviet aid. If the relationship is more a mix of cooperative influence and assertive power, with influence or power flowing both ways between A and B on diverse issues, then less totally dominant Soviet control is suggested. Under these conditions, the Cubans may have attempted to exert influence over the Soviets on some issues, such as the appropriateness of armed struggle rather than peaceful change in Latin America during the 1960s and late 1970s, or at minimum they pursued foreign policies adopted to meet their own perceived interests.

CONCEPTUALIZING THE INTERESTS
AFFECTED BY INFLUENCE

Beyond identifying the types of influence applied by A against B, we need to understand the kinds of vital interests affected by influence. To probe the realm of interests at stake in an influence action allows us to capture the richness and complexity of the A-B influence network and to approach more accurately the realities of how influence operates. A focus on interests suggests clues to why A seeks influence in the first place, how it does so, and the effects of A's pressure on B in terms of why B does or does not modify its behavior.

To begin with, the significant interests involved in an A-B influence setting cluster within areas associated with A and B's essential concerns relative to the survival of the state.[17] These vital interests—or goals and objectives as depicted in Table 1.1—fall into the categories of security, economic (economic viability), and political (sovereignty) interests.[18] Within each category, some interests are more important than others, lending themselves to a classification of first, second or third level of importance—or saliency.[19] Whether or not the interest is of first, second or third level saliency is in effect how significant, sensitive or vulnerable it is to A and B in their survival. At what level of priority is the specific interest? When it comes to an A-B influence situation, A seeks to influence B typically because it wishes to change or sustain B's behavior relative to strengthening an interest within A's vital security, economic or political priorities. It does so by applying pressure on one of B's major interests.

The variety of salient interests at work in A and B's domestic and foreign policies help explain several operative aspects of an A-B influence setting. First, A can influence B through reward or denial only insofar as the reward or denial is relevant to one of B's vital interests. We learn more about the focus of influence between A and B by looking at the operative interests for both countries.

Second, the interests at stake when A tries to influence B need not be the same nor are they necessarily at the identical level of salience for A and B. Moscow tried to influence Cuba to abandon its emphasis on armed struggle rather than peaceful change by denying oil to the Cubans in 1967-68. In this case, Cuba's insistence on armed struggle affected Moscow's Latin American diplomacy, most likely a second level priority, while denying oil to the Cubans impinged on a Cuban first level concern, namely the country's economic survival.

Third, as this case of assertive Soviet oil pressure on Cuba illustrates, the intended modified behavior of B is closely related to an interest within B's vital security, economic or political goals. In the well-known statement about influence, "A getting B to do x," the "x" (influenced action), is a function of various interests of different importance within B's domain.

How and why B modifies its behavior under A's pressure is likely to result from three aspects of vital interests in the A-B situation: (1) the

Table 1.1. Vital Interests and Salience, Hypothetical Case

Salience	Security	Political	Economic
First Level	Protection of homeland Strong military force Alliance maintenance Border security	Political sovereignty protection Political control over internal decision making Political order and unity	Economic development and welfare Resource access, e.g., energy, food, natural resources
Second Level	Power projection abroad Maintenance of country's military prestige	Leadership prestige in international system Settlement of regional conflicts Political support against third party adversaries	Acquisition of hard currency Favorable balance of trade and payments
Third Level	Arms control and disarmament	Advancement of ideological goals	Signing broad international agreements, e.g., Law of the Seas

type of pressure exerted by A, (2) the level of importance of the interest against which A's pressure is applied, and (3) the impact of B's modified behavior on its other vital interests. We can examine each of these aspects briefly in turn.

As to the first point—the type of pressure exerted by A—we need to identify *issues* as opposed to interests. Pressure can occur over any number of kinds of issues through which A channels its action. Relevant issues might include, for example, oil supplies, foreign aid credits, guaranteed commodity purchases from B or assistance to B's armed forces. It is helpful analytically to think of these issue-oriented actions by A toward B, not as the vital interests previously discussed, but rather as issues through which A can apply pressure to B. Interests lie in the realm of fundamental goals, shaped by the values held by a state's political leaders and typically one highly relevant to the state's survival.[20]

Interests are to be distinguished from issues when we analyze the A-B influence relationship. Interests lie in the minds of the actors as kinds of "ideal types" against which daily policies are measured.[21] Interests are basically stable, long term and enduring. They constitute the reasons that A initiates an influence action and how B responds. Issues are the acts that affect interests. They constitute the actions or policies in the external world through which influence is exercised by A against B. Issues are an "outside" manifestation of A and B's interests because they occur in the external world, yet are linked to political leaders' internal goals. Issues vary from situation to situation and typically are short term in duration.

Because issues are so closely linked to interests and because they constitute the record of historical events, we can study them as a means to learn more about A's influence-seeking and B's responses. Insofar as issues are "windows" to A and B's internal interests and the channels through which A applies pressure on B, we have an available source of historical information about A-B relations. A look at how A uses a specific issue and how B responds to A's pressure allows us to infer what is the level of importance (saliency) attached to an interest, how sensitive and vulnerable is B to A's specific pressure, and why A is successful or not in applying pressure. Interests and issues help illuminate the diversity of an A-B influence network.

In terms of the second aspect, B's modified behavior, the level of priority against which A applies pressure will vary from one situation to the next in the A-B relationship. In some cases, B's leadership may envision a first level interest affected, in others a second or third level interest. How B responds to A's pressure will depend in part not only on the level of salience B's leadership attaches to a particular interest affected by A's action. Country B's response will depend in part also on the nature of the issue through which A seeks influence. For it is in B's perception of how, and in what ways, an issue is attached to its vital interests that leads B to modify or not its behavior, just as A's application of pressure against B is a product of how A envisions an issue's significance to B's key needs. Issues come in a vast array of forms. What is or is not an issue, and how an issue affects vital interests, lies in the minds of both A and B's leadership.

As a third point, country B typically must evaluate the impact of its behavior on its other vital concerns in deciding whether or not to modify behavior. In the case of Soviet oil sanctions in 1967-68, this was a form of assertive influence expressed through an energy issue and applied against a first level Cuban priority—economic survival. Yet the modified behavior—putting Cuba's foreign policy more in alignment with the Soviet emphasis on peaceful change in the Third World rather than stressing armed struggle—was in effect a second level interest, because it did not negatively affect Cuba's very survival. For this reason, Cuba acquiesced in A's favor.

Should country B believe that its primary interests would not be served in terms of changed behavior on some specific issue, as a response to sanctions imposed by A, then B is less likely to change, although it still may be forced to do so. Here again it is a question of what kind of sanction is applied, what issues are affected and what will be the overall impact of B's changed behavior on its other vital interests. Castro was asked in January 1984 if he would stop supporting Nicaragua, Angola and other revolutionary movements in return for a U.S. promise to open diplomatic, economic and technical links with Cuba. He replied that he would not. Castro said the United States "would be asking a price too high for our honor and for our principles in exchange for material benefits that we are not too interested in."[22]

Country B may agree to changes desired by A if B can avoid a negative impact on its first level interests, such as maintaining continued control by B's leadership over its political system. As a case in point, Cuba changed its behavior, under Soviet pressure, during the early 1970s, toward economic decision making more along the Soviet model and a restructuring of the political system to give the Cuban Communist Party (PCC) widened participation in decision making. Here the Soviets clearly cooperatively influenced the Cubans. Fidel Castro and the 26th of July Movement, however, retained ultimate political control (first level saliency for the Cubans), and massive Soviet economic and military aid continued to flow to Cuba (first level importance).

Table 1.1 is a suggested model of how a country's vital interests might be arranged in terms of the basic objectives at stake in each category and the level of saliency for these goals. An interest's saliency is naturally a function of the importance assigned to the interest by A and B's leaders.[23] One country's leaders may assign the country's prestige in the Third World a higher importance than another country. Cuba's leaders undoubtedly give this goal higher value than the Haitian leadership because the Castro government sought a strong Third World leadership position from the early 1960s onward. Similarly, the Cuban leadership assigns a higher saliency to support for the regional economic objectives of the New International Economic Order (NIEO)—an agenda of demands formulated by the Third World developing countries, than does the Soviet Union which is not a part of the southern developing countries.

Table 1.1 is meant as a heuristic depiction of possible kinds of in-

terests, with varying saliency, in a country's different vital objectives categories. Although Table 1.1 by no means exhausts the possible interests
on a country's agenda, it does illustrate the basic point that not all interests
are of the same importance for a given political leadership. Some interests,
notably those in the first level category are especially important to a country's survival, are highly sensitive, and are less likely to be traded off.
Here it is critical for the analyst to try to put himself into the shoes of
the policy-maker, following the admonitions of the historian, R.G. Collingwood, in an effort to see the situation as the actor saw it at the time.[24]
We need to try to understand the perceptions of the actor in order to assess both interests and issues. Country B, for example, likely will be especially protective of its first level goals in relations with A, but might
accept the pressure to modify its behavior over priorities in the second
and third levels. Castro seemed willing to modify his structure of economic decision making in the early 1970s (second level issue) under Soviet pressure, as long as it did not threaten his ultimate political control
(first level saliency). In modifying economic decision making, Castro acted
in a manner that soon ended Soviet petroleum deprivations and guaranteed first level priorities of continued Soviet economic and military aid.

Castro's actions suggest how, and in what ways, Cuba clearly benefits
from its Soviet ties. It also suggests that in the Soviet-Cuban relationship,
the Soviets are able to influence Cuba at an economic security level, while
the Cubans are less able to influence the Soviets at their economic security level. This is not to say that the Cubans do not influence the Soviets
on other issues, especially within the Soviet political domain on second
and third level issues. In this sense it is not a contradiction to say that
the Soviets and Cubans potentially can influence each other, given the variety of interests and issues of different saliency at work in their relationship. One of the tasks in analyzing Soviet-Cuban relations is to try to identify at what specific level of saliency a given interest falls in the hierarchy
of A and B's central goals and how a particular issue affects that interest.

The criterion for placing an interest at a specific level is how central is it to the survival of the regime in the perceptions of the leadership?
How does it affect a country's security, economy and political sovereignty.
How sensitive and vulnerable is the country's leadership to pressure applied through a specific issue? Will the behavioral change desired by A
negatively affect B's vital interests? First level interests will be especially
important to A and B on these types of questions.

A caveat associated with Table 1.1 is that in the day-to-day dynamics
of foreign and domestic policy making, the security, economic and political interests are more closely interlinked than depicted by Table 1.1,

just as the distinction between first, second and third level salience is more blurred. The arrangement of interests in levels two and three, moreover, are likely to shift from country to country and from situation to situation between countries—more so than first level interests. Yet organization of interests into fundamental goals categories, arranged in different levels of saliency, helps to explain the variations in a country's objectives and why influence is a relative matter. It suggests why A seeks and B responds to pressure, demonstrating the kinds of interests that become targets of influence-seeking and the types of issues through which pressure might be channeled and over which action x is likely to occur for B. Placing interests into divergent levels of salience helps illuminate the dynamics and complexity of influence between A and B, rather than interpreting influence as a simple zero-sum game. Soviet-Cuban relations form an appropriate laboratory for this type of investigation.

Table 1.1 is also instructive in depicting how cooperative relations between two countries, such as the Soviet Union and Cuba, may support their various vital interests, as well as what interests are at stake when influence is sought by one country or the other. The fascinating aspect of these goals and their first, second and third levels of saliency is that not only are they the objects of beneficial trade-offs in a cooperative relationship, but they become subjects of influence when A or B seeks to affect the behavior of the other.

Turning back to our earlier discussion of the multiple types of influence (indirect, cooperative, assertive and coercive), it is relevant to ask a number of questions when attempting to identify the parameters of influence. What type of influence did A use against B in a specific situation? What capabilities were brought to bear? Was the type of influence appropriate, given the salience of the interest to B? Did A apply influence in a rational manner and how did B respond?

Answers to these questions shed additional light on the A-B relationship, the kind of interactions at work, and the effectiveness of the influence-seeking by A or B. The point here is that different kinds of pressure can be applied by A on B's varying interests at different levels; their results in terms of influence depend on how sensitive B is to the pressure and what overall effect B's modified behavior will have on its major goals. To state it differently, the effects of A's type of pressure (cooperative, assertive, coercive) depends in great measure on the level of interest saliency the influence operates. What we attempt in this book is to break up "influence" into both their methods and interests affected. Through this kind of study, we at least learn that "influence" is a distinctly relative matter.

GENERAL RULES ABOUT INFLUENCE

With these conceptualizations of the methods and interests involved in an influence relationship in mind, a number of general rules suggest the dynamics at work when influence occurs. As a first rule of thumb, influence entails the calculation of costs and benefits in policies pursued by the political elites of A and B. Influence occurs when A moves B to act, where the action is conceived by A's political elites to produce benefits that outweigh the costs. But what about costs and benefits in B? If B, like A, also believes the benefits to outweigh the costs in taking a specific action, then it cannot be said that A coerced B to act, even though that action advances A's benefits. In this type of situation, B's political elites made their decision based upon their own internal calculation of the benefits and costs associated with the policy. If, however, the costs outweigh the benefits on a specific issue for B, then the elements of influence or power are introduced. It should be noted that A and B are likely to assign different costs and benefits to different issues, depending upon the importance of the issue to each country's leadership, and we must try to assess these differences in order to infer if, and under what circumstances, "influence" did or did not occur.

A second general rule is applicable in assessing Soviet influence: once a donor country begins an aid program, it is politically useful to continue the program rather than curtail it.[25] A continuing aid program may not indicate that country A is receiving enormous dividends in its relations with B, but rather that the aid continues to flow irrespective strictly of B's behavior. This is so for several reasons, not least of which is that as state A becomes more committed to a course of action (foreign aid), it continues to pursue that path in order to protect its integrity and the original decision to support state B in the first place. This pattern of consistency in action is reinforced over time in order to justify the increasing level of A's investment of resources, which may or may not be producing actual "influence" of A over B.[26]

Third, valued resources, as discussed above, are utilized as sanctions in exerting power by one country over the other.[27] Valued resources include a wide variety of both objective and subjective factors, which can be used to reward or punish, supply or deny. Objective factors include key economic resources, for example, petroleum and food, purchasing and lending capabilities, military weapons, armed forces fighting capacity, and technical aid. Subjective factors involve an equally wide domain, such as the prestige of a country in the international or regional setting, its reputation as a revolutionary leader, morale, nationalism, quality of the country's leadership, and the population's work ethic. While not all valued resources are convertible into direct positive or negative sanctions, many nonetheless operate as a basis of influence in the relations between two countries.

In the case of Soviet relations with Cuba, it is important to examine the less obvious valued resources possessed by the latter, which increase its leverage with the apparently "stronger" country. Cuba's nationalism, revolutionary past, morale, prestige as a Third World leader against the United States, commitment to defying the United States in its own backyard, geographic location, and charismatic leadership by Castro are resources insofar as the Soviets perceive them as important issues of value to the Soviet foreign policy interests. Cuban potential influence, or resistance to Soviet pressures, includes previous Soviet investments of money, commitment, and prestige in Cuba which, over time, it could ill-afford to lose. There exists a kind of supply and demand link between the Soviets and Cubans, with different estimates of valued resources affecting the outcomes of their relationship. The point is that both the Soviets and Cubans have different types of leverage, based upon different valued resources as perceived by each country *vis à vis* the other.

Perceptions, therefore, are extremely critical in attempting to estimate where and how influence occurs, for what constitutes a valued resource lies in the perceptions of A and B's political leaders.[28] Valued resources are not necessarily the same for each country, yet are no less significant in the influence relationship. The Cubans depend on Soviet economic and military aid—highly valued resources in terms of Cuba's vital interest issues, and potential sanctions from the Soviet viewpoint. But Cuba's political, diplomatic and strategic importance to the Soviets are also valued resources with utility for Soviet foreign policy, made all the more valuable over time as Moscow's huge economic and military investments tied them ever more closely to this small island so near to the United States. From Cuba's perspective, these factors provided them with leverage in dealing with the Soviets, for as the Soviet Union increasingly invested in the island's future, they could ill afford to run the risk of alienating Castro.

Perceptions involve attributed influence or power. If a country's leaders attribute influence or power to another country, then the second country has the potential to actualize its resources if need be. In the case of Soviet-Cuban relations, perceptions and attributed influence suggest that country B, Cuba, may have resources available to influence the Soviets, depending upon Soviet perceptions. This notion allows the investigator to pay more attention to the smaller and seemingly "less powerful" country in a superpower-client state relationship.

Influence in Soviet-Cuban affairs leads to other questions about Soviet and Cuban foreign policy objectives and capabilities. These need to be answered if we are to perceive influence at work over specific issues and under particular conditions. What objectives does the Soviet Union pursue in its relations with Cuba? What capabilities and techniques does the Soviet Union possess to produce changed or sustained behavior in Cuba? What conditions are favorable for the Soviet pursuit of influence and why? Can it be demonstrated, conversely, that Havana has influenced Moscow in specific situations that promoted Cuban objectives? What situations suggest that Cuban behavior, while advancing Soviet aims, did not result from Soviet influence but rather from more *sui generis* Cuban origins? What objectives have the Cubans pursued *vis à vis* the Soviets, and what changed or sustained behavior resulted from Cuban influence? Overall, what can be learned from the study of the Soviet/Cuban behavior?

WORKING HYPOTHESES

Drawing upon other studies of Soviet-Third World relations, and of influence and power in world politics, a number of working hypotheses guided the research for this book. First, influence may flow: (1) from A to B, (2) from B to A, or (3) simultaneously between A and B—depending upon the issue(s), it(s) saliency, the capabilities used to influence and the impact of the modified behavior on the affected actor's vital interests. In this model of influence, the direction of pressure is not automatically a unilinear flow from A to B. State B may be fully capable of "influencing" A, depending upon the circumstances. These possibilities suggest that influence is by no means an automatic zero-sum game, where A has all the power over all the issues and B has none.[29]

Second, influence is an interdependent process over time, where the shaping of behavior in A and B is occurring simultaneously. This is so because influence is issue specific and situation specific, where A may induce B to act in a desired manner on one issue in one situation but not in others, while B simultaneously may be affecting A's behavior on another issue.[30] Country A may pursue cooperative influence on one issue, assertive influence on another. In this sense, the interdependent relationship between A and B has different influence dimensions on different issues.

Third, influence exerted by A or B on a specific issue is typically short-term in effect.[31] State A may be successful in compelling B to do x at one point in time, but the period of influence is unlikely to be of long duration. Yet the effect of A's "influence" on a specific issue at one point in time also can set up the conditions for B to seek to regain its perceived loss of control over a foreign policy issue to A by looking for the time, place and circumstances when it can regain its power. Moscow, for example, was successful in persuading Castro to remove the Soviet missiles from Cuba in November 1962, but this pressure on Castro led him later to assert his own independent line of action on the role of armed struggle in Latin America during the mid-1960s, which the Soviets did not like.

Fourth, a relationship between A and B matures over time. It creates a learning process between both parties. Castro's experience with the Soviet Union, and vice versa, has evolved over more than two decades, which suggests that Moscow's unfolding policies toward Havana were in part shaped by past experiences. The 1960s, a period of volatile strains affected the rapprochement-oriented 1970s. Castro's capability to use the Cuban military to advance both Cuban and Soviet interests in Africa from the Angolan adventure of late 1975 onward, moreover, may have influenced the Soviets to increase their military aid to Cuba in the early 1980s because they perceived Cuba as a valuable ally over time.

Fifth, in assessing influence we must evaluate the roles played by other states. To understand the reasons for and means of A seeking influence over B, or vice versa, we need to know A and B's assessment of their relations with states C and D, especially when C and D are either another superpower or a significant great power in the game of world politics.[32] Soviet-Cuban relations are affected sharply by Soviet and Cuban perceptions of U.S. foreign policy throughout the period examined in this book. And the People's Republic of China plays a significant role in Soviet-Cuban relations, especially during the initial period of the relationship during the 1960s. Soviet attention to Cuba stems largely from Soviet-U.S. competition and the Soviet drive to reduce U.S. power in Third World regions without a direct military confrontation with the United States. Cuba's attraction to the Soviet Union arises no less from perceived economic and military threats directed by the United States. We need to probe these and other roles of the United States in coming to grips with Soviet-Cuban ties.

CONCLUSION

A simple characterization of influence in Soviet-Cuban affairs does not adequately explain the richness of this bilateral relationship. The Soviets undoubtedly exerted major influence on Cuba over the years. That this will continue seems plausible in view of Cuba's substantial dependency on the Soviet Union for economic and military aid to serve Havana's vital interests. Cuba's economic and military needs place the country in a vulnerable and sensitive position relative to Soviet pressures. But at the same time it seems equally plausible that Cuba could have exerted influence on the Soviet Union, in view of the role Cuba played in serving Soviet interests, especially within the political category. A careful conceptualization of "influence" helps in untangling where, when, how, and under what circumstances influence may have been flowing both directions over diverse issues.

A systematic look at influence in Soviet-Cuban affairs is useful in understanding this relationship from other perspectives. It suggests that both the Soviets and Cubans derive mutual benefits from the relationship and that influence-seeking is likely to be utilized in an effort to balance the benefits with the costs if and when either Cuba or the Soviet Union believes they have become unbalanced. And this point suggests, in turn, that much of Soviet-Cuban relations are not necessarily a case of one side influencing the other, but rather of both sides enjoying the fruits of close association, where A and B promote each other's vital interests at first, second and third levels.

A final useful aspect of studying "influence" in Soviet-Cuban relations will hopefully emerge from our inquiry. If the Soviet-Cuban case is an example of shared costs and benefits, adjusted at various points in time by influence-seeking, then we can learn more about the management of influence. When either the Soviets or Cubans resorted to influence, how did they manage their relationship during this period? The stresses associated with influence between A and B call for effective diplomacy. Were the Soviets and Cubans effective from the diplomatic perspective?

NOTES

1. Cole Blasier, "Comecon in Cuban Development," in *Cuba in the World,* edited by Cole Blasier and Carmelo Mesa Lago (Pittsburgh: University of Pittsburgh Press, 1979), p. 225.

2. Ibid.

3. Fidel Castro, *La Primera Revolucion Socialista en America* (Mexico, 1976), pp. 55–56.

4. Statement by Professor Luis E. Aguilar, Department of History, Georgetown University, *Impact on Cuban-Soviet Ties in the Western Hemisphere, Spring 1980.* U.S. Congress, House Committee on Foreign Affairs, Hearings before the Subcommittee on Inter-American Affairs, May 14 (Washington, D.C.: U.S. Government Printing Office, 1980), p. 98.

5. By November 1959, just 11 months after Fidel Castro assumed power, a number of observers in the United States had begun to comment on Castro's activities as suiting "communist aims." See *The New York Times,* November 29, 1959 Section IV, p. 1:7. By July 1960, President Dwight D. Eisenhower warned that the United States would never permit international communism to set up a regime in the Western Hemisphere, and he argued that Nikita S. Khrushchev aimed to make Cuba serve Soviet ends in the hemisphere. See *The New York Times,* July 10, 1960, p. 1:8. See also similar comments by a number of senators, including John F. Kennedy, *The New York Times,* July 10, 1960 pp. 3:1, 2, 4, and 5. On scholarly works emphasizing Soviet dominance of Cuban decision making, see Leon Goure and Morris Rothenberg, *Soviet Penetration of Latin America* (Miami: University of Miami, Center for Advanced International Studies, 1975), pp. 63–69; James D. Theberge, *The Soviet Presence in Latin America.* (New York: Crane, Russak, 1974), pp. 65–66; David Rees, *Soviet Strategic Penetration of Africa* Conflict Studies No. 77 (London: Institute for the Study of Conflict: November 1977), pp. 1–21; Irving Louis Horowitz, "Military Outcomes of the Cuban Revolution," in *Cuban Communism,* edited by Irving Louis Horowitz (New Brunswick: N.J.: Transaction Books, 1977), p. 94; and Hugh Thomas, "Cuba's 'Civilizing Mission': Lessons of the African Adventures," *Encounter* (February 1978), pp. 51–55.

6. See V. Vasilyev, "The United States' 'New Approach' to Latin America." *International Affairs* (Moscow) 6 (June 1971): 43.

7. Roger Kanet, *The Soviet Union and the Developing Countries* (Baltimore: Johns Hopkins University Press, 1974); Jacques Levesque, *The USSR and the Cuban Revolution: Soviet Ideological and Strategic Perspectives, 1959–77* (New York: Praeger, 1978); Herbert Dinerstein, *The Making of a Missile Crisis: October 1962* (Baltimore: Johns Hopkins University Press, 1976); W. Raymond Duncan, *Soviet Policy in the Third World* (New York: Pergamon Press, 1980).

8. For this contrasting view, see Nelson P. Valdes, "Revolutionary Solidarity in Angola," in Blasier and Mesa Lago, eds., *Cuba in the World,* pp. 110–13; Cole Blaiser, "The Soviet Union in the Cuban American Conflict," ibid., pp. 37–38; testimony of William M. LeoGrande, School of Government and Public Administration, American University, U.S. Congress, House Committee on Foreign Affairs, *Hearings before the Subcommittee on Inter-American Affairs,* pp. 94–95; and Mark N. Katz, "The Soviet–Cuban Connection," *International Security* 8, 1 (Summer 1983): 88-112.

9. The question of converged interests, as well as other schools of thought on Soviet–Cuban relations, are discussed in Stephen T. Homer and Thomas W. Wolfe, *Soviet Policy and Practice Toward Third World Conflicts* (Lexington, Mass.: Lexington Books, 1983), pp. 100–3. Hosmer and Wolfe settle on a concept of "cooperative intervention" to explain much of Soviet–Cuban interventions in Third World conflicts.

10. See evaluations of this third view in Edward Gonzalez, "Cuba, the Soviet Union and Africa," in *Communism in Africa,* edited by David Albright (Bloomington: Indiana University Press, 1980), pp. 147–65; Jorge I. Dominguez, "Cuban Foreign Policy." *Foreign Affairs* (Fall 1978): 91–95, 98; Michael A. Samuels et al., *Implications of Soviet and Cuban Activities in Africa for U.S. Policy* (Washington, D.C.: Center for Strategic and International Studies, Georgetown University, 1979), pp. 43–50; Jorge I. Dominguez, "The Armed Forces and Foreign Relations," in Blasier and Mesa Lago, *Cuba in the World,* p. 73.

11. William J. Durch, "The Cuban Military in Africa and the Middle East: From Algeria to Angola." *Studies in Comparative Communism* (Spring/Summer 1978). For ad-

ditional discussion of this third interpretation, see Hosmer and Wolfe, *Soviet Policy and Practice,* chap. 8.

12. For a discussion of sanctions, influence, and power, see David V.J. Bell, *Power, Influence, and Authority: An Essay in Political Linguistics* (New York: Oxford University Press, 1975), pp. 20–24. Also Harold D. Lasswell and Abraham Kaplan, *Power and Society: A Framework for Political Inquiry* (New Haven: Yale University Press, 1950); pp. 48-49.

13. Bell distinguishes between influence and power in terms of sanctions. Power employs sanctions, influence does not. Power, therefore, is influence with sanctions. Bell, *Power, Influence and Authority,* pp. 17-24.

14. Ibid., p. 17. Also Lasswell and Kaplan, *Power and Society,* chap. 4; and K.J. Holsti, *International Politics: A Framework for Analysis* (Englewood Cliffs, N.J.: Prentice-Hall, 1967), chap. 6-11.

15. See Bell, *Power, Influence and Authority,* pp. 17-24.

16. On the cooperative and coercive aspects of influence, see Klaus Knorr, *The Power of Nations: The Political Economy of International Relations* (New York: Basic Books, 1975). For other studies of power as an influence relationship, see Michael P. Sullivan, *International Relations: Theories and Evidence* (Englewood Cliffs, N.J.: Prentice-Hall 1967); Holsti, *International Politics;* Karl W. Deutsch, *The Analysis of International Relations,* 2nd. ed. (Englewood Cliffs, N.J.: Prentice-Hall, 1978); and Hans J. Morgenthau, *Politics Among Nations,* 5th ed. (New York: Alfred A. Knopf, 1973).

17. Determining the importance of interests and their position within a leadership's policy perceptions is well discussed by Richard W. Mansbach and John A. Vasquez, *In Search of Theory: A New Paradigm for Global Politics* (New York: Columbia University Press, 1981), chap. 6. See also William D. Coplin, Stephen Mills, and Michael K. O'Leary, "The PRINCE Concepts and the Study of Foreign Policy," in *Sage International Yearbook of Foreign Policy Studies,* vol. 1, edited by Patrick J. McGowan, (Beverly Hills, Calif.: Sage, 1973); p. 74.

18. See Holsti, *International Politics,* chap. 5; William D. Coplin, *Introduction to International Politics,* 3rd ed. (Englewood Cliffs, N.J.: Prentice-Hall, 1980), chap. 4; John Spanier, *Games Nations Play,* 5th ed. (New York: Holt, Rinehart and Winston, 1984), chaps. 4 and 5.

19. This conceptualization is stimulated by the work of Mansbach and Vasquez, *In Search of Theory,* chap. 6.

20. On the connection between values, which lie in the policymaker's head, and interests related to decision making, see Christopher Hodgkinson, *The Philosophy of Leadership* (New York: St. Martin's Press, 1983), pp. 9, 29. As Hodgkinson argues, "it is impossible to free decision processes of the value component." (p. 29).

21. For a discussion of "ideal" types versus the "real" of daily life, see Edward S. Corwin, *Higher Law Background of American Constitutional Law* (Ithaca, N.Y.: Cornell University Press, 1955).

22. *Newsweek,* January 9, 1984, p. 40.

23. Saliency is well analyzed in Mansbach and Vasquez, *In Search of Theory,* pp. 102–10, 189–90, 192, and 202–203.

24. R.G. Collingwood, *The Idea of History* (New York: A Galaxy Book, 1956).

25. See Alvin Z. Rubinstein, ed., *Soviet and Chinese Influence in the Third World* (New York; Praeger, 1975), p. 5.

26. Consistency of action approaches to the study of international politics is exam-

ined in Robert Jervis, *Perception and Misperception in International Politics* (Princeton University Press, 1976). Rubinstein explains this behavior from still another perspective. State A's political elites may continue their heavy foreign aid program in country B because of internal bureaucratic pressures in country A, where that group which has a vested interest in continuing the policy in state B persuasively lobbies for its program. Rubinstein, *Soviet and Chinese Influence*, p. 5. In any case, what seems clear in past U.S. relations with the Third World, as well as in numerous cases of Soviet activities in the developing countries, is that superpower presence in a "weak" Third World country does not always result in superpower control over the "weak" state.

27. Bell, *Power, Influence and Authority,* pp. 16-31. Lasswell and Kaplan, *Power and Society,* chap. 4; Holsti, *International Politics,* chaps. 6-11.

28. On the question of psychological perceptions as they affect issues and capabilities, see Mansbach and Vasquez, *In Search of Theory,* pp. 213-21; and I. William Zartman, ed., *The 50% Solution* (Garden City, N.Y.: Anchor, 1976), where he argues that influence constitutes a psychological relationship between actors. Also Lasswell and Kaplan, *Power and Society),* pp. 18-28; and John G. Stoessinger, *Why Nations Go To War* (New York: St. Martin's Press, 1974), chap. 7.

29. David A. Baldwin, "Power Analysis and World Politics: New Trends versus Old Tendencies." *World Politics, The Power of Nations,* 31, 2 (January 1979): 162-96; Knorr, chap. 1.

30. Baldwin, *"Power Analysis and World Politics";* also Oran R. Young, "Interdependencies in World Politics," *International Journal* (Autumn 1969): 726-50.

31. Rubinstein, *Soviet and Chinese Influence,* p. 10; Mansbach and Vasquez, *In Search of Theory,* pp. 467-68.

32. Rubinstein, *Soviet and Chinese Influence,* pp. 15-18.

2

MUTUAL INTERESTS
AND EARLY STRAINS:
1959–64

Mutual interests, soon followed by early strains, characterize the Soviet-Cuban relationship during 1959-64. These years mark the beginning of Fidel Castro's leadership of the Cuban Revolution in January 1959 until the overthrow of Nikita S. Khrushchev in late 1964. The 1959-64 period is a natural era to explore because Leonid Brezhnev's leadership after 1964 introduced new Soviet approaches to the Third World and new tensions in Soviet-Cuban relations. An overview of the early years illustrates the types of interests that produced the Soviet-Cuban alliance and which continued to affect their ties through the years. A look at the strains in their relationship suggests how, and in what ways, their interests sometimes clashed through specific issues, and how each country pursued its interests through different kinds of influence.

Compatible interests initially brought the Soviet Union and Cuba together in February 1960, when they signed their first trade agreement. This event occurred after over a year of rapidly deteriorating relations between Cuba and the United States. The Soviets demonstrated little early faith in Fidel Castro's revolutionary movement during 1957-58, nor much belief in his staying power against U.S. opposition during 1959. They grew progressively more interested in Cuba's brand of radical nationalism, anti-Americanism, and revolutionary capacity during 1960-61. As for Castro, he at first held the Soviets and local Cuban communists at arms length as he consolidated his power, but adversarial relations with the United States encouraged him to seek outside economic aid and military support against a perceived growing security threat from the United States.

Soviet attraction to Cuba stemmed largely from Khrushchev's optimistic new approach to the Third World as an arena to compete for influence against the "imperialist" West and Communist China in the drive to strengthen a Soviet-led world socialist system. Table 2.1 illustrates Soviet vital interests and their salience levels; it suggests the importance of Cuba to the USSR's second level political and security interests. The role of Cuba in this global context was especially important to Khrushchev, because the Latin American region had not previously been a progressive arena for national liberation movements, and Soviet successes in gaining a foothold in this part of the world were greatly limited. Cuba's Revolution marked a significant change in Soviet opportunities to expand their presence in the Western hemisphere and to bring it into the broader Third World domain.

Cuba's attraction to the Soviet Union lay in Moscow's economic and military capabilities, paralleled by its competition on the world stage with the United States. As the United States increasingly threatened Castro's Revolution after the U.S.-led Bay of Pigs invasion of April 1961 and the missile crisis of October 1962, Moscow's willingness to extend economic and military aid to Cuba during this period of great need well served Castro's first level economic and security interests. These and other vital Cuban interests are depicted in Table 2.2. With these benefits in mind, it was not unusual that Castro would begin to envision the role Marxism-Leninism might play in Cuba as a unifying ideology of change, one compatible with Cuba's growing anti-American nationalism. During this period Castro also needed to organize Cuba politically, a goal that he could promote by utilizing the old pro-Soviet communist party of Cuba (Popular Socialist Party, PSP), as long as Castro remained in control of Cuba's internal political decision making.

The underlying *leitmotiv* in Soviet-Cuban relations in the early years is a concern to shore up each country's vital interests, pursued in large part through policies adopted in the context of the U.S. threat. Moscow and Havana began their affair because each country calculated the foreign policy benefits in doing so to outweigh the costs. Rather than trying to influence each other immediately at the outset, Moscow and Havana seemed more concerned in advancing their own foreign policy interests in their local, regional and global contexts. One way to accomplish this end lay in agreements on mutually beneficial issues. This rationale of attempting to advance their foreign policy goals, especially, but not exclusively, in terms of their U.S. perceptions (noting Moscow's continuing concern with communist China), conditioned the two countries' foreign relations toward each other well after 1960.

As the Soviets and Cubans joined hands in pursuit of their national interests and ideological goals, they soon experienced discord over a variety of issues—undoubtedly the result of a certain amount of influence

Table 2.1. Soviet Vital Interests and Salience Levels

Salience	Security	Political	Economic
First Level	Strong defense Weapons and armed forces development (conventional and nuclear) Border security	Political sovereignty Internal control over decision-making Political stability and unity	Economic growth Resource access, e.g., energy, natural resources, food
Second Level	Extended security parameters abroad Military power projection abroad, especially in geographically proximate arenas, e.g., Eastern Europe, but also Third World Alliance maintenance, e.g., Warsaw Pact Attention to state's military prestige	Extended political influence abroad into specific countries and regions, e.g., Eastern Eur. and South Asia; next, other Third World arenas Political support against third party adversaries, e.g., U.S. and China Leadership prestige in international system Focus on East-West struggle	Improve state's trade and commercial rels with other countries Economic alliance maintenance, (e.g., CMEA after 1972) Increase state's economic prestige in international system
Third Level	Reduce threat of war Arms control and disarmament Avoid nuclear proliferation	Extend political influence abroad through international intergovernmental organizations (IGOs), e.g., U.N. Extend ideological influence abroad, e.g., local communist parties	Improve state's trade and development position through attention to world trade setting in terms of East-West trade Encourage socialist models of development

Table 2.2. Cuba's Vital Interests and Salience Levels

Salience	Security	Political	Economic
First Level	Strong defense Weapons and armed forces development Border security	Political sovereignty Internal control over decision-making Political stability and unity; survival of the Revolution	Overcoming economic underdevelopment Resource access, e.g., energy, natural resources Access to development aid and trade
Second Level	Extended security parameters abroad Military power projection abroad; support for armed national liberation movements in Third World Attention to state's military prestige	Extended political influence abroad to help proletariat internationalism Political support for national revolutionary movements; quest for international status Political support against third party adversaries, e.g., U.S. Leadership role in nonaligned movement	Improved aid and trade abroad with communist and noncommunist countries Technical aid and other aid for national liberation movements Focus on North-South relations
Third Level	Reduce threat of regional or world war	Extended political influence in global international governmental organizations, e.g., U.N.	Modification of international economic system to improve Cuban and other Third World countries' economic development potential, e.g., in NIEO

seeking. Issues of discord included: Soviet displeasure with Cuba's economic performance despite Moscow's material aid, Cuban doubts about the scope of Soviet economic and military support, Moscow's early reluctance to recognize socialism in Cuba, the outcome of the October 1962 missile crisis, and Castro's stress on armed struggle as the road to change versus the Soviet emphasis on united fronts and peaceful parliamentary change. Havana also opposed Moscow's commitment to peaceful coexistence and its attempts to ease relations with the United States. Within this context, Moscow's limited support for Vietnam did not set well with the Cubans.

These strains in foreign policy issues, as Carla Anne Robbins appropriately notes, were linked to basic differences in how the Cubans and the Soviets characterized the nature of the present epoch.[1] The Cubans interpreted the era as a fundamental struggle between imperialist countries and the underdeveloped countries, namely the North-South debate. But for the Soviets, the central issue was the clash between the socialist camp and the imperialist camp, or the East-West conflict. It was the differences in foreign policy priorities over these and other issues that led to influence-seeking by both Moscow and Havana during the 1960s.

Castro's discord with old communists in the pro-Soviet PSP is one example of influence seeking, in this case Cuban pressure on the Soviets. In March 1962, Fidel Castro denounced and purged several old-line Communists, including one of its top members, Aníbal Escalante, who were identified with Moscow, for attempting to capture his revolutionary organization.[2] Underlying this event was Castro's displeasure with the Soviets over their inattention to Cuba's economic needs, demonstrated by the lack of a commercial agreement for 1962. Nor was Castro certain of what kind of actual protection the Soviets would provide against the United States other than symbolic statements of the type issued by Khrushchev in July 1960.[3] In addition to Moscow's default on delivering their economic aid to Cuba, the Soviets were becoming more friendly with the Americans and had failed to officially recognize Cuban socialism—the term Castro used to label his Revolution in April 1961. Meanwhile, Escalante seemed to be organizing old-line pro-Soviet Cuban communists in an apparent bid to gain control of Castro's revolutionary movement.

Castro's purge of Escalante's microfaction may be seen not only as a means to assert his own leadership. It appears to have been an influence move to encourage the Soviets to deliver on matters of importance to Cuba. As it turned out in this case, Cuba's efforts were successful, for the Soviets soon recognized Cuban socialism, condoned the ouster of Escalante, and signed a definitive commercial treaty with Cuba in May

1962.[4] In September 1962, the Soviets announced that they would supply arms to Cuba and provide technical specialists to train Cuban forces.[5]

This example suggests that Cuba, a small state, at times under specific conditions could wield influence against its superpower patron. Like other issues in the Soviet-Cuban relationship, who influences whom is not necessarily weighted totally in favor of the Soviets, despite their superiority in military strength, economic resources, and trading power. As other students of international relations have argued, Moscow's commitment to the smaller client, its stakes invested in making Cuba a viable socialist state and its prestige placed on the line, curiously provide Cuba with leverage against the Soviet Union.[6] Indeed, David Ronfeldt of the Rand Corporation describes this type of relationship as a "superclient," where the client wields power owing to its strategic location, previous investments by the patron that require safeguarding, and the consequent need to defend it.[7] It is analogous to the United States courting Iran and Vietnam during the 1960s.

But all this is getting ahead of the story. In an effort to explore cases of influence seeking in Soviet-Cuban foreign relations, it is useful to examine several major forces at work in the Soviet-Cuban relationship during 1959-64 and after. They are: (1) Soviet Third World policy under Khrushchev; (2) Soviet policy in Latin America before the Cuban Revolution; (3) Cuba's Revolution and evolving Soviet contacts; (4) Soviet foreign policy goals and the Cuban Revolution; and (5) Cuba's foreign policy and the Soviet connection. The forces at work within these dimensions in turn shaped how and why influence seeking between Moscow and Havana occurred during 1959-64.

SOVIET POLICY TOWARD THE THIRD WORLD UNDER KHRUSHCHEV

The Cuban Revolution erupted at a time of expanding Soviet interest in the Third World. While Soviet attention to Third World developments under the post-World War II leadership of Joseph Stalin was not altogether passive, the years following his death in March 1953 soon evolved into enthusiastic support for a number of regimes in the newly independent countries. Once Nikita S. Khrushchev came to power in 1954-55, the Soviet Union approached the Third World as an arena for competition for influence *vis à vis* the imperialist West, where favorable trends for these countries to advance toward communism in the post-colonial period seemed evident, and where bourgeois nationalist leaders would promote the interest of national liberation movements.

These Third World perceptions were based upon a number of assumptions held by the Soviet political elite during the period of Khrushchev's leadership, which lasted until late 1964.[8] First, the drive toward independence for many Third World countries, coupled with the Soviet Union's own increasing economic, military, and technical strength, produced a wave of optimism in the Soviet Union over these trends. Khrushchev appeared convinced that the new national revolutionary movements in Africa and Asia were highly favorable to advancing the correlation of forces between socialism/communism, on the one hand, and on the other, capitalism/imperialism, in favor of the former. This prognosis spelled out a weakening of the imperialist West with the added benefit of strengthening Soviet security. That the Soviets could support these movements in Africa and Asia, to advance the East-West struggle in favor of the former, stemmed from the growth in the Soviet economy, developments in the military and space technology fields, and the emerging East-West *detente.*[9]

Second, the Soviets perceived the newly independent states as inherently anti-imperialist in nature, thus establishing the conditions for a major weakening of the forces of imperialism within the international economic and political arena. As Khrushchev stated in his "Report of the Central Committee of the C.P.S.U. to the 20th Party Congress" (February 1956), the postwar "disintegration of the imperialist colonial system" is of "world historical significance."[10] Besides the progressive weakening of the forces of imperialism, Khrushchev also stressed that the newly emerging nonaligned countries of the Third World, along with communist states, created a "vast peace zone" that opposed Western "imperialism" and thereby helped to prevent the outbreak of world war.[11]

Third, Khrushchev's new approach to Third World states stressed the role of bourgeois national leaders, rather than local communist parties, in leading national liberation movements and revolutionary struggles for more complete economic and political independence from the imperialist and colonialist powers.[12] This perception of Third World leadership again reflected Khrushchev's optimism about socialist development possibilities in the developing countries, although Soviet ideological formulations on just how this transition was to come about in "revolutionary" or "progressive" states was admittedly vague.[13]

In any case, the Soviets developed a theory of the national democratic state to account for these optimistic possibilities for the transition to socialism that seemed to be emerging in Africa and Asia.[14] National democratic states were neither a part of the imperialist nor of the socialist camp. Politically independent, they could choose between the capitalist and non-capitalist path of development. The national democratic state selected the latter, stemming from its anti-imperialist and anti-colonialist posture. Further, the national democratic state, as viewed by the Soviets, did not oppose Communist party organization, ensuring thereby progressive development into succeeding stages of socialist construction.

These enthusiastic assumptions about positive conditions in the newly independent states of Africa, Asia, and the Middle East led Khrushchev to an ebullient courting of several Third World countries through military and economic aid programs. Egypt became the first arms aid recipient in September 1955, while Iraq received Soviet military aid in November 1958, and India in November 1960. By late 1959 and early 1960, just as Cuba was into its first and second year of Revolution, the Soviets began to extend moderate military aid to Guinea, followed shortly thereafter by military aid to Ghana and Mali. Between 1955-60, Moscow provided military aid to a total of 11 countries, while six countries (Egypt, India, Indonesia, Iraq, Afghanistan, and Syria) received over 90 percent of Soviet-bloc economic aid commitments between 1954-1960.[15]

Cuba's ties with the Soviet Union began with an economic agreement in April 1959, followed by their trade agreement of February 1960. They were formulated in the context of these Soviet assumptions about and relations with the Third World, rather than as an isolated event between the Cubans and the Soviets. As Cuba increasingly combated the United States and moved toward nationalization of U.S. property and centralized state control over the economy and polity during 1959-61, it was natural for the Soviet Union to see in this Revolution a remarkable opportunity to expand its presence in the broader Third World context. This conclusion must have seemed especially exciting in view of Moscow's previous record in Latin America.

SOVIET PERCEPTIONS OF LATIN AMERICA

As Moscow's interest in the Third World mounted during the late 1950s, most of Soviet writings about Latin America during this period were far less optimistic. They did not include Latin America as a progressive part of the Third World nor was Latin America incorporated as a part of Khrushchev's "zone of peace" formulation at the 1956 20th Party Congress.[16] The Soviets, to be certain, concluded a three year trade agreement with Brazil worth $214 million and were able to extend a $100 million credit to Argentina in 1958. But approaches to Mexico and Colombia for expanded trading relations met with little response. At the risk of oversimplifying the record, Soviet policy in Latin America before 1959 had established few significant and lasting diplomatic, economic, or political contacts.

During these years of Soviet foreign policy, Moscow's leaders were too focused on other matters to concern themselves with Latin America.[17] Vladimir Ilyich Lenin was basically ignorant of Latin American affairs, and Karl Marx's perceptions of the region were based upon the memoirs of a disgruntled French soldier of fortune rather than upon more objective and informed sources.[18] Lack of knowledge about Latin America undoubtedly contributed to Moscow's low success rate in forging and maintaining close ties with the region's governments before 1959. Ignorance led to a contemptuous attitude toward Latin American traditions, coupled with inappropriate tactics in the communist movement.[19]

Ignorance was not Moscow's only problem. Other obstacles to influence faced Moscow's foreign relations in this part of the world. The Soviets had trouble trying to reconcile their efforts to seek influence through support of communist activities by way of the Comintern (1919-43), while attempting to forge solid relations with the very governments that opposed communism. The Soviets established diplomatic relations with Mexico in 1924, but these were broken in 1930 because of Comintern meddling in Mexico's internal affairs.[20] Uruguay, where the Soviets had diplomatic relations and a trading agency (*Yuzhamtog*), broke relations with the Soviets in 1935 out of fear that Moscow's mission in Montevideo had promoted an uprising in Brazil. While the Comintern continued its activities with Latin America's traditionally pro-Soviet communist parties, most of these parties were banned or lacked influence.[21]

Nevertheless, the Latin American communist parties remained loyal to Soviet doctrine and practices. Their ideological positions and policies were imported from the Soviet Union, and their successes and failures stemmed essentially from Soviet leaders rather than local party officials in the host country. The Latin American communists pursued the Comintern's ultra-Leftist and combative tactics after 1928, and they continued this approach until 1935, when the Comintern initiated the Popular Front at the 7th Comintern Congress.[22] Moscow's historic control over its pro-Soviet followers in Latin America became a key feature of later Soviet influence seeking in relations with Cuba. Once Castro began to challenge the tactics and strategy of the pro-Soviet communist parties in Latin America during the early and mid-1960s, the Soviets drew upon their past ties to resist Cuba's efforts to advance the armed struggle thesis as the only truly revolutionary path to change.

Beyond the weakness of the pro-Soviet communist parties within the

Comintern framework, the Soviets faced other major limits to their potential influence. The region's authoritarian political cultures and structures, Hispano-Catholic traditions, conservative land-holding classes, legacy of strong military rule, and even opposition from some segments of workers and peasants all resisted Soviet penetration. The area's geographic proximity to the United States and its association with the Monroe Doctrine, warned against outside influence, just as U.S. economic penetration, political ties, and military presence in the region served as *de facto* bulwarks against Soviet inroads. Indeed, the United States had demonstrated in Guatemala in 1954 its determination to intervene against regimes that represented the possible extension of communism in the Western hemisphere.[23] These types of barriers continued to plague the Soviet Union after relations with Cuba had been established and the Soviets began to expand in Latin America during the 1960s.

THE CUBAN REVOLUTION AND EVOLVING SOVIET CONTACTS

It was an understandably cautious and pragmatic Soviet Union that first greeted the Cuban Revolution. The Soviets were well aware of the Guatemala episode in 1954, a failed Revolution undermined by a determined United States, which indicated to Soviet observers the continued strength of U.S. imperialism in this part of the world. Indeed, the U.S. economic presence was larger in Latin America than elsewhere in the Third World, the large landowners supported "reactionary" military rulers also backed by the United States, and U.S. multinational corporations were interlocked with the local upper bourgeoisie—not an attractive setting for the success of Cuba's radical nationalist movements as Guatemala so vividly demonstrated.[24]

Castro's 26th of July Movement, first defeated in its ill-fated assault on the Moncada Army Barracks in July 1953, and back in Cuba as a guerrilla movement since December 1956, by no means enjoyed active Soviet backing, much less influence seeking, nor did it receive support from the Cuban communists in the Popular Socialist Party (PSP). The Soviets at first viewed Castro as unlikely to succeed, believing that the United States would sooner or later snuff him out, or that he might even accommodate the imperialists.[25] As late as November 1958, Khrushchev observed in an interview that everybody remembered the fate of Guatemala and although the Cubans were heroic in their struggle, it was an unequal affair.[26] And until the summer of 1958, the PSP still insisted that only a popular uprising of Cuban workers, led by the communists, could insure Batista's overthrow.[27]

Not surprisingly, when Castro assumed power in January 1959, the coalition government did not represent the PSP, and when the Soviet Union recognized the new Cuban government on January 10, 1959, Cuba did not reciprocate. Indeed, in the beginning, Castro made clear that he "was not a communist," and that the PSP would not have a dominating role in running Cuba.[28] Without going into all the details of this early period, it should be noted that the Soviets were not optimistic about Castro's staying power, and Castro, fearing possible intervention against him, kept both the PSP and the Soviet Union at bay.

Philip W. Bonsol, U.S. Ambassador to Cuba at the start of Castro's long rule, accentuates the independence of Castro from the old line (PSP) communists. He argues that in 1959 Castro's thrust was distinctly nationalistic, and that Castro was anxious to dispel any impression that the communists were gaining influence in his regime. Castro, he said, was not an admirer of the old line communists with "all that it had to live down in the past politics of Cuba, including its reluctance to support Castro until the summer of 1958."[29]

Soviet-Cuban relations ultimately jelled in the context of Cuba's deteriorating relations with the United States during 1959-60. In answer to an official invitation, Vice Premier Anastas Mikoyan arrived in Havana in February 1960 to open a Soviet Exhibition, the same one he had opened in Mexico the previous November. This was more than one year after Castro's advent to power. The Soviets and Cubans concluded this visit on February 15 with a trade agreement for the purchase by the Soviet Union of 425,000 tons of sugar in 1960 and one million tons in each of the following four years.[30] Moscow also agreed to loan Cuba $100 million at 2 1/2 percent interest to allow Cuba to purchase machinery and materials. The Soviets also offered "whatever technical assistance may be required in 1961-1964 in the construction of plants and factories undertaken by the government of the Cuban Republic."[31] Additional agreements between Cuba and Eastern Europe were made in a subsequent tour of the Soviet Union and Eastern Europe by Antonio Nunez Jimenez, the head of Cuba's National Institute of Agrarian Reform.

The Soviet-Cuban trade pact of February 1960 illustrates an action of mutual benefit for the Soviets and Cubans relative to each country's posture toward the United States. By supporting the Cubans, the Soviets could help strengthen a movement only 90 miles off U.S. shores that challenged U.S. economic and political power in the Caribbean Basin and Latin America. It offered the Soviet Union its first real opportunity to gain potential strategic leverage in the East-West struggle in a region previously impervious to Soviet efforts. For the Cubans, the pact provided needed economic support, a demonstration that the Cubans could survive without the old U.S.-dominated economic ties, and potentially more economic and military support in the years ahead.

SOVIET FOREIGN POLICY GOALS AND CUBA'S REVOLUTION

Cuba's importance to the Soviet Union is best understood in the context of Khrushchev's general foreign policy goals and his enthusiastic adoption of the Third World as an arena for competition with the "imperialist" west. Soviet foreign policy objectives ranged from the projection of Soviet power to guarantee territorial security to an expanded Soviet Third World presence as a means to an enlarged role within the global arena. Castro's anti-American and anti-imperialist posture in the United State's "strategic backyard" (a Soviet phrase), lent enormous support to Khrushchev's optimistic assumptions about the nature of the trends at work in the Third World, its anti-imperialist character, and the role played by bourgeois national leaders in the national liberation movements.

These assumptions were strengthened by the transition occurring in Cuba's Revolution during 1959-61. Castro independently directed Cuba through various stages of great promise to the Soviets. The Cuban Agrarian Reform Law of 1959, which expropriated domestic and foreign-owned estates, fit Soviet theoretical thinking about the need for land reform throughout Latin America.[32] Castro expropriated over $912 million in North American petroleum, manufacturing, public utilities, and sugar holdings; discharged the Military Advisory and Assistance Group, and eventually separated economically from the United States by early 1962. Behind these events were long years of North American influence in Cuban affairs paralleled by Castro's deep frustration with a consistently corrupt and inefficient Cuban political system partially identified with North America.

Castro's description of the Cuban Revolution as "socialist" in April 1961, with its anti-North American bias and in the tradition of Latin American nationalism, provided a new basis for pro-Soviet PSP and communist respectability inside Cuba.[33] Khrushchev welcomed this turn of events, and in September he said that he would be pleased if Castro became a communist.[34] Castro's description of himself and his revolution as precisely of this ideological persuasion in December 1961 set up the conditions for another optimistic revision in Soviet thinking about the nature of newly independent states, namely that some could become "revolutionary democracies." Based on the Cuban experiment, this meant that, with the Soviets in the vanguard, providing economic aid and military support, a transition to Marxism-Leninism could occur under bourgeois national leadership rather than the leading role played by a local communist party.[35]

Cuba's successful defense against the U.S.-backed Bay of Pigs invasion of April 1961 gave proof of Castro's staying power in this new Latin American national liberation movement so close to U.S. shores. At the same time, it provided apparent evidence in Moscow that Soviet threats had deterred the United States from direct invasion. After the U.S. fiasco, Khrushchev perceived new advantages opening in Latin America, although they were tempered with continuing Soviet caution about Cuba's vulnerability.[36] While the missile crisis of late 1962 forced Khrushchev to remove the missiles from Cuba, the island nonetheless became a forward base for Soviet troops, training and naval facilities as a result of Soviet aid to Castro.

The evidence in this string of events suggests that Castro made these decisions as his relations with the United States forced him to seek new options to insure the survival of his Revolution and a new international status for Cuba.[37] From the Soviet perspective, Cuba had survived, rapidly consolidated its anti-American and anti-imperialist credentials, and, the biggest surprise of all, declared itself to be Marxist-Leninist—all of which strongly reinforced Khrushchev's optimistic perceptions about trends in the Third World.

Cuba became the chief anti-American and anti-imperialist critic in Latin America during the Khrushchev period, reduced U.S. economic power through its expropriation, adopted Marxism-Leninism as its leading ideology, and merged the old Cuban Communist Party (PSP) with Castro's 26th of July Movement. The island's transformation was so persuasive that it led Soviet theorists to modify their notions about the national democratic state, their previous formula about the newly independent countries in Africa and Asia in 1960, into the updated version of socialist transformation identified as "revolutionary democracy"—which underscored just how important the Soviets deemed Cuba's Revolution by 1961.[38]

CUBAN FOREIGN POLICY AND
THE SOVIET CONNECTION

If Cuba attracted Soviet interests, the Soviets served Cuban objectives. In an effort to understand why, and under what circumstances, Cuba became interested in the Soviet Union as a means to advance Havana's goals, we need to examine the latter. Like all countries, they were formed in terms of Cuba's size, geographic location, culture, and history. These "determinants of foreign policy orientations," to use the language of James N. Rosenau, help explain Cuba's version of its vital interests.[39]

Cuba's vital interests seem reasonably clear from the historic record. They include the island's national security, survival of the Revolution, overcoming economic underdevelopment, support for national revolutionary movements, and the quest for international status.[40] Table 2.2 illustrates these major, as well as other, first, second and third level salient interests.

Cuba's national security after January 1959, when Castro came to power, turned increasingly on the need for substantial military power to counteract U.S. military strength. This lesson stemmed not only from U.S. policies toward Cuba and the Central American region after January 1959, but also from Cuba's history of military struggle against external intervention and its recognition of the role historically played by U.S. military power in neighboring states. It was quite natural that Castro's version of how to survive in an unstable regional and global system assumed a predominant military emphasis. How else might the small island defend itself against the northern threatening neighbor?[41] And as discussed below, Castro's emphasis on armed struggle as the path to change in Latin America and the Third World not surprisingly also stemmed from his historic view of U.S. military power toward Cuba and Central America.

History, as Cuba's Vice Minister of Foreign Relations, Ricardo Alarcón, told the author in April 1983, is a foremost factor in shaping the national image of Cuba's past, present and future foreign relations.[42] The Cuban leadership is acutely conscious of their legacy of the struggle for independence dating back to 1868, when the first campaigns against external Spanish control broke out in what Alarcon describes as a "true national and popular war" of "all the people" against the "oppressor nation."[43] When the United States entered the 1895-98 version of this struggle, Cuba once again fell under foreign control, but by then thousands of Cubans had perished in the bloody battles to gain independence. From the turn of the century onward, the United States replaced Spain as the external enemy intervening in Cuban internal affairs. The legacy of United States policy in Cuba, especially during the Platt Amendment years until 1934, which gave the United States the "right" of intervention in Cuban domestic life, cannot be underestimated in shaping contemporary Cuban perceptions and expectations relative to its major foreign policy priorities.

Cuba's security consciousness, already steeped in a history of frustrated independence and external interventions, assumed magnified proportions from the Cuban perspective shortly after Castro's assumption of power in 1959. Alarcón writes that "since early 1959, the U.S. adopted a hostile attitude and very shortly after promoted activities intended to overthrow the Revolutionary Government."[44] The long list of U.S. threatening activities cited by the Cubans include: sheltering criminals from the Batista era in the United States, allowing them to conduct acts of sabotage and harassment against Cuba, the imposition of an arms embargo against Cuba, opposition to the Cuban Agrarian Reform law of May 17, 1959, C.I.A.-backed counterrevolutionary action in Cuba, and the U.S.-sponsored Bay of Pigs invasion in April 1961. Interestingly, in a number of informal discussions inside Cuba in January 1983, the memories and felt insecurities spawned by the 1961 Bay of Pigs invasion were still very much alive over two decades later.[45] Indeed, one is struck by the size of the U.S. military shadow when one stands on shores around Havana, looking northward, as opposed to gazing southward from Miami, Florida.

The Cubans stress that their insecurity was heightened greatly by other U.S. actions. The United States severed relations with Cuba and imposed an economic, commercial, and financial blockade against Cuba by 1961. Under U.S. pressure, Cuba was suspended from the Organization of American States (O.A.S.) in January 1962. Continued U.S. pressure helped produce greater O.A.S. pressure in 1964, when the inter-American organization levied sanctions against Cuba that isolated it from all the Latin American countries, except Mexico.[46] These actions in turn convinced the Cubans that their foreign policy in support of security and other radical nationalist movements must adopt the armed struggle approach. Reinforcing the specter of the United States as a geographically constant enemy against which the island must mobilize militarily were other events: the efforts of the Central Intelligence Agency (C.I.A.) to assassinate Castro during the 1960s and the continuous exile opposition to the Cuban Revolution.[47] In light of these events, national security to preserve territorial independence became a deeply sensitive issue for the Castro regime, one measured against the U.S. presence.

National security is naturally equated with survival of the Revolution.

This is especially so for Cuba, because the *Fidelistas* identify their goals with revolutionary aspirations of past Cuban heroes who battled for independence, dating back to 1868. Castro and his followers see in their 1959 Revolution a continuation of the national revolutionary struggle carried on by the precursors to Castro's victory: José Martí, Antonio Macéo, Ignacio Argramonte, Carlos Manuel de Céspedes, and Máximo Gómez—all nineteenth century Cuban national heroes.[48] As Castro stated in 1968, alluding to the ties between his Revolution and previous revolutionary battles:

> What does October 10, 1968, signify for our people? What does this glorious date mean for the revolutionaries of our nation? It simply signifies the beginning of one hundred years of struggle, the beginning of the Revolution in Cuba because in Cuba there has been one revolution: that which was begun by Carlos Manuel de Céspedes on October 10, 1868, the revolution which our people are still carrying forward.[49]

These historic roots of Castro's Revolution carried an enormous sensitivity to external influence, a glorification of the past independence struggles and an increasing anti-Americanism associated with the first decades of the twentieth century and subsequently with the U.S. opposition to Castro's version of the Revolution. It must be said that the anti-American aspects of Castro's Revolution easily blended with Marxism-Leninism, with its own unique version of the United States as the leader of the capitalist/imperialist camp.[50] These historic nationalist roots of Castro's 1959 Revolution, to state it simply, accentuated the new regime's desire to preserve it as well as providing a national historic image on which Castro could draw for popular support against the U.S. threat.

Cuba's national history provides a natural link between the Castro leadership and the Cuban population. As Marshall R. Singer writes, "many of the decisive inputs into foreign policy processes of small states are the values, attitudes, identities, and goals of the domestic elite."[51] Cuba's revolutionary historic roots assuredly shape the attitudes and values of Cuba's 26th of July Movement elites, giving direction to foreign policy behavior. Even more it forms a national image among the population, a real and potential source of communication between the leaders and the led that can be manipulated to legitimize leadership decision making in foreign policy. This tie between Castro's revolutionary elites and the masses provides a source of order and unity within the policy, thus strengthening elite negotiating power in relations with other countries, including the Soviet Union. Castro, always the consummate politician, has demonstrated over the years a unique ability to utilize national symbols—as well as Marxism-Leninism—to build legitimate authority, to institutionalize the Revolution and to mobilize grass roots support for decisions made at the highest level. The role of nationalism in the context of Cuba's Marxist-Leninist thrust is of enormous importance in the calculation of Cuban foreign policy and most definitely in its evolving relations with the Soviet Union.

Overcoming economic underdevelopment became a third key foreign policy objective. This goal was clear in the early revolutionary pronouncements of Castro and his 26th of July Movement in the late 1950s. In declaring his Revolution as a continuation of the revolutionary generation of the past, Castro attacked the colonial mentality in Cuba and excessive foreign economic domination.[52] Castro's emphasis on past foreign economic control of Cuba was notably quite consistent with a number of Cuban historians' assessment of Cuba's colonial dependency prior to the 1959 Revolution.[53] Castro stressed that his Revolution was a struggle to gain higher levels of economic development that would benefit all of Cuba's citizens. It intended to achieve this goal through modernization of agriculture, industrialization, nationalization of private property, and the expansion of foreign trade. Deterioration of relations with the United States, with the break in diplomatic relations in January 1961 and the subsequent closure of U.S. markets to Cuba, propelled the United States even more into the role of Cuba's natural enemy.

Support for Third World revolutionary movements experiencing conditions similar to those faced by Cuba formed a fourth foreign policy goal.[54] This sense of internationalist solidarity, quite clear in Castro's foreign policy from the outset, did not arise strictly from an identification with Marxist-Leninist ideology. Castro's commitment to internationalist duty and solidarity rests upon Cuba's own national history of revolutionary struggle against colonialism, which predates the Russian Revolution and the birth of Marxism-Leninism on a global scale. It is here that we see a clear distinction between Castro's approach to the developing countries from a North-South perspective as opposed to the Soviet emphasis on the East-West struggle.

A quest for international status is a fifth foreign policy goal which meshes neatly with and reinforces the others. It is an understandable objective in view of Cuba's small island status and past subjugation to other countries, followed by a successful Revolution against these conditions. Following Castro's assumption of power, it is as if the new leadership determined to break Cuba's position in the stratified international system described by Johan Galtung as essentially feudalistic with "top dog" countries (the United States and the Soviet Union) ranked in power at the top, with other states following in descending order as "underdogs."[55] The new Cuban leadership seemed no longer content to lie at the lower levels of this hierarchical system as a consistent "underdog," rather than to attempt to elevate its status.

This motivation in Cuban foreign policy is complemented by Castro's own charismatic personality, his sense of revolutionary activism, and his pronounced global perceptions.[56] And as a consummate political opportunist and pragmatic leader, Castro is more than capable of playing the game of power politics, of seeking political leverage in an effort to gain influence abroad, and of maximizing his limited power capabilities as leader of a small, but important, Third World country. The quest for international status began to appear very early in Cuban foreign policy, with outreaching contacts to other Third World countries, insistence on Cuba as a model for revolutionary change elsewhere, and in its United Nations policies.

The record of early and continuing Cuban foreign policy, including Havana's relations with Moscow, indicates the forces of both historic nationalism and newer Marxism-Leninism behind Cuban decision making. The nationalist dimensions especially merit our attention, because Marxism-Leninism is frequently cited as a major force behind Cuba's activities. The nationalist forces began to take many forms inside Cuba as Castro consolidated his control. They included: (1) Castro's 26th of July Movement followers in prime positions of decision making, even when they were merged with the old communists in the PSP; (2) forging a sense of a national consciousness among the Cuban people in an effort to build *Cuban* unity and purpose; (3) establishing a sense of defense for the *patria* or fatherland; (4) organizing the Cuban population with a new nationalist ethic of work and struggle for the people and the homeland; and (5) infusing the Cuban population with a new sense of pride, not only in domestic policies, but also in foreign policy as Cuba entered a new brand of twentieth century diplomacy.[57]

The Soviet Union offered Cuba a variety of avenues to pursue these foreign policy objectives after 1960. To begin with, Soviet economic and military aid insured the economic survival of the Cuban Revolution and contributed greatly to its physical security.[58] Moscow made Cuba's physical security possible by providing most of the equipment for the Cuban army, navy, and air force, an amount estimated at $933 million between 1961 and 1975.[59] Since 1962, the country has experienced a deficit economy, unable to export enough goods to pay for needed imports, and only

Soviet aid has spared Cuba from bankruptcy.[60] The grand total of Soviet assistance to Cuba between 1961 and 1967 is estimated at $2.025 billion.[61]

As to international solidarity and the drive for international status, here again the Soviet Union served Cuba's purposes. By joining with the Soviet Union, Cuba could draw upon Soviet economic and military support to increase its own capabilities to project power abroad. The stronger the Cuban economy and military, the more likely Cuba's support for national liberation movements could be asserted at the regional and global levels. Cuba's ties with the Soviet Union as a socialist great power also brought added dignity and status to the island, through international conferences, the ceremonial functions associated with sending and receiving delegations within the socialist (and nonsocialist) community, and through high level meetings held in Havana.

Cuba's benefits from its Soviet connection can be summarized as follows. They received: (1) a vast reservoir of economic, military, organizational, and technical resources which made possible Cuba's survival and pursuit of Third World interests; (2) support for Cuba's own negative nationalist reactions to foreign capitalism and imperialism associated with Cuba's national historic legacy and its subsequent attraction to socialist principles even before the adoption of Marxism-Leninism; and (3) backing from other small and medium socialist states that added to Cuba's efforts to achieve international status through Third World leadership aimed at weakening the world capitalist system through the strengthening of national liberation movements in the postwar period.

When these benefits derived by Cuba from the Soviet embrace are measured against the gains Havana provided Moscow, the basis for compatible objectives and policies between the Cubans and the Soviets seems clear. From the outset, it appears that much of Soviet and Cuban interactions turned less on issues of persistently sought after influence by the Soviets over the Cubans, or *vice versa,* than on a situation of shared compatible interests in mutually reinforcing policies worked out, as discussed by K.J. Holsti, through "discussion, exchange of information, or joint study."[62]

But a number of cases of influence seeking did erupt in Soviet-Cuban relations during this early period. For as Holsti also states,

> where objectives and actions are less compatible, the act of influencing may involve...*persuasion* (e.g., demonstrating benefits to be received by changing or sustaining behavior), (2) *offers of rewards,* (3) *compellence,* through (a) threats or (b) application of sanctions, or

(4) *deterrence,* by making threats of retaliation; or it may involve some combination of these.[63]

In the influence typology adopted for the present study, Holsti is pointing to the application of cooperative influence, assertive power, and coercion as possible types of interaction when discord began to ensue over a number of issues between the two countries that affected their vital interests.

DISCORD AND INFLUENCE IN SOVIET-CUBAN RELATIONS: 1959–64

While mutual interests brought the Soviet Union and Cuba together and sustained the relationship over time, discord soon developed as one country's policies began to conflict with the other's essential priorities. This led to different types of influence seeking, based upon different sets of capabilities, applied in an effort to get the other country to do, continue doing, or not to do, some specific behavior. Most of these situations, but by no means all, were of the *cooperative* type not involving the use of sanctions and producing outcomes of mutual benefit. Coercive sanctions were less applied by the Soviets against the Cubans, such as a trade blockade, a boycott, or threat of direct military invasion. These types of influence seeking were more applicable to relations between the United States and Cuba rather than the Soviet-Cuban affair.

Nevertheless, cooperative influence quite clearly occurred in several incidences. Early economic and military relations illustrate the point. On economic matters, it seems clear, as Jacques Levesque, one student of early Soviet-Cuban relations argues, that from the early 1960s onward the Soviets were concerned with the pace and efficiency of Cuban economic planning, especially their over-rapid nationalization of the private sector.[64] The Soviets believed it necessary to preserve a private sector for a lengthier period of time in order to facilitate the transition to wider state planning and development. Above all, the Soviets were constantly concerned about the Cuban regime's vulnerability. They were not enthusiastic about added economic responsibilities in Cuba, if its leaders were bent upon a total rupture of supplies from western, notably the United States, trading partners.

That the Soviets continued their aid, despite the deterioration in Cuban-U.S. economic relations, suggests how politically important the Cubans became to the Soviets from 1960 onward. Continued Soviet economic support over time created leverage for the Cubans, given Moscow's investments, prestige and credibility in keeping the Cuban economy a going concern.[65] While Cuba became economically dependent on the Soviets, the latter developed their own kind of political dependency on the Cubans.[66] By the summer of 1962, preceding the October missile crisis, world attention still focused on numerous economic strains between the Soviets and the Cubans.[67]

Under these conditions of Soviet aid at a time of obvious Cuban economic development problems, evidence of Soviet cooperative influence can be identified. After the trade protocol of May 1962 was concluded, only some of the promised twelve shiploads of food had arrived by mid-August, suggesting either normal shipping bottlenecks or calculated delays.[68] During this period the Soviets recalled its ambassador to Cuba, Sergei Kudriatsev, one of the Soviet's famous top diplomats, and replaced him with Aleksei Alexseiev, a specialist in Latin American cultural affairs, who arrived in Havana in August with a group of Soviet economic experts.[69] And earlier in May 1962, Premier Khrushchev told a group of 1,000 Cuban students returning home that Soviet aid alone would not solve Cuba's problems, a form of subtle persuasion with the Cubans.[70] Khrushchev's actions suggest pressure on Cuba to work harder on more efficient use of Soviet aid, a point directed at first level economic interests for the Cubans and a particularly sensitive and vulnerable issue for them in future years.

Military relations between the Soviets and Cubans produced other strains and influence seeking. While the Cuban leaders were increasingly conscious of their military vulnerability *vis á vis* the United States, one of their highest priority interests as depicted in Table 2.2, Washington's role in the April 1961 Bay of Pigs invasion brought home just how painfully insecure Cubans were—just 90 miles off U.S. shores and in a region traditionally dominated by the United States. Following the invasion, Castro swiftly moved from his earlier identity with socialism to declaring himself Marxist-Leninist, clearly hoping to encourage the Soviets to admit Cuba into the socialist camp and thus making Cuba worthy of Soviet military protection—at a level beyond cloudy verbal commitments.[71] As other scholars note, this is exactly what the Soviets did not wish to do, owing to the island's vulnerability in the U.S. shadow. Despite Castro's efforts to win socialist identity from Khrushchev, it was not until April 1962 that the Soviets began to speak of Cuba as on the path of "socialist construction."[72]

The timing of the April 1962 Soviet recognition of Cuba's "socialist character" is noteworthy on the issue of influence, for it came just one month after the much publicized denunciation and purge of Aníbal Escalante, identified as a pro-Soviet communist, as discussed above. The Escalante affair suggests Cuba's *assertive power* against the Soviets, the sanction one of political pressure and embarrassment. In this case, Cuban pressure appears to have worked, because the Soviets shortly recognized Cuban socialism, supported Escalante's ouster, and concluded a definite commercial treaty with Cuba in May 1962.[73]

The missile crisis of October 1962 underscores continued security strains between Moscow and Havana. Although the evidence is contradictory about whether the initial decision to place the missiles in Cuba originated with Castro or with Khrushchev, the move clearly served both countries' interests.[74] They would add greatly to Cuba's protection in the wake of the Bay of Pigs invasion, especially since Castro in early 1962 "felt sure that the U.S. were preparing a military invasion of Cuba," as did the Soviets.[75] The Soviets could hope to add to their international prestige in guaranteeing Cuban security given its desire for protection, and at a relatively low risk given the U.S. defeat in the April 1961 Bay of Pigs episode.[76]

But the evidence also indicates that Khrushchev placed the missiles in Cuba more for his own strategic and political objectives than for Cuba's security concerns, and Khrushchev removed the missiles without prior consultation with Castro.[77] This action resulted in serious tensions between Moscow and Havana because Castro rejected any form of inspection of the withdrawal of the Soviet weapons from Cuba, and he submitted his own list of conditions for their removal quite separate from Soviet agreements with the United States.[78] In an effort to deal with this situation, Khrushchev sent Mr. Mikoyan to Cuba in early November in an attempt to persuade Castro to adopt a more flexible attitude on the matter. The difficulty in this task is illustrated by the length of time Mikoyan remained in Cuba, 24 days, not even returning to Moscow when his wife died. Eventually the missiles were removed, and Castro agreed on November 19, during Mikoyan's visit, to the added removal of Soviet IL-28 bombers stationed on the island. Mikoyan's persuasion evidently worked, for he departed Cuba stating that Havana had "complete support of the Soviet Union."[79]

But just how firm was the Soviet-Cuban relationship following the missile crisis? As noted previously, the Cubans fundamentally disagreed with the Soviet commitment to peaceful coexistence in the East-West context and with Moscow's efforts to calm relations with the United States. Would such a policy not lead the Soviets to abandon their new Cuban allies? At the same time the Cubans were strongly committed to armed struggle, drawing upon their own historic experiences, on behalf of the developing countries against the imperialist powers. This commitment did not easily fit with Soviet efforts on behalf of peaceful coexistence. Not surprisingly, then, the Cubans did not allow U.N. personnel into Cuba to monitor the missile removal, despite such an understanding between Khrushchev and President John F. Kennedy. As Carla Anne Robbins states, the Cubans emerged from this crisis with several key questions about their alliance with the Soviets, notably how committed the Soviets were to the Cubans under U.S. pressure.[80]

As a result of Castro's deep displeasure with the whole affair, he determined to keep up his own version of influence against the Soviets, directed at their second level political interests, as depicted in Table 2.1, in pursuit of more tangible economic aid from the Soviet Union. He did so through three discernible tactics, which proved effective in the aftermath of the missile crisis. First, Castro began to use the Sino-Soviet rift to his advantage by not committing himself to either side. Second, he began to insist on the role of armed struggle as the fundamental path to change in Latin America. The basis for this insistence lay in the history of Castro's successful guerrilla struggle against the Batista government, a record enshrined in the Second Declaration of Havana of February 1962.[81] Third, the Cubans publicly criticized the Soviets for giving insufficient aid to Vietnam. Each of these tactics was used to extract more assistance from the Soviets as the reward for continued allegiance and participation in their mutually beneficial relationship. Insofar as rewards (sanctions) are implied in the Cuban pressure, it appears that the smaller country used its own version of *assertive influence*.

These tactics were especially effective after the missile crisis, because of Soviet embarrassment over its outcome, its lowered global image as defender of national liberation movements, and the criticism heaped upon the Soviet Union by the People's Republic of China for capitulating to the "imperialists."[82] After the missile crisis, Moscow was on the defensive with Peking in the deepening schism between the two countries, while Peking was declaring its constant solidarity with Havana. So Castro pursued studied neutrality in the Sino-Soviet rift rather than siding with the Soviets, and he attacked the pro-Soviet communist parties in Latin America for spreading "false interpretations" of the Cuban revolution to legitimize their policy of "peaceful transition" to socialism.[83] Given Castro's prestige in the world communist movement, these were not idle accusations.

These influence efforts proved successful, because in February 1963, the trade agreement for that year was finally signed on impressively favorable terms for Cuba. The agreement included higher prices for Cuba's sugar and the opportunity for Cuba to sell more sugar, previously scheduled for shipping to the Soviet Union, on the open market for dollars instead of selling to the Soviets for rubles.[84] During late April through early June 1963 Castro made his first trip to the Soviet Union, which produced Soviet recognition of Castro's Cuba as a full-fledged member of the "socialist camp," thus entitled to more Soviet economic assistance and military concessions—which the Cubans in fact received. The joint communiqué published on May 23 also indicated some compromises made by Castro, especially on toning down his dictatorial approach to the pro-Soviet Latin American communist parties on their proper political role.[85] It would appear, then, that the Cubans indeed exercised political leverage in playing the role of "superclient."[86]

Castro's general insistence on the primacy of armed struggle as the proper path to change in Latin America continued to plague easy relations with the Soviet Union. During the latter part of 1963, the Cubans increasingly emphasized the value of armed struggle, and the Cuban press wrote of favorable conditions for armed struggle in Latin America. Cuban volunteers were in fact known to be participating in guerrilla activities on the continent.[87] Although the Soviet Union opposed this position, Khrushchev tried to maintain cordial relations with the Castro government, which was not an easy task.

A second trip by Castro to the Soviet Union in January 1964 led to another communiqué like the one signed the previous year. It approved both peaceful and nonpeaceful means to abolish capitalism, suggesting that the Soviets and Cubans were cooperating with each other in attempting to reach a compatible understanding on this delicate issue.[88] But the debate over armed struggle continued through the last days of Khrushchev and was by no means resolved by the time of his demise in late 1964. The issue became especially delicate for Khrushchev, who was attempting to relax tensions with the United States following the missile crisis, a goal not made any easier by Castro's insistence on armed struggle at a time of close embrace with the Soviet Union.

Neither was Castro's role in the Sino-Soviet dispute fully satisfactory for the Soviet Union during Khrushchev's rule. As the Soviet premier more and more turned his attention to the condemnation and ousting of China from the Communist movement after the missile crisis, he attempted to establish a compromise between the Castro regime and the Latin American communist parties as a means to unify support against the Chinese. For all Khrushchev's efforts, including the economic concessions and recognition of Cuba as a member of the socialist camp, Cuba did not enter the Sino-Soviet rift on the side of the Soviet Union during Khrushchev's term in office, and Castro continued to complain about the low level of Soviet support for the Vietnamese.

CONCLUSION

The early 1960s illustrate vulnerabilities and sensitivities for both the Soviets and the Cubans when it comes to the question of who influenced whom. Each country had key vital interests at stake, and despite the Soviet Union's clear economic and military power which could be applied against major Cuban interests, for example, its economic survival and need for military security, the Cubans wielded diplomatic and political influence over the Soviets. Soviet vulnerability arose from its public commitment to Cuba, its interest in and need to maintain this relationship with its new client state, and the prestige it had on the line. Cuba's own prestige among the developing countries, the Cuban leadership negotiating skills, political conditions in Cuba, for example, the Cuban leadership's ties with the population through the national revolutionary legacy, and the leadership's determination to make a place for itself within the international system offered additional sources of potential power in Cuba's relations with the Soviets. The apparent inequality in power between the two countries, in this sense, was less totally unequal than surface features indicated.

The use of different types of interests, at distinct levels of saliency, helps in probing what goals brought the Soviets and Cubans together in the first place as well as what issues deeply affected Soviet and Cuban foreign policy behavior. Mutual interests that produced and sustained Soviet-Cuban relations after 1959 helped the alliance hold together despite the obvious sources of discord. But the discord was there, and we now turn our attention to how, and in what ways, Soviet and Cuban policies were pursued after the fall of Khrushchev, how they coincided or diverged, and what types of influence seeking occurred from Khrushchev's demise into the beginning of the decade of the 1970s. We will examine the outcomes of these efforts and how they shaped Soviet-Cuban relations.

NOTES

1. See Carla Anne Robbins, *The Cuban Threat* (New York: McGraw-Hill, 1983), pp. 44–46.

2. Escalante's dismissal occurred when Castro was in the process of merging the old PSP with his 26th of July Movement which led the guerrilla struggle against Batista. Castro attacked Escalante for placing old PSP members into key political positions, for "counter revolutionary activities," and for advancing his personal aims in the new merged organization, the Integrated Revolutionary Organization (ORI). Castro clearly was determined to maintain his own leadership against any power plays by the old communists. An incisive account of this event is given by Herbert S. Dinerstein, in his *The Making of a Missile Crisis: October 1962* (Baltimore: Johns Hopkins University Press, 1976), pp. 169–70; 172–73; see also Andrés Suárez, *Cuba: Castroism and Communism, 1959[8] 1966* (Cambridge: Massachusetts Institute of Technology Press, 1967), pp. 146–52. On the subsequent positive Soviet support for Castro's actions, see *Pravda*, April 11, 1962.

3. Khrushchev's belief in the great strength of Soviet nuclear capabilities spilled over to Cuban relations. In a speech at a schoolteachers' convention in July 1960, he warned that Soviet missiles could be used against the United States if it intervened against Cuba. See *Pravda*, July 10, 1960. On the background to this statement, made July 9, 1960, see Dinerstein, *Making of a Missile Crisis*, pp. 80-98.

4. The Soviets thus officially recognized Cuban "socialism" one year after Castro had described his movement as "socialist." *Pravda*, April 15, 1962. On the commercial agreement of May 1962, see *The New York Times*, August 19, 1962. Also see the article by Jacinto Torras, in *Cuba Socialista*, no. 10, June 1962, on the development of Soviet–Cuban relations, as translated in Stephen Clissold, ed., *Soviet Relations with Latin America* (London: Oxford University Press, 1970), pp. 266-71.

5. The announcement of increased economic and military aid in September was carried in *The New York Times*, September 3, 1962. Also see the joint statement on additional Soviet and economic aid signed by the Soviet and Cuban governments, September 2, 1962. *Pravda*, September 3, 1962.

6. Carla Anne Robbins cites the relevance of Albert Hirschman's thesis on "dependency management," where small states wield more influence in their alliance with a large state than the inequalities of surface features lead one to believe. See Robbins, *The Cuban Threat*, p. 166; also Hirschman, "Beyond Asymmetry: Critical Notes on Myself as a Young Man and on Some Other Old Friends," *International Organization* 32 (Winter 1978): 45-50.

7. As quoted in Robbins, *The Cuban Threat*, p. 166; David Ronfeldt, "Superclients and Superpowers," p-5945 (Rand Corporation, 1978). See also Jacques Levesque, *The USSR and The Cuban Revolutions: Soviet Ideological and Strategic Perspectives, 1959-77* (New York: Praeger, 1977), where Levesque observes that while the Cubans depended on the Soviets for economic aid, the Soviets became politically dependent on the Cubans, p. 20.

8. On background analysis of the Khrushchev approach to Third World relations, see R.A. Yellon, "Shifts in Soviet Policy Towards Developing Areas 1964-1968," in W. Raymond Duncan, ed., *Soviet Policy in Developing Countries* (Waltham, Mass.: Ginn-Blaisdell, 1970), pp. 225-86; and *The Soviet Union and the Third World: A Watershed in Great Power Policy?* Report to the Committee on International Relations, House of Representatives, Congressional Research Service (Washington D.C.: U.S. Government Printing Office, May 8, 1977); and Roger Kanet, ed., *The Soviet Union and the Developing Countries* (Baltimore: Johns Hopkins University Press, 1974), chaps. 1 and 2.

9. Yellon, "Shifts in Soviet Policy" in Duncan, *Soviet Policy*, pp. 226-32.

10. Report of the Central Committee of the Communist Party of the Soviet Union

to the 20th Party Congress. Speech of the First Secretary of the C.C.C.P.S.U., Comrade N.S. Khrushchev, *Pravda* February 2, 1956, pp. 1ff.

11. Ibid.

12. Kanet, *Soviet Union and Developing Countries*, chap.2.

13. Yellon, "Shifts in Soviet Policy" in Duncan, *Soviet Policy*, pp. 230-32.

14. Ibid., pp. 234-39.

15. Leo Tansky, "Soviet Foreign Aid to the Less Developed Countries," in *New Directions in the Soviet Economy*, Studies Prepared for the Subcommittee on Foreign Economic Policy of the Joint Economic Committee, 89th Congress, 2nd Session, Part IV, *The World Outside* (1966), pp.947-74.

16. On Soviet perceptions of and experiences with Latin America prior to the Cuban Revolution, see Clissold, *Soviet Relations*; and Stephen Clissold, "Soviet Relations with Latin America between the Wars," in J. Gregory Oswald and Anthony J. Strover, eds., *The Soviet Union and Latin America.* (New York: Praeger, 1970), chap. 1.

17. Oswald and Strover, *Soviet Union and Latin America*, p. 2.

18. Clissold, "Soviet Relations with Latin America Between the Wars," in Oswald and Strover, *Soviet Union and Latin America*, p. 16.

19. Oswald and Strover, *Soviet Union and Latin America*, p. 2.

20. Clissold pp. 17-19 in Oswald and Strover, *Soviet Union and Latin America*, "Soviet Relations with Latin America Between the Wars."

21. Ibid., pp. 19-21. See also William E. Ratliff, *Castroism and Communism in Latin America, 1959-1976* (Stanford: Hoover Institution Press, 1976), Introduction.

22. Clissold, *Soviet Relations*, p. 19.

23. See Dinerstein's excellent analysis of this event, *Making of a Missile Crisis*, chap. 1.

24. On this pessimistic Soviet overview of Latin America, see Jacques Levesque, *USSR and Cuban Revolution*, Introduction; also Edward Gonzalez, *Cuba Under Castro; the Limits of Charisma* (Boston: Houghton Mifflin, 1974), pp. 121-22.

25. Another reason for the lack of Soviet enthusiasm stemmed from Soviet–American relations, for at this time Soviet–American relations were shaded by an optimistic "Spirit of Camp David"—where Khrushchev and Eisenhower had met in September 1959. See Suarez, *Cuba*, p. 83.

26. As quoted in Dinerstein, *Making of a Missile Crisis*, p. 35.

27. Ibid., pp. 36-47; Gonzalez, *Cuba Under Castro*, pp. 96-100.

28. Gonzalez, *Cuba Under Castro*, pp. 96-100.

29. Bonsol also concluded that the Soviets had no other choice but to come to Castro's aid in view of U.S. actions. Philip W. Bonsol, *Cuba, Castro and the United States* (Pittsburgh: University of Pittsburgh Press, 1971), p. 67.

30. Joint Communiqué on Soviet–Cuban commercial agreement, *Pravda*, February 16, 1960; also see *Survey of International Affairs, 1959-60* (London: Oxford University Press, 1964), pp. 489-90.

31. *Survey of International Affairs*, pp. 489-90.

32. Levesque, *USSR and Cuban Resolution*, p. 405.

33. See Dinerstein, *Making of a Missile Crisis*, chap. 4.

34. *Pravda*, September 10, 1961, p. 1.

35. That the Soviets would revise their concept of the national democratic state into a new model of "revolutionary democracy," based upon Cuban developments in 1961 and 1962 illustrates just how significant the Cuban revolution had become to the Soviet

Union. See Levesque, *USSR and Cuban Revolution*, pp. 61-68.

36. Dinerstein, *Making of a Missile Crisis*, pp. 127-35; Levesque, *USSR and Cuban Revolution*, pp. 27-30.

37. On the events of U.S.-Cuban relations, in addition to previously cited sources, see *Cuba, the U.S., and Russia, 1960-63* (New York: Facts on File, Inc., 1964).

38. For additional discussion of "revolutionary democracy," see Roger Kanet, "Soviet Attitudes Toward Developing Nations since Stalin," in Kanet, *Soviet Union and Developing Countries*, pp. 27-50.

39. James N. Rosenau, "The Study of Foreign Policy," in Rosenau, Kenneth W. Thompson, and Gavin Boyd, eds. *World Politics: An Introduction*. (New York: The Free Press, 1976), pp. 19-22.

40. On Cuban foreign policy objectives, see Jorge Dominguez, "The Armed Forces and Foreign Relations," in Cole Blasier and Carmelo Meso Lago, eds., *Cuba in the World* (Pittsburgh: University of Pittsburgh Press, 1979), pp. 53-86; Dominguez, "Cuban Foreign Policy," *Foreign Affairs*, 57 (Fall 1978), pp. 83-108; Edward Gonzalez, "Institutionalization, Political Elites and Foreign Policies," in Blasier and Mesa Lago, *Cuba in the World*, pp. 3-35; and W. Raymond Duncan, "Cuba," in Harold E. Davis and Larman C. Wilson, eds., *Latin American Foreign Policies* (Baltimore: Johns Hopkins University Press, 1975, pp. 155—77.

41. The historic role of U.S. military power in the Caribbean is examined by Walter LaFeber, *Inevitable Revolutions; the United States in Central America* (New York: W.W. Norton, 1983). In looking at the Central American setting at the outset of the 1960s, LaFeber notes that, given U.S. intervention in the Dominican Republic in 1954 and in Vietnam from the 1960s onward, "no one could claim that North Americans reluctantly used military force." He states that the resemblance of the Caribbean area and Central America "occupied the same place in Washington's geopolitical plans that Czechoslovakia (1968, author's note) did in Moscow's." LeFeber stresses that this resemblance was not lost on Central American revolutionaries. "If they hoped to transform their countries," he writes, "they had to do it in the face of overwhelming U.S. military power" (p.158).

42. Informal discussion with Ricardo Alarcon, Bonn, West Germany, May 15, 1983.

43. Ricardo Alarcon, "Cuba: La Politica Interior y Exterior de una Revolucion: Que Ha Logrado y Cuales son sus Expectativas?" Paper prepared for the "Cuba in the 1980s" Conference organized by the Friedrich Ebert Stiftung, Bonn, West Germany, May 16 and 17, 1983, p. 6.

44. Alarcon, "Cuba-United States Relations: Behavioral Patterns and Options." Paper prepared for the "Cuba in the 1980s" Conference, p. 2.

45. Informal discussions between the author and numerous individuals inside Cuba, January 2-8, 1983.

46. See G. Pope Atkins, *Latin America in the International Political System* (New York: The Free Press, 1977), pp. 332-33.

47. On these and other C.I.A. activities, see *Final Report of the Select Committee to Study Governmental Operations with Respect to Intelligence Activities*, Vol. IV, 1976 (Washington, D.C.: Government Printing Office, 1976).

48. See W. Raymond Duncan, "Nationalism in Cuban Politics," in Jaime Suchlicki, ed., *Cuba, Castro and Revolution* (Coral Gables, Fla.: University of Miami Press, 1972), chap. 1.

49. Speech by Fidel Castro in Manzanillo, Oriente Province, October 10, 1968. *Granma Weekly Review in English* (October 13, 1968), pp. 2-4.

50. See W. Raymond Duncan, "Moscow and Cuban Radical Nationalism," in Duncan, *Soviet Policy in Developing Countries*, pp. 109-18.

51. Marshall R. Singer, "The Foreign Policies of Small Developing States," in Rosenau et al., *World Politics* p. 276.

52. See Castro's *Manifesto programa del Movimiento 26th de Julio*, issued in November 1956, as cited in Rolando E. Bonachea and Nelson P. Valdes, eds., *Cuba in Revolution* (Garden City, N.Y.: Anchor Books, Doubleday, 1972), pp. 113-40.

53. See, for examples, Ramiro Guerra y Sanchez, *Sugar and Society in the Caribbean; An Economic History of Cuban Agriculture*. Translated from the Spanish by Marjory M. Urquidi and with a foreword by Sidney W. Mintz (New Haven and London: Yale University Press, 1964), Mintz's foreword, pp.xxvi-xxvii; Herminio Portell-Villa, *Historia de Cuba en sus relaciones con los Estados Unidos y Espana*. 4 vols. (Havana: 1938–1941); and Alberto Lamar Schweyer, *La Crisis del Patriotismo* (La Habana: Editorial Marti, 1929). The historical backdrop, utilizing Cuban authors, is the subject of Ramon Eduardo Ruiz's penetrating study, *Cuba; the Making of a Revolution* (Amherst: The University of Massachusetts Press, 1968).

54. Dominguez, "The Armed Forces and Foreign Relations," in Blasier and Meso Lago, *Cuba in the World*, pp. 53-56.

55. Johan Galtung, "International Relations and International Conflicts: A Sociological Approach," International Sociological Association plenary session, September 4-11, 1966, cited in his "East-West Interaction Patterns," *Journal of Peace Research*, 3 no. 2 (1966): 146-77, as cited by Singer in "Foreign Policies" in Rosenau et al., *World Politics*, p. 271.

56. Gonzalez, "Institutionalization and Political Elites," in Blasier and Mesa Lago, *Cuba in the World*, p. 19.

57. On the importance of nationalism in Cuba's revolution, see Ramon Eduardo Ruiz, *Cuba*; and W. Raymond Duncan, "Nationalism in Cuban Politics," in Suchlicki, *Cuba, Castro and Revolution*, pp. 23-42.

58. The extensive Soviet economic aid on which Cuba became dependent is explored in Cole Blasier, "COMECON in Cuban Development," in Blasier and Mesa Lago, *Cuba in the World*, pp. 225-56.

59. Cole Blasier, "The Soviet Union in the Cuban–American Conflict," in Blasier and Mesa Lago, *Cuba in the World*, p. 41.

60. Ibid., pp. 40-46.

61. Ibid., p. 44.

62. While Holsti is not referring specifically to Soviet–Cuban relations, his analysis of interactions between countries A and B, where objectives are basically compatible, is relevant. See Holsti, "The Study of Diplomacy," in Rosenau et al., *World Politics*, p. 299.

63. Ibid.

64. Levesque, *USSR and Cuban Revolution*, p. 22.

65. After examining early Soviet–Cuban relations, Levesque makes this point in the strongest of terms. *USSR and Cuban Revolution*, p. 20.

66. Ibid.

67. Ibid., pp.21–22.

68. *The New York Times*, August 19, 1962, p. 1.

69. Ibid.

70. Ibid.

71. Levesque, *USSR and Cuban Revolution*, p. 32.

72. Ibid.

73. See note no. 4.

74. Castro has provided a variety of explanations as to who asked that the missiles be installed in Cuba. These range from "the Russians desired them," to the Cubans asked for them, Castro personally desired the missiles, and they were the result of joint consultation between the Soviets and the Cubans. Hugh Thomas, *Cuba, the Pursuit of Freedom* (New York: Harper and Row, 1971), pp. 1391–93.

75. Ibid. p. 1391.

76. For the Soviet rationale for placing missiles in Cuba, see Dinerstein, *Making of a Missile Crisis*; also Elie Abel, *The Cuban Missile Crisis* (Philadelphia: Lippincott, 1966); Graham T. Allison, *Essence of Decision: Explaining the Cuban Missile Crisis* (Boston: Little, Brown, 1971); and Davis Bobrow, *International Relations* (New York: The Free Press, 1972).

77. Dinerstein, *Making of a Missile Crisis*, chaps. 5 and 6.

78. Ibid., pp. 216-17; Suarez, *Cuba*, chap. 7.

79. Suárez, *Cuba*, p. 174.

80. Robbins, *Cuban Threat*, pp. 18, 111-12.

81. Fidel Castro, *Second Declaration of Havana* (Havana: Imprenta Nacional Unidad, 1962). Castro stated in this declaration that "the duty of a revolutionary is to make revolution," by direct implication a distinctly negative comment on the activities of the pro-Soviet communist parties in Latin America. See Dinerstein's treatment of the Second Declaration of Havana in Dinerstein, *Making of a Missile Crisis*, pp. 162 ff.

82. Suárez, *Cuba*, pp. 171-85.

83. Ibid., p. 177.

84. *Pravda*, May 24, 1963; *Hoy*, May 25, 1963.

85. Suárez, *Cuba*, op cit., pp. 171-75.

86. Ronfeldt, "Superclients and Superpowers."

87. Blanca Torres Ramirez, *Las relacions cubano–sovieticas (1959-1968)* (Mexico: El Colegio de Mexico), pp. 77-80.

88. Levesque, *USSR and Cuban Revolution*, p. 97; see also *Pravda*, January 23, 1964.

3

ESCALATING TENSIONS AND NEW ACCOMMODATIONS: 1964–70

The Soviet-Cuban alliance from 1960 onward is best described as a complex and interdependent network of actions and reactions, not a simple extension of Soviet power over a compliant and obedient surrogate. Within the context of shared goals, both the Soviets and Cubans used periodic influencing techniques, based upon available capabilities and the vulnerabilities of the other country, in attempting to maximize the benefits and minimize the costs of their relationship. This characterization of Soviet-Cuban relations during the Khrushchev years seems equally evident once Leonid Brezhnev and Alexei Kosygin assumed the Soviet leadership following Khrushchev's ouster in October 1964.

Never a passive ally during Khrushchev's rule, Castro proved even less so at times once Brezhnev and Kosygin came to power. Indeed, Soviet-Cuban relations were so strained during 1966-68 that a break in relations seemed possible over the question of armed revolution in the Third World, especially in Latin America. For a number of reasons, including, but not limited to, the application of Soviet economic leverage on Cuba, Castro realigned his foreign policy with Moscow during the summer of 1968, an accommodation that extended well into the next decade. But the strained relations of the mid-to-late 1960s quite clearly illustrate that Soviet-Cuban ties were not some modern version of older Spanish patrimonial power over a colonial subject, replete with coercive rule and applied sanctions. It was rather a situation of each country maneuvering to advance its foreign policy which meant, at times, trying to influence the behavior of the other country.

Soviet-Cuban tensions resulted from differences of policy priorities on a number of key issues. These included the role of armed struggle, the capacity of communist parties in leading revolution in Third World countries, how to treat bourgeois reformist governments, the appropriate economic development model for Cuba, the required level of Soviet military commitments, and continued differences over Soviet aid to Vietnam. Soviet-Cuban conflict over these issues illustrate not only the role of geographic-strategic differences, leadership personalities, and decision-making systems of the two countries, but also the recent histories experienced by each state.

As for the Cubans, they viewed armed struggle as the appropriate path to revolution, downgraded the leadership of Third World communist parties, and were disinclined to support bourgeois reformist governments in Latin America. These perceptions, which centered around the priority of military strength, stemmed from Castro's rise to power through the guerrilla army built by himself and his brother Raúl, and from their perceptions of the historic role played by U.S. military power in the Caribbean Basin. They generally downgraded the unrevolutionary communist parties, based upon their direct experience with the old Cuban Communists, and they believed that revolutionary interests would be little served by consorting with bourgeois-reformist regimes, given their continued ties with the United States and their painfully slow process of change.

These assumptions and beliefs clashed with Soviet policy perceptions as they emerged after the demise of Khrushchev. The incoming Brezhnev-Kosygin leadership of October 1964 turned toward a more pragmatic and cautious approach to the Third World, which was ill-timed to mesh with the Castro version of armed struggle and limited contacts with bourgeois governments. Following the fall of Khrushchev, the Soviets faced numerous difficulties in the Third World which were not helped by the increasing volatility and destabilization in the world Communist system, brought on largely by the Sino-Soviet dispute, but abetted by Castro's brand of radical nationalism. Soviet global aspirations for superpower status and a projected presence throughout the Third World, based upon expanded state-to-state relations through normal trade and diplomatic ties, were undermined by Castro's insistence on armed struggle at a time of his own growing leadership aspirations within the Third World.

Added to Soviet-Cuban discord over ideology and national interests were their differing perceptions of third party states. Consistent factors in the Soviet-Cuban alliance from the outset and actions by the United States and China strongly conditioned both Moscow and Havana's policy imperatives during the latter half of the 1960s. The Sino-Soviet conflict, in the open by 1960, contributed to the disarray in the international socialist system over which the Brezhnev-Kosygin team sought to bring some order. The U.S. bombing of Vietnam, initiated in early 1965, aggravated

Soviet relations with China, and had a fragmenting impact within the Communist camp where Moscow competed with Peking for Third World leadership. U.S. bombing of North Vietnam brought Chinese criticism of the Soviets for their ineffective responses to the U.S. threat. And Cuba's call in 1966 for "taking all the necessary risks" to combat the United States in Vietnam did not help the Soviet image as leader among embattled Third World movements.[1]

Moscow's relations with an "armed struggle" oriented and maverick communist ally like Cuba were difficult enough under these conditions. They were made more complex by the U.S. invasion of the Dominican Republic in April 1965, which soured Moscow on armed struggle possibilities in Latin America, but convinced Castro all the more that the violent path was necessary in the face of U.S. military power. From the Cuban perspective, the U.S. invasion of the Dominican Republic was simply another manifestation of U.S. military strength in support of the economic, social and political *status quo* in the Caribbean Basin, which they had broken with their own military strength in 1959.

The Dominican Republic episode constituted a distinct security threat for Cuba, coming in the wake of the October 1962 missile crisis and the April 1961 Bay of Pigs invasion, and this time just a few nautical miles off Cuba's shores. The United States had launched the Dominican invasion, fearing that a communist-led movement was at work there, leading to the possibility of "another Cuba" emerging in the Caribbean Basin—something the Lyndon Johnson Administration simply was not prepared to endure. Cuba could not be sanguine about Johnson's legitimizing the U.S. invasion because "the American nations...will not prmit the establishment of another Communist government in the Western Hemisphere."[2] While the fear of communism in the Dominican Republic was enormously exaggerated, the U.S. fear of it led the Johnson Administration to violate its noninterventionist pledge in the Organization of American States Charter, signed in 1948. This violation later produced a sharp negative reaction to U.S. policies in Latin America.[3] In light of Johnson's justification of the invasion in the name of anticommunism, and given his violation of the OAS charter through U.S. unilateral intervention, Castro, like other Central Americans, might logically expect that another round of gunboat diplomacy stalked the region.[4]

The priority of military power and the armed path to change assumed new proportions following the 1965 Dominican Republic episode. If Central and South American political conditions were to be changed as the basis for socioeconomic transformations, the Cubans and their revolutionary allies realized they would have to achieve this feat, as Walter LeFeber stresses, through a mass base and armed struggle against overwhelming U.S. military power.[5] As the decade of the 1960s progressed, the Cubans could judge their possibilities for victory through armed struggle were increasing, for in the wake of negative Latin American reactions to the 1965 intervention, Johnson had begun to stress that the Latin Americans must help themselves, especially in economic integration, the Alliance for Progress was failing, and the region's revolutionary conditions were increasing.

These conditions in Central and South America, coupled with the history of Castro's own armed struggle, help explain the Cuban determination to stress armed struggle as the essential policy for change. In the debate with the Soviets over armed struggle, who better understood the significance of military power in view of the U.S. geopolitical presence and overwhelming military strength? As the Soviets continued with their version of "peaceful coexistence" with the United States, the Cubans were driven to essentially different conclusions, not least by virtue of the geographic-historic position they occupied in the U.S.-dominated Caribbean Basin. The Cubans lived next door to the United States, the Soviets did not.

In spite of the differing policy priorities and consequent strains between the Soviets and the Cubans, neither would cut the relationship. The Soviets had already invested too much in the Cuban regime, an investment over time that argued against breaking relations because of the losses involved and undoubtedly because of competing bureaucratic interests back in the Kremlin. In light of their negative experiences with other Third World leaders, the Soviets needed the Cubans for political legitimacy as the Third World's natural ally, as well as leverage in their global ambitions *vis à vis* the United States and mainland China. Castro, in turn, needed the Soviets to sustain Cuba's economic survival and physical security, as well as to support the pursuit of his own Third World foreign policy objectives.

These years nevertheless were extremely tense, testing the outer boundaries of the relationship. The alliance's limits proved flexible, owing largely to the ways in which each country served the other's vital interests. The limits were capable of absorbing the shocks of influence seeking and power pressures by both the Soviets and Cubans, as long as neither country threatened a combination of the other's first level salient vital interests through assertive or coercive power. The policies that threatened to overload the alliance's capacity to absorb strains were those associated with severe costs *versus* perceived benefits for either party in continuing the affair, e.g. the Soviets exerting too severe coercive economic and military power that could threaten Cuba's very survival, such as sanctions of denied economic and military support or direct intervention in Cuba's political decision making against Castro's will, or massive Cuban inflexibility on the question of armed struggle versus the peaceful path to change, which would greatly threaten second level Soviet vital interests.

This chapter examines influence seeking in the Soviet-Cuban alliance in an effort to disentangle the realities of the Soviet presence in Cuba during the latter half of the 1960s in contrast to the illusion that Soviet power consistently dominated the Cuban government. To do so, we probe the following key dimensions of Soviet-Cuban international relations: (1) emerging Soviet-Third World objectives after Khrushchev; (2) Soviet policy toward Latin America under the Brezhnev-Kosygin leadership; (3) the Soviet-Cuban compromise over armed struggle: the December 1964 agreement; (4) the Tricontinental Conference of January 1966 as a turning point; and (5) tensions between the Tricontinental Conference and the Soviet invasion of Czechoslovakia of August 1968 and renewed Cuban accommodation to Soviet foreign policy.

EMERGING SOVIET-THIRD WORLD
OBJECTIVES AFTER KHRUSHCHEV

Khrushchev's ebullient and optimistic assessments about socialist development potential in the Third World and the benefits in courting these countries produced a mix of successes and failures by the time Brezhnev and Kosygin came to power. On the positive side, Khrushchev established a global strategic presence for the Soviet Union during 1955-64, brought Moscow out of its Stalinist isolation, and inaugurated an era of great power competition with the United States.[6] Khrushchev began to penetrate the developing countries, previously a uniquely Western-influenced arena, with Soviet ideas and material assistance in the quest for new clients in virtually all parts of the globe and in so doing transformed the Third World into an area of great power competition. He raised Soviet prestige as an international actor by turning to developing country needs, and began to develop a sensitivity to the role of nationalism in the Third World and how its anti-Western dimensions might be used to advance Soviet global strategic interest in weakening U.S. power.

But the Khrushchev years led to numerous setbacks for Soviet policy, which deeply challenged the new Soviet leadership and provided the overall context for subsequent tensions with Fidel Castro's Cuba. For one thing, Khrushchev's unorthodox ideological formulations about rapid transformation toward socialist development in the newly independent African and Asian countries proved oversimplified and overoptimistic.[7] Comprehensive ideological conclusions about the diverse economic and social processes evolving in these countries defied easy Marxist-Leninist formulations owing to the enormous variety of countries and their different cultures and stages of development. Nor had scientific socialist development proceeded as rapidly as anticipated in 1955-56 when Khrushchev began to court them. Leaders in a number of these countries, for example, Algeria, Ghana, Guinea, Mali, the U.A.R. and Burma, rejected the idea of allowing communist parties uncontrolled activities in their countries, as implied in Khrushchev's "national democratic state" formula, even though they continued to press the Soviet Union for recognition of their own paths of development. On this basis they could request greater foreign aid from the Soviet Union.[8] In light of these conditions, it is not surprising that the Soviets had begun to feel a certain loss of ideological initiative on the broad question of the future course of national liberation movements toward the end of Khrushchev's rule.

Second, the new Soviet leadership faced increasing disunity within the international socialist movement which affected their evolving policy formation toward Third World countries in general, and Cuba in particular. The Sino-Soviet split formed the greatest source of disunity, but others had emerged in Western Europe (the Italian Communist Party), Eastern Europe (Albania, Rumania), and among Third World states courted by the Soviet Union, as in India's dispute with Pakistan.[9] The Soviets were preoccupied with this disunity because they were deeply concerned with their own domestic development where they needed to concentrate resources. Disputes within the international socialist system, or among Moscow's client states, tended to drag in the Soviets, with a consequent drain on resources needed for development and further erosion of ideological unity. Insofar as Castro's emphasis on armed struggle naturally generated conflict and disunity among Latin American communists and guerrilla revolutionaries, it was much out of tune with Moscow's emerging global policy priorities.

Third, by the time Brezhnev and Kosygin came to power, the Soviets had experienced only limited returns on their economic and political investments in Third World countries. Soviet economic aid had not produced notable economic development in much of its Third World recipients, as in Ghana, Indonesia, Burma, Guinea, Mali, Syria or Iraq.[10] Cuba itself had cost the Soviet Union at least $300 million in credit commitments, plus about $750 million in balance-of-payments assistance by the autumn of 1964, so the prospect of many other "Cubas" economically dependent on the Soviet Union was not a welcome thought in the Kremlin. Meanwhile, many of the aid recipients had not changed their neutral and nonaligned posture toward the Soviet Union, and they had demonstrated little appreciation for Soviet assistance.[11] Added to these shortcomings was the lack of staying power of some leftist regimes, recipients of large-scale Soviet economic and military aid who were overthrown in less than a decade. Cases in point were Mohammed Ben Bella in Algeria (1965); President Sukarno in Indonesia (1965); Kwame Nkrumah in Ghana (1966); and Modibo Keita in Mali (1968).[12] Taken together, these developments contributed to a new caution, pragmatism, and realism which began to emerge in the Kremlin from 1965 onward.

In facing these conditions the Brezhnev-Kosygin team initiated new policies designed to continue Moscow's ambitions as a global power in competition with the United States and China, but with more cautious, pragmatic, and realistic assessments of opportunities for an expanded Soviet presence in the Third World. On the question of regaining ideological initiative, the Soviets adopted more orthodox concepts, such as the important vanguard role played by communist parties, the use of broad united fronts for peaceful change, participation in mass organizations led by the party, and clarity of socialist goals. In dealing with revolutionary states in the Third World, the Soviets became less optimistic about the rapidity of socialist transformation, stressed the problems of socialist development, reassessed Khrushchev's vague ideological formulas, and refused to recognize any country as building socialism that was under noncommunist leadership.[13]

These adjustments provided increased flexibility for the Soviets in dealing with progressive Third World regimes, because even though a revolutionary state may not have been designated as building socialism, depending upon the roles played by the communist party in the movement, they might still be identified as on the noncapitalist path of development. Embarked upon a noncapitalist path of development, a Third World country could be designated as playing an important role in the anti-imperialist movement, making strides toward the prerequisites for socialist development, and yet making it possible for the Soviets to avoid unwelcome economic or political commitments.[14]

At the same time, Moscow began to broaden the base of its relations with nonrevolutionary Third World states on the assumption that they would be around for a long time and might serve shifting Soviet foreign policy objectives. This transition led to new aid, trade, and diplomatic relations with a larger number of developing countries in Africa, Asia, the Middle East, and Latin America. This approach allowed the Soviet Union greater representation in national liberation movements, provided them the opportunity to ride the tides of radical nationalism at work in the post-World War II setting, and allowed for greater flexibility and detachment in world affairs befiting Moscow's aspirations for superpower status. Thus Moscow established relations with Pakistan, the Philippines, Malaysia, Singapore, Sierra Leone, the Ivory Coast, Jordan, and Kuwait, and increased its contacts with Morocco, Libya, Tunisia, Syria, Iraq, and Tanzania. In addition to trade benefits and access to important raw materials, these evolving contacts provided bridge-building contacts throughout the world where the Soviets might acquire foreign port facilities and bases in friendly countries—so necessary in Moscow's growing global power status. The expanding aid, trade, and diplomatic relations in the Third World under Brezhnev-Kosygin vividly illustrate how Soviet national interests as a superpower in quest of strategic parity with the United States increasingly took precedent over the ideological goal of expanding communism.[15]

Accompanying the trend toward broadened contacts in the Third World was the increasing desire by Soviet leaders to avoid entanglement in international disputes involving developing countries.[16] They tended to emphasis peace and stability, avoidance of disputes not directly concerned with fundamental Soviet interests, and the pacific settlement of disputes once they arose. In addition to conserving Soviet resources through this approach, it had the additional benefit of casting the Soviet Union as a responsible and disinterested superpower, advocating peaceful international relations, compared to a militant United States involved in the Vietnam conflict after 1965 and an ultramilitant China as the other extremist in the world. Such a policy seemed well constructed to maximize Soviet prestige among the substantial number of moderate developing countries.

While expanding Soviet trade and diplomatic relations in the Third World, the new leaders determined to hold new aid commitments to a minimum. The $2.1 billion committed in Africa and Asia between 1965 and 1968, albeit equaling the total pledged between 1957 and 1960, was actually a lower amount when expressed as a percentage of the Soviet national product, and fractionally lower than for 1961-64.[17] The Soviets also began to enforce more careful analysis of development projects and to ensure that aid was channeled to those countries best able to utilize it. As might be expected, aid projects also became reflective of changing Soviet national security interests—containment of China (aid to India, Pakistan, North Vietnam, the Philippines, Malaysia, Singapore), maintenance of peace and stability (to allow concentration on economic growth at home), and emphasis on peaceful settlement of disputes. Such an approach to economic policy abroad would help the Soviet Union to promote its own socialist production, facilitate Soviet investments in their strategic and conventional military forces to gain parity with the United States, and avoid becoming overcommitted in potential disaster areas such as Algeria, Indonesia, and Ghana during 1965-66.

SOVIET POLICY TOWARD LATIN AMERICA UNDER BREZHNEV-KOSYGIN

The application of Moscow's Latin American version of its changing Third World diplomacy under Brezhnev-Kosygin provides a fascinating case study of the conditions and issues that could stimulate discord between Moscow and Havana. This post-Khrushchev period, especially during 1966-68, provides additional insight into the techniques and capabilities utilized by each country to attempt to influence the other, the range of benefits and costs each country apparently attached to specific foreign policy issues, and how each country adapted its behavior not only out of response to the other's pressure, but also for reasons less related to influence seeking by one or the other state. These aspects of Soviet-Cuban relations are best assessed by now turning our attention to Soviet objectives and policy techniques adopted for Latin America that generated a number of difficulties for Moscow in trying to manage its special relationship with revolutionary Cuba. What emerges from this Soviet perspective of Latin America, a region in which Cuba formed a growing and significant presence, is how and why Soviet diplomacy in pursuit of Moscow's fundamental national interests conflicted at times with Cuban policy priorities which were in turn linked to Havana's perception of national interests.

Soviet policy in Latin America mirrored the cautious and pragmatic innovations pursued by the Kremlin elsewhere in the Third World. In terms of ideology, the Soviet leaders were at first willing to compromise with Castro's insistence on armed struggle as the correct path to change, increasingly turned against the prospects of guerrilla warfare, especially as the United States escalated its bombing of Vietnam after February 1965 and in the wake of the U.S. invasion of the Dominican Republic in April 1965. This willingness to compromise, recognizing that armed struggle provided a relevant alternative to peaceful change (with communist party participation) is illustrated by the Soviet-Cuban agreement of the December

1964 Communist party conference held in Havana. But as the 1960s progressed, the Soviet Union increasingly stressed the role of broad united fronts, including Communist party participation, and peaceful change toward socialism through parliamentary reforms with an automatic downgrading of armed struggle.[18]

This by no means suggests that Moscow began to stress the role of revolutionary states under active communist party leadership over nonrevolutionary states under bourgeois reformist leadership. The Soviet Union rather sought to expand its trade and diplomatic relations with a range of Latin American countries, matching Kremlin practices in other Third World nonrevolutionary states.[19] The net effect of expanded trade and diplomatic relations with Latin America from 1965 onward is evident in available statistics. Trade rose from $157 million in 1965 to $260 million in 1968, and overall Soviet trade representation also increased.[20] By 1969 Moscow was making firm trade inroads in Argentina, Brazil, Ecuador, Peru, and Uruguay. A more dramatic indication of Soviet focus on Latin America was increased aid, despite Moscow's basic desire to hold new aid commitments in developing countries to a minimum. Moscow extended $85 million in credits to Brazil in 1966, the first large credit to that country; $55 million to Chile in 1967, the only major Soviet aid to developing countries that year and one under bourgeois-reformist leadership (the Christian Democratic government of Eduardo Frei); and a $20 million credit for machinery purchases to Uruguay in 1969.

The Soviets also stepped up their diplomatic activity. Moscow established relations with Peru in January 1969, the first exchange of ambassadors since the Bolshevik Revolution. One year earlier, in January 1968, Colombia had announced the establishment of diplomatic relations with Moscow. Shortly after his election in 1964, Chilean President Eduardo Frei opened diplomatic channels with Moscow after a nineteen year lapse. These ties were in addition to the embassies in Argentina, Brazil, Mexico, and Uruguay. And in late 1969, Bolivia and Ecuador announced plans for the exchange of ambassadors.[21]

These expanded Soviet links with nonrevolutionary countries in Latin America were made possible not only by Moscow's new approach to the Third World. The new leadership's positive attitude toward nonrevolutionary developing countries coincided with evolving trends in Latin America which amounted to great opportunities for the expansion of a Soviet presence. A number of states (Bolivia, Chile, Colombia, Argentina, Brazil, Ecuador, Peru, and Uruguay) either displayed interest in broadening their trade patterns beyond traditional trade partners or began reform programs detrimental to U.S. foreign investments. Chile initiated a powerful domestic reform program in late 1964 after Frei's election, leading to partial nationalization of the copper industry. The new Peruvian government of General Velasco Alvarado expropriated the installations of the International Petroleum Company (IPC) in October 1968. General Alfredo Ovando Candia, who assumed power in Bolivia in September 1968 through a bloodless coup d'état, announced annulment of the petroleum code as an opening step to nationalizing the Gulf Oil Company subsidiary in that country. These events strongly indicated the erosion of the old U.S.-dominated Pan Americanism and as such an opportunity for the Soviets to support these nationalist forces with their anti-American currents.

A SOVIET-CUBAN COMPROMISE OVER ARMED STRUGGLE: THE DECEMBER 1964 AGREEMENT

The problem for the Soviet Union lay in balancing its widening relations among the nonrevolutionary states of Latin America with continued, but more conservative, support for the key revolutionary state, Cuba. The nature of the region's international politics compounded this problem during the latter 1960s. Cuba—the revolutionary state supported by Moscow and in which considerable Soviet investments had been made (including prestige as well as economic and military aid)—was separated from much of Latin America not only by geography. It was excluded from the Organization of American States (OAS) since Februrary 1962. It was the object of U.S. and other Latin American economic sanctions since July 1964. And many Latin American leaders increasingly feared Cuba's insistence on export of violent revolution, as demonstrated by additional O.A.S. resolutions against Cuba in 1967.

None of these situations helped the Soviets in their budding relations with established governments in Latin America, as Cuba increasingly talked about overthrowing them through armed struggle. During and after the Tricontinental Conference, held in Havana in January 1966, Castro moved steadily toward support for violent left-wing guerrilla movements throughout Latin America and condemned the region's pro-Soviet communist parties for lacking in revolutionary leadership. Under these conditions, Cuba's foreign policy priorities, in the context of the Soviet Union's cautious and pragmatic overtures to many Latin American countries on a broadened peaceful state-to-state basis, produced inevitable strains for Moscow. Indeed, the conflict between Moscow and Havana over armed struggle reached confrontation proportions during 1966-68.

A number of perceptive works on Cuban foreign policy document the growing discord between Moscow and Havana from the mid-1960s through the summer of 1968.[22] Essentially it is a story of a period of compromise over armed struggle versus the peaceful path, which began with the December 1964 Conference of Latin American Communist Parties, held in Havana, and lasted for a while thereafter. The compromise held for most of 1965, followed by growing strains initiated during the January 1966 Tricontinental Conference, also held in Havana.

The December 1964 Conference convened at the instigation of the Soviet leaders who sought to achieve three objectives: (1) to isolate China in its continuing bid for Third World leadership over the Soviet Union, by excluding pro-Chinese groups from the Conference, (2) to counter China's relations with Cuba, and (3) to help establish Cuba's leadership in the Latin American communist movement.[23] The first two objectives were important for Moscow insofar as Cuba, following Castro's great displeasure with the outcome of the 1962 missile crisis, had not taken sides in the Sino-Soviet dispute, had continued its friendly relations with China and its pressure on the Soviets for more assistance in return for moderate allegiance to them.[24]

If they could achieve the third objective, the Soviets might be able to neutralize Castro's continued stress on armed struggle after the missile crisis and to moderate his vociferous condemnation of the pro-Soviet Latin American communist parties who were advocating peaceful change. Castro accused these groups during 1963, following the Soviet pullout during the missile crisis and maneuvering to get the most out of the Soviets, of fearing revolutions and of adhering too closely to peaceful transitions, by implication a challenge to the Soviet Union. These parties, Castro said, "are not revolutionary; they are satellites."[25]

Castro's insistence on armed struggle produced notable discord between Havana and Moscow, as well as within the Latin American communist movement. As a consequence, Castro and Khrushchev discussed their differences during their talks in April-June 1963, which resulted in a compromise formula expressed in the joint Soviet-Cuban communiqué of May 23, 1963. In the May 1963 communiqué, Castro and Khrushchev acknowledged that:

> the question of the peaceful or nonpeaceful road toward socialism in one country or another will be definitely decided by the struggling peoples themselves, according to the practical correlation of class forces and the degree of resistance of the exploiting classes to the socialist transformation of society.[26]

But the two governments also agreed that they adhered "to the principle of the noninterference of states in the internal affairs of other countries," a distinct Cuban accommodation to the Soviets.[27]

Castro had good reason to compromise with the Soviets because he was able to use his independent emphasis on armed struggle to extract extremely favorable economic concessions from the Soviet Union. Prior to the May 1963 communiqué, the Cubans had received long-range credits for irrigation and drainage works, another credit for the impending trade imbalance with the Soviets, an agreement to take one million tons from the annual quota assigned to Moscow and sell it on the market in order to earn badly-needed hard currency, and the Soviets had also agreed in the February 1963 trade agreement to pay higher prices for Cuban sugar.[28] As André Suárez notes, Castro, the young rebel, was capable of negotiating with the skill of a horse trader.[29] And the communiqué issued at the conclusion of Castro's second trip to the Soviet Union in January 1964 produced a repeated promise by the Soviets to come to the aid of Cuba in case of aggression.

The Cubans, as appropriately stressed by D. Bruce Jackson, did not abide by their compromise, for by September 1964, Castro again argued openly on the "inevitability" of armed struggle almost everywhere in Latin America.[30] Given the Soviet determination to expand its contacts with the nonrevolutionary states in Latin America, the policy line coming out of Havana could only cause serious irritation. And unlike other socialist countries in the Moscow-led world socialist system, Cuba continued to refrain from criticism of China, and the Cubans refused to sign the treaty on the limited banning of nuclear tests.

The December 1964 Conference of Latin American Communist Parties represented a Soviet compromise with Cuba, because the final Declaration recognized Communist support for armed struggle in six Latin American countries (Venezuela, Colombia, Guatemala, Honduras, Paraguay, and Haiti), where the Cuban counterpart compromise with the Soviets lay in the final Declaration's recognition of the peaceful road as a legitimate path for pro-Soviet communist parties to follow in the rest of Latin America.[31] While many accounts of the 1964 Declaration approach it strictly as a compromise between Moscow and Havana, the "influence" model suggests a different insight into the arrangement worked out between the Soviets and the Cubans, allowing us to discern more the complexity of the interactions occurring between the two countries' political leaders.

The 1964 Declaration actually indicates Soviet influence on Cuba and Cuban influence on the Soviets, a two-way flow of influence over the basic issue of armed struggle versus peaceful change. The Cubans influenced, that is, modified the behavior of the Soviets, just as the Soviets modified the behavior of the Cubans in this December 1964 situation. As for Cuban influence on the Soviets, it is reasonable to assume that the Cubans were instrumental in moving the Soviets to a recognition that armed struggle indeed was appropriate in some cases. Without Cuban pressure, the Soviets undoubtedly would have stressed essentially the peaceful road, emphasizing strictly broad united fronts with Latin American communist party participation, across the board. The Cuban factor modified this behavior in a pronounced direct manner. The Soviets influenced the Cubans, on the other hand, because Castro needed continued economic and military assistance, which the Soviets could deliver. Influence flowed both ways: the influence path from Moscow to Havana also ran from Havana to Moscow, with each country utilizing its available leverage on the other.

It is possible to view the December 1964 accord also as a case of Moscow and Havana checking each other with power, so that the type of influence executed in this case was more *assertive* than *cooperative*. By this is meant that each country modified the behavior of the other through the threat of implied or potential sanctions. Assertive influence, or *power* need not be exercised with applied sanctions, as long as the threat of their application is conceivable and where the threat involves a valued resource.

Khrushchev, by not compromising on the armed struggle with Castro, stood to lose his leverage with this socialist maverick whose insistence on the violent option was contributing to disunity in the communist movement, polarization of debate within the Soviet Union, and a loss of control by the Soviets over the communist parties of Latin America. Given Cuba's prestige in Third World affairs, Castro's position on the relevance of armed struggle and his unwillingness to criticize the Chinese were forms of political power to be used against the Soviets. One can speculate that bureaucratic factions within the Soviet decision-making structure also had a stake in identifying with the Cuban position, which provided another source of influence for Havana. Once the Soviets had initiated their investments in Cuba, moreover, it was crucial to keep the country afloat with economic and military aid in order to maintain it as a model for socialist development. Should the Cuban model fail, it could become an economic and political burden to the Soviets, all of which gave the Cubans leverage over Moscow. The Cubans, meanwhile, could lose much needed economic and military aid, should the Soviets seek to cut it off.

Each country faced potential negative deprivations by not compromising, while a compromise (modified behavior) would protect against these negative outcomes. By modifying their behavior, each country stood to gain specific rewards: continued material aid for Cuba; Soviet leverage over Castro to encourage unity in the communist camp, potentially getting him on the Soviet side against the Chinese and reducing the splitting among the Latin American communist parties. Behind the "compromise" we see struggles for influence at work. The influence analytic framework suggests that the Soviet-Cuban connection demonstrates how, and under what conditions, influence and power can flow both ways, over a specific issue, even when it appears on the surface of events that the superpower "controls" the lesser power.

The Soviet-Cuban compromise over armed struggle versus peaceful change held relatively firm throughout 1965. For the Soviets, their agreement reached in December 1964 seemed to be producing positive outcomes. The Cubans began to show increased displeasure with the Chinese in the Sino-Soviet dispute, Havana attended the important Conference of Communist Parties held in Moscow in March 1965, called largely to isolate China, and in October 1965, Castro converted the United Party of the Socialist Revolution (PURS) into the Communist Party of Cuba (1965), which meant that finally a Communist Party was introduced formally into Cuba, albeit still under the control of Castro and the July 26th Movement. The new PCC followed the model of Communist organizations and must have pleased the Soviets because Cuba had now begun to institutionalize the Cuban Revolution as called for in the new Soviet approach to revolutionary states.

Here we see a case of anticipated reaction on Cuba's part: taking steps on a cooperative influence basis, where Cuba expects to influence Soviet behavior positively through rewards of continued aid to Cuba, the results of which would benefit both Cuba and the Soviet Union. This anticipated response was enhanced by the simultaneous disappearance from public view of Ernesto "Che" Guevara, which aided Cuba's relations with the Soviets. For "Che" Guevara, as one of Fidel's highest decision-making colleagues within the 26th of July Movement, had continued to stress armed struggle imperatives, despite the December 1964 agreement, and notably criticized Soviet trade practices with Third World countries.[32]

But another trend of events during 1965 revealed gathering storm clouds in Soviet-Cuban relations. The Soviet response to U.S. escalated bombing of North Vietnam in February 1965 did not satisfy the Cubans, as indicated by Castro's statement in March 1965 that "we are in favor of the socialist camp taking all the necessary risks for Vietnam."[33] And as noted previously, a Cuban delegate stated at the Twenty-Third Congress of the C.P.S.U., held in March 1966, that in combating U.S. imperialism, one needed to "use all the available means" and must take "the necessary risks." This speech was greeted without applause and even with scattered boos to the more explicit Cuban criticism of Soviet restraint in Vietnam, but the Cubans made their point.[34] Despite the economic and military aid flowing from Moscow to Havana, it is clear that Castro still maintained his independent foreign policy posture on issues of deep sensitivity to the Cubans and that he persistently pressured the Soviets on these matters.

Then came the late April 1965 U.S. invasion of the Dominican Republic, which initially produced only limited Soviet and Cuban reactions—basically protests at the United Nations. This feeble reaction from a notoriously revolutionary Cuba brought Chinese and Trotskyite accusations of Moscow *and* Havana as "revisionists" and not worthy of respect by true Third World and Latin American revolutionaries. As other observers have noted, Castro's embarrassing position undoubtedly made him uneasy and in psychological need of demonstrating his independence of the Soviets as a means to regain favor among Latin America's insurrectionist groups who had provided Castro with his most powerful backing.[35]

These Cuban perceptions must have been enhanced by Moscow's subsequent efforts to press the older popular front tactics and peaceful road thesis, since by then their primary objective of isolating China at the December 1964 Conference seemed to have been achieved as demonstrated by the growing Cuban-Chinese conflict and the declining role or pro-Chinese groups in Latin American politics. In any case, the Soviet-backed international communist apparatus sharply escalated the theme of popular fronts and peaceful change after the April 1965 Dominican crisis.[36] Soviet activities suggest decreasing belief in the potential of armed struggle, an attitude reinforced by the U.S. action in the Dominican Republic and the series of guerrilla defeats in Latin America throughout 1965, despite their emphasis on the armed struggle approach. It must be said, however, that the Soviets continued to pay a certain degree of lip service to the concept of armed struggle in specific Latin American countries, for example, Venezuela, Peru, Colombia, and Guatemala, during late 1965 and early 1966.[37] As for Cuba, their actions at the January 1966 Tricontinental Conference suggest a growing determination to accentuate once again the preeminence of armed struggle.

THE TRICONTINENTAL CONFERENCE OF JANUARY 1966: A TURNING POINT

From the Tricontinental Conference of January 1966 to the Soviet invasion of Czechoslovakia in August 1968, the Soviet-Cuban relationship entered a period of intense strain over conflicting policy priorities centered on armed struggle versus peaceful change. This era offers a unique opportunity to study the relations between a great power and "weaker" power, in terms of not only the power capabilities of the "dominant" country, but also of the "weaker" state. What emerges are a number of insights: (1) that the apparently "weaker" country in fact possesses valuable resources which can be utilized in an influence setting; (2) that the dominant power is limited and checked in its influence seeking by its client's own influence capabilities which render it less susceptible to the patron's apparent power; and (3) that the "weaker" state can enjoy a margin of independence in its foreign policy—provided a wide range of other factors (beyond its relations with the dominant power) do not necessitate a realignment of its foreign policy more in tune with the wishes of the donor country.

What type of influence resources did Cuba possess as it entered the period of conflict with Soviet foreign policy at the outset of 1966? The answer lies in a key aspect of the influence relationship, namely the *perception* of each country's capabilities *vis à vis* the other's policy priorities. The exercise of actual influence by either the Soviet Union or Cuba over the other is in part a function of attributed power capabilities that either country's leaders perceives in the other. These perceptions are in turn a consequence of past events in both countries, the nature of the contemporary situation, and the type of interests and issues at stake at any specific moment in time.

A number of Cuba's influence capabilities relative to the Soviets came into play during this period. Recall that the December 1964 conference of Latin American Communist parties was organized in Havana under the leadership of Cuba's new PURS. This event established Cuba's primacy among the Latin American communist parties, not a small matter in terms of Havana's political power. Castro and his 26th of July Movement followers also continued to dominate Cuba's communist party, despite its outward manifestations of appearing more in the socialist mold espoused by Moscow. And within the 26th of July Movement, Castro was the *líder máximo*, a charismatic figure with devoted followers prepared to support his decisions. Here again we see a source of Castro's political strength, in this case the power of *personalismo,* a phenomenon familiar in the Hispano-Catholic culture which produces political parties and interest groups more around strong charismatic leaders than in terms of party platforms and bureaucratic organization.

Castro could draw upon other sources of leverage. Numerous Marxist-Leninist groups in Latin America sided with the Cubans on the role of armed struggle versus peaceful change. These included the Chilean Socialist Party, some elements in the Colombian Communist Party, and various guerrilla groups throughout Latin America, notably in Venezuela under Douglas Bravo's leadership. In the debate over armed struggle, Castro was distinctly not without his political resources. And while Cuba was dependent on Soviet economic and military aid, the Soviet Union's influence over Havana was greatly limited by its need of Cuba in the continuing Sino-Soviet rift and long-run desire to weaken U.S. imperialism.[38]

The Tricontinental Conference is the subject of considerable discussion in other studies, and we need not detail its daily meetings and internal conflicts again here.[39] But by highlighting the Soviet-Cuban foreign policy conflict at the Conference, we can capture the essence of the divergent trends set in motion during those days. The Soviets intended to use the Conference once again to pursue their old objectives: to reduce Chinese influence in the Third World, to check China's influence with Cuba, and to strengthen Cuba's prestige in Latin America and elsewhere in the Third World, which in turn could help solidify Soviet-Cuban relations.[40]

Given the state of Soviet-Cuban affairs, which on balance must have seemed favorable to the Soviets during much of 1965, Moscow apparently did not suspect a radical departure in Cuban foreign policy. The Soviets hoped that the Conference would lead to the formation of a new three-continent organization to replace the previous Afro-Asian People's Solidarity Organization (AAPSO), founded in the early 1960s, which did not include Latin America and in which the Chinese competed vigorously with the Soviets for influence. The new organization would include Latin America under vanguard leadership provided by Cuba and thus a counterpoint to the Chinese. As it turned out, the Cubans did not buy the idea, electing instead to create a parallel organization entitled the Latin American Solidarity Organization (LASO), and thus avoiding all the tensions associated with the creation of a new organization. A Cuban-Chinese rift did develop during the Conference, but over Cuban-Chinese bilateral relations when the Chinese lowered their rice supplies to Cuba.[41]

Cuba entertained foreign policy objectives at the Tricontinental Conference distinctly different from the Soviets, which became clear in Havana's reassertion of armed struggle as the dominant path to change for national liberation movements. Castro hoped, first, to impress the Soviets with the continued importance of armed struggle, which he had long advocated. What was new in the shift was Cuba's assertive emphasis on the issue, not the issue itself. Castro's new militancy on armed struggle occurred for good reasons, most notably the need to keep the leverage on Moscow for continued economic and military support of Castro's Revolution. For Castro could see by early 1966 that Moscow's commitment to Cuba's brand of armed struggle was lagging, made evident by the Soviet's unimpressive reaction to U.S. activities in Vietnam and the Dominican Republic. The pro-Soviet Latin American communist parties, moreover, were disassociating themselves with Cuba.

Other causes for concern in Havana by the end of 1965 can be identified.[42] The Cubans, despite Soviet public pronouncements, still had no absolutely certain security guarantees from the Soviets, neither in the form of a bilateral defense treaty nor membership in the Warsaw Pact. Previous trade arrangements with the Soviets left the Cubans under conditions of continuing uncertainty, because the yearly levels of trade had to be negotiated through annual trade protocols, with the Castro government left in an unfavorable bargaining position.[43] These signs of a lag in Soviet support of the Cuban position, coupled with the previous Soviet missile crisis behavior, from the Cuban perspective meant that some means was necessary to keep the pressure on Moscow for continued support of Cuba, which was still engaged in a survival struggle with the United States, which by now had greatly stepped up its armed intervention in Vietnam—a matter of no small urgency from Cuba's highly salient security interests, as discussed in Chapter one. Castro, meanwhile, was eager to move on with his own brand of economic development, which required massive external aid. Emphasis on armed guerrilla struggle was one way to put pressure on the Soviets in pursuit of Cuba's domestic and foreign policy objectives.

The Cubans also felt pressed to demonstrate to other Third World revolutionaries that they had not become passive within the Soviet embrace, thereby reinforcing Havana's vanguard revolutionary credentials in Latin America and the Third World. In strengthening Havana's revolutionary leadership, the Cubans also hoped to improve their bargaining position with the Soviets, who would be reminded publicly of their internationalist responsibilities to this leading Third World communist regime—no small matter in the Soviet's ongoing polemics with the Chinese over leadership of the socialist camp. Finally, the Cubans must have felt a need not necessarily to influence the Soviet Union so much as to assert a certain independence from Moscow, as a natural result of the history and dynamism of their own nationalist-communist revolutionary process and Castro's charismatic leadership.

In probing the origins of these goals and the Cuban switch to militant support of the armed struggle path, consider the following. The previous months had produced growing Cuban sensitivity to accusations that the Cuban Revolution had sold out to the Soviets, making it no longer a leader of revolutionary principles and actions.[44] Fidel's closing speech at the Tricontinental Conference denounced what he perceived as a campaign against the Cuban Revolution, which characterized it as "Sovietophile."[45] Cuba's aspirations for greater leadership within the Third World seemed undermined by Havana's close association with Moscow and the compromises reached by the two countries on the issue of armed struggle versus peaceful change. Cuba's participation in AAPSO, along with North Vietnam and North Korea, likely inspired Castro in this direction. A stepped-up emphasis on armed struggle, the Cuban leadership could reason, would recapture revolutionary leadership, demonstrate independence from the Soviet Union, and allow Cuba to take a vanguard Third World position in the heritage of previous AAPSO hosts as Gamal Abdel Nasser, Sékou Touré, Julius Nyerere, and Kwame Nkrumah.

As Cuba's public statements at the Tricontinental Conference progressed in their militancy, the Soviets looked on in virtual confusion.[46] The Cubans pressed the matter of the Soviet Union's *duty* to aid "liberation movements" through specific commitments, tried in various ways to strengthen the status of the visiting guerrilla delegation from Venezuela (now deep in internal differences with the pro-Soviet Venezuelan Communist Party), and increased their emphasis on the armed struggle thesis. As the Soviets listened to Castro's closing speech, it was clear that Havana had launched a militant brand of revolutionary leadership at odds with Soviet caution. Castro said that

> ...sooner or later all or almost all peoples will have to take up arms to liberate themselves....What with the ones who theorize and the ones who criticize those who theorize while beginning to theorize themselves, much energy and time is unfortunately lost; we believe that on this continent, in the case of all or almost all peoples, the battle will take on the most violent forms.[47]

BETWEEN THE TRICONTINENTAL CONFERENCE AND THE SOVIET INVASION OF CZECHOSLOVAKIA: CUBA ON THE OFFENSIVE

Cuba's foreign policy efforts following the Tricontinental Conference indicate continued goal seeking along the lines identified above. The Cubans began to participate in international communist front organizations, in which they previously absented themselves, organized the LASO, to be located in Havana, and strengthened relations with other radical nationalist countries like North Korea and North Vietnam. Throughout this period they insisted on the preeminence of armed struggle, while lashing out against the pro-Soviet Latin American communist parties and bourgeois reformist governments courted by the Soviet Union.

Numerous sources of evidence illustrate this new militancy in Cuban foreign policy. In July-August 1966, the Castro government castigated the socialist countries for their relations with Eduardo Frei of Chile, and in early 1967 renewed its criticism of the Soviet Union for maintaining relations with the "oligarchies" of Latin America, which included Colombia and Venezuela.[48] Throughout 1966 Havana broadcasted a series of interviews with Latin American guerrilla leaders from Guatemala, Colombia, Venezuela, and the Dominican Republic, stressing in each interview that the predominant struggle for national liberation must be armed struggle. And throughout 1966 the Cuban government continued a drive for recognition of the Venezuelan guerrilla movement rather than the Communist party, which was now advocating the more conventional "broad front" tactics. In addressing the Venezuelan and other pro-Soviet communist parties, Castro argued that " . . . what defines a Communist is his action against the oligarchies, action against imperialism and, on this continent, action in the armed revolutionary struggle."[49] Havana repeatedly called on the peoples of Haiti and the Dominican Republic to revolt.

When the Cuban-sponsored Latin American Solidarity Organization (LASO) meetings convened in Havana in August 1967, its participants were left-wing extremists from throughout the hemisphere. The Cuban-initiated final declaration made clear Havana's continued pressure on and independence from the Soviets on the question of armed struggle. The final declaration stated:

> . . . that making the Revolution constitutes a right and a duty of the peoples of Latin America. . . . That armed revolutionary struggle constitutes the fundamental course of the Revolution in Latin America. . . . That all other forms of struggle must serve to advance and not to retard the development of this fundamental course, which is armed struggle. . . . That, for the majority of the countries of the continent, the problems of organizing, initiating, developing and crowning the armed struggle at present constitutes the immediate and fundamental task of the revolutionary movement.[50]

The final document ended with the declaration that "the duty of every revolutionary is to make the revolution."

During most of 1966 the Soviet Union surprisingly reacted to Castro's challenges in a relatively low-key manner, apparently reluctant to enter too sharply into a debate with the Cuban leader, perhaps not wishing to alienate this highly valuable client in the western hemisphere. But in January 1967 the Cuban challenge to Soviet theory about the peaceful path to socialist reached a new level of intensity, a higher level of Cuban pressure, that is, with the publication of Regis Debray's book *Revolution within the Revolution,* which laid out in detail the Cuban thesis about armed struggle. In systematically expounding the theory of armed struggle, emphasizing the mobile guerrilla unit, the guerrilla *foco,* Debray's book essentially postulated the method used by Cuba to attain victory. Thus the Cuban model was now advanced as the most significant method for revolutionary change in Latin America. This new Cuban challenge was destined to stir Soviet reactions, for it criticized the subjection of the guerrilla movement to the pro-Soviet communist parties of Latin America, advancing military and political action as more appropriately placed under guerrilla control rather than under communist party control. With this new assertion of Cuban authority, the compromise reached back in December 1964 clearly was relegated to the dust bin—at least as far as the Cubans were concerned.[51]

Debray's book challenged the Soviet and pro-Soviet communist parties' positions on the importance of Marxist-Leninist principles, downgraded the need for guerrillas to know Marxism-Leninism as the key to their military pursuits, and promoted a global policy demanding submission to the Cuban model of revolutionary struggle.[52] From this point onward, it became increasingly difficult for the Soviets to remain passive about Castro's growing insistence on the primacy of armed struggle, especially following the LASO conference. Here was a Cuba now seeking to assume the vanguard position in the Third World revolutionary movement in opposition to the Soviet tactics, shifting its policies toward Vietnam and the Latin American movements and challenging basic precepts of Marxism-Leninism. By 1967 Castro's assertive power was beginning to penetrate higher level salient interests of the Soviet Union, namely its own leadership position in the socialist community and Third World revolutionary movements. Certainly Castro challenged the Soviet theory of revolutionary democracy, because Castro now had placed revolutionary democrats in opposition to, rather than compatible with, the communists.[53] And this situation was unfolding while Soviet economic aid continued to flow—not an especially enviable position in which the Soviets found themselves.

The year 1968 began with continued Soviet-Cuban strains. Castro purged a group of Cuban communists, a "microfaction" allegedly led by the old pro-Soviet disciple, Aníbal Escalante and several "old guard" pro-Soviet communists. The highly publicized purge produced a report by Major Raúl Castro to the Central Committee of the Cuban Communist Party that contained direct anti-Soviet statements and supported, by clear implication, sources of attempted Soviet influence in Cuban domestic and foreign policy—not surpising in view of Cuba's challenge to Soviet control of the Latin American communist parties.[54] One of the major accusations against the microfaction was its contacts with officials of "foreign governments," which included the Soviet Union. In responding to this situation, the Cuban attorney general summarized his argument as follows:

> As for the USSR, no one can fail to respect Lenin's party and that heroic country that bravely withstood the shock of the terrible wars that afflicted it. However, when our revolution demands to think with its own head, we are not failing to pay that respect; we are merely requesting the right to think and act for ourselves.... If there is anything that irritates us, it is the servility of these gentlemen who want to deny our fatherland the right to think about and decide its own problems and those of the world. Our revolution was born among our own people and developed by them by their own effort.... *No one can call us a satellite state and that is the reason we are respected in the world.*[55]

The February 1968 trial reconfirmed Castro's commitment to revolutionary violence in Latin America, strengthening the new alliance of many noncommunist revolutionary groups under his control through the Cuban-led LASO, challenging the vanguard role of the pro-Soviet communists, and attacking reform regimes and Soviet efforts to improve relations with these governments.[56]

Independence from Soviet influence, as underscored by the microfaction affair, became a predominant theme in Cuban policy statements and actions in 1967 and 1968. When Soviet Premier Aleksei N. Kosygin visited Cuba in late June 1967, the first ever to do so, he received a remarkably cool reception. He was met at the José Martí airport with little fanfare, no crowds and no cheering, a prelude for lacklustre treatment by the Cuban news media of the entire visit.[57] Several days after Kosygin's visit came two notable speeches, one on July 24 by Commandante Raúl Castro (Second Secretary of the Central Committee of the Cuban Communist Party) and another by Fidel Castro on July 26th. On Cuban-Soviet relations, Raúl Castro stated:

...relations between Cuba and the USSR can only exist on the basis of the strictest mutual respect and absolute independence, and it is on this basis that they were born, are maintained today, and will always be maintained...we do not have a daddy; our nation does not have a daddy....Must the security of a people, in this case its very existence, depend exclusively on aid from abroad? We think not. Why? Because this would bring our people to the dangerous habit of having others solve our problems.[58]

This concept of Cuban independence in foreign policy was followed two days later when Castro spoke of national commitment and motivation in moving Cuba forward, not dependence on outside aid:

That essential characteristic of the revolutionary movement which began that day (July 26 attack on the Moncada barracks) is today also the essential characteristic of our revolution; the confidence of the people in themselves, the faith of the people in their cause....[59]

In both of these speeches, the Castro brothers went on to stress that external support is good, but nothing will ever be better than Cuba's own efforts and that if Cuba were in a war situation, it would have to fight alone.

How did the Soviets react to Castro's assertive power seeking? It is clear that the Soviets began to utilize their economic and diplomatic pressure during 1967 and 1968, in ways beyond the microfaction evidence, to modify Castro's foreign policy. Castro announced on January 2, 1968 that gasoline rationing and other curbs on oil consumption were necessary because of the inadequacy of Soviet deliveries. He emphasized that Cuban oil needs rose 8 percent during 1967, while Soviet supplies rose only 2 percent. In early January, the Soviets also appointed one of its senior diplomats, Alexander A. Soldatov, a former ambassador to Britain, to be the new Soviet representative in Cuba. This appointment can be interpreted as a major attempt to improve relations with Castro, although not to pacify him. *Pravda* had by this time made quite clear that Moscow did not agree with Castro's position on armed struggle by vigorously defending Soviet trade with the very countries Castro sought to overthrow through revolutionary violence.[60] And when Moscow and Havana eventually signed their trade agreement in March 1968, it called for an increase in trade of only 10 percent, compared to the 23 percent in the trade agreement of 1967.[61] In May 1968, *Pravda* launched a broad condemnation of worldwide student violence, which by implication included Cuba's armed struggle thesis. *Pravda* condemned the "New Left" and all "reactionaries who follow the writings of men who call for revolutionary change of the entire social system" and praised the nonrevolutionary call of the French Communists for a united front with all forces favoring democratic change.[62]

The Soviets reacted to Castro's challenge with their own form of assertive power, which took the form of a reduction in Soviet supplies. The Soviets might have reacted more intensely with coercive power, for example, a dramatic shut down of economic support; that they did not illustrates the continuing significance of Cuba to the Soviets and the Soviet desire to mend relations owing precisely to that significance. But here we see the importance of *perceptions* in foreign policy behavior, because from Castro's perspective, the Soviet's limited sanctions were received in Havana as a major economic reprisal.[63] Indeed the "microfaction" affair of February 1968 was one method utilized by Castro to vent his anger over Soviet economic santions that had led to gas rationing in January.

That the Soviets did not resort to coercive power against Cuba during 1966-68 undoubtedly stemmed in part from Moscow's own improving relations with the rest of Latin America during this period, coupled with Cuba's growing isolation in the region relative to established governments. Soviet trade, aid, and diplomatic relations expanded in Latin America from 1965 onward, as evident in available statistics. Trade rose to $157 million in 1968, and overall Soviet trade representation increased.[64] By 1969 Moscow was making new trade inroads in Argentina, Brazil, Ecuador, Peru, and Uruguay. Aid extensions also increased, with the Soviet Union extending $85 million in credits to Brazil in 1966, the first large credit to that country; $55 million to Chile in 1967, the only major Soviet aid to developing countries that year; and a $20 million credit for machinery purchases went to Uruguay in 1969.[65]

Soviet diplomatic activity improved with Latin America during this period. In 1964, the Chilean President, Eduardo Frei, opened diplomatic channels with Moscow, after a nineteen year lapse. Colombia announced the establishment of diplomatic relations with the Soviets in January 1968, and in January 1969 the Soviets and Peruvians exchanged ambassadors for the first time since the Bolshevik Revolution. In late 1969, Bolivia and Ecuador announced plans for the exchange of ambassadors. These improved relations, in the context of Cuba's growing isolation, left the Soviets in a unique position to allow the Castro government to generate it own negative pressures in Latin America which sooner or later might bring the Cubans back toward policies more compatible with those of Soviet Union—which began to happen by the middle of 1968.

THE SOVIET INVASION OF CZECHOSLOVAKIA IN AUGUST 1968: RENEWED ACCOMMODATIONS

The Cubans surprisingly declared their support of the August 1968 Soviet invasion of Czechoslovakia. This was remarkable evidence of the beginning of a new rapprochement in Soviet-Cuban relations, that the competing types of assertive influence on each other by Moscow and Havana were soon to be moderated in yet another round of accommodation to the vital interests of each country. The two states began to praise their "fraternal friendship," and they demonstrated a new accord through formation of a Cuban-Soviet Friendship Association in April 1969. Seven Soviet warships visited Havana to help celebrate the 26th of July and in November 1969, 650 Soviet technicians and diplomats participated in one day's work in the Cuban cane fields. Much fanfare attended the Soviet naval fleet visit, itself a demonstration of Moscow's interest in Cuban security, as was the visit of Andrei A. Grechko, Defense Minister of the Soviet Union, in November—all a sharp contrast to the low-key treatment of Soviet Premier Alexei Kosygin's June-July visit in 1967.

Evidence of this new phase is clear in other events. Major speeches during 1969 relegated acknowledged problems between Moscow and Havana to the past.[66] Second, a defector from Castro's intelligence network reported in July 1969 that Castro had signed an accord with Moscow in 1968 committing himself to a pro-Moscow line, in return for which the Soviet Union agreed not to diminish its economic support to Cuba and would supply 5,000 technicians to work in Cuba's faltering economy— in which the Soviets had a clear prestige stake as noted earlier. Third, party events inside Cuba began to urge the necessity to strengthen the party and its mass organizations at all levels, referring in some cases to the Soviet experience as the example to be followed.[67] A stress on party unity and renewed building of base organizations, rather than on the differences of Cuban communism from other brands of Marxism-Leninism, which Castro had accentuated in 1968, revealed a surprising convergence of Soviet and Cuban views.[68] It is difficult to find direct evidence of Soviet influence on Cuba's party organization; the orthodoxy advocated by Moscow was gradually beginning to be reproduced in Cuba.

The big question is whether or not the Soviet assertive power forced Castro to moderate his insistence on armed struggle and return to the fold of Soviet socialist orthodoxy. Certainly Soviet power applied to Cuba's first and second level of salient vital interests cannot be ignored. But to leave the matter simply at that does not adequately reflect the dynamics at work during this period.

It was not Soviet influence alone that so distinctly modified Cuban behavior from the Soviet invasion of Czechoslovakia onward. For various domestic and external regional pressures on the Cuban leadership had been building up for some time, which led to a revision of policy toward accommodation with the Soviets. On the domestic front, the 1968 sugar harvest by mid-March was almost a million tons below the previous mid-March total for 1967, and a far cry from the eight-million ton sugar harvest goal set for the year. And as reported later in 1969, a number of social and economic problems were besetting the government. These included worker apathy bordering on passive resistance, absenteeism, lack of discipline, shoddy work, low labor productivity, disorganization and carelessness with equipment.[69] Other difficulties ranged from juvenile delinquency to crime, truancy and growing illiteracy.[70] These internal difficulties, in light of Castro's desire to produce a ten million ton sugar harvest in 1970 helped condition a new predilection toward accommodation with the Soviets in order to ensure continued and higher economic aid from the Soviet Union.

The regional international setting of mid-1968 undoubtedly contributed to Castro's reassessment of his foreign policy tactics. Castro's theory of armed struggle in the hemisphere produced strong condemnation from other Latin American governments, while the theory of armed struggle had not been translated into notable victories. Ernesto "Che" Guevara's activities had failed in Bolivia, illustrating a misinterpretation of the specific conditions for revolution in that country. Bolivian peasants did not respond well to Che's plans, while support from the Bolivian Communist party was lukewarm at best. Che's death in October 1967 helped confirm Moscow's and the pro-Soviet Latin American communist parties' argument that power could best be attained, at least in this period, through peaceful united fronts. Meanwhile, as if to add credence to this argument, other guerrilla movements were not doing well. The guerrillas in Venezuela were less numerous and less active than previously, the guerrillas in Guatemala were on the defensive, and LASO had become noticeably ineffective. Castro may well have concluded from these events— added to Soviet pressures—that a shift in policy toward accommodation with the Soviet Union was in Cuba's best long-range interests.

The renewed accommodation with the Soviets soon began to take form after Castro gave his backing to the Warsaw Pact's invasion of Czechoslovakia on August 23, 1968. Cuba's criticism of Latin America's reformist governments became less frequent and more circumspect. Havana even began to laud Peru's new military regime, which deposed President Fernando Belaúnde Terry in October 1968. This reorientation coincided with the first Soviet-Peruvian accord of February 1969. Decreased criticism of Chile followed, as it did with Venezuela. These steps were inspired not only by Soviet pressure, but undoubtedly as a means to overcome Cuba's hemisphere isolation.

In an effort to restore good relations with the Soviet Union, other steps were taken. Beginning in November 1968, *Granma Weekly Review* began a positive approach to Soviet domestic and foreign policies. And in a press conference held in Lima, Peru, by Carlos Rafael Rodríquez, a high ranking member of the Cuban Communist party, Cuba's new orientation to armed struggle became public:

> Cuba believes that armed struggle is the fundamental instrument for the advancement of the revolutionary process in the vast majority of the Latin American countries. This concept has often been misinterpreted in the belief that it means that armed struggle is indispensable in each and every country of Latin America. *We consider that there may be cases in which this is not so. Uruguay has been cited as such a possibility. In the specific conditions of Latin America there is even the chance of electoral victories. This is the hypothetical case of Chile.* . . . [71]

This statement placed Cuba much more in line with the traditional pro-Soviet Latin American communist parties and with the Soviet Union itself. And in June 1969, Cuba attended the Conference of Communist Parties in Moscow, called to line up international communist support behind the Soviets in their running battle with the Chinese. Cuba's representative at this conference, Carlos Rafael Rodríguez, stated that, like the other pro-Soviet communist parties of Latin America,

> The Communist Party of Cuba is convinced of the importance of the unity of action of the Communists, of all anti-imperialist forces in order to develop, utilizing all new possibilities, to the maximum degree, a broader offensive against imperialism and the forces of reaction and war. . . [72]

In April 1970, Castro honored the Soviets again by noting that it would have been impossible for Cuba to become the first socialist country in Latin America without Soviet aid. He praised the Soviets for their supportive help to Vietnam, the Middle East, and Cuba. He stated that Cuba's ties with the Soviets were unshakeable, and he observed that his government had received $1.5 billion in Soviet arms, free of charge over the years. [73]

The Cubans reaped economic benefits from their new accommodations to Soviet policy. The Soviets signed trade protocols with the Cubans in 1969 and 1970, providing long-term Soviet credits to cover Cuba's rising trade deficits with the Soviet Union. This marked a change from the 1968 trade protocol, which clamped down on the volume of Soviet-Cuban trade, as discussed above. Given Cuba's need for Soviet assistance to continue its high powered developmental programs, Castro's shift in policy paid handsome dividends. Given the Soviet position as Cuba's chief trading power—even during the 1966-68 period of stress—Cuba's new accommodation illustrates pragmatic decision making in Cuba.[74]

CONCLUSIONS

In assessing the results of the overall events during 1966-68, several points merit attention. First, the influence capacity of the weaker state must be evaluated in relations between a presumed "dominant" state and the lesser client. Cuba enjoyed a certain leverage over the Soviet Union, which it attempted to use during this period. That the Soviets did not break relations with the Cubans, but rather continued their economic and military assistance, suggests substantial influence on the part of the lesser country.

Second, although Cuba exerted its influence, the Soviets did not modify their behavior to fit Cuba's asserted policy priorities on armed struggle. Thus, although Cuba enjoyed a certain leverage with the Soviets, they reached the other limits of their influence, as the Soviets began to respond with their own brand of economic and diplomatic influence on Cuba. In the end, Cuba modified its behavior, largely out of need for sustained, even increased, Soviet economic support in order to continue their ambitious developmental goals and to guarantee Cuba's physical security against the United States. Clear limits to Cuba's influence over Moscow emerged during these years, just as the limits to Moscow's influence on Cuba were apparent during the period.

Third, Castro altered his behavior not strictly as a result of Soviet pressure but as a result of other third party forces and internal pressures. These included Cuba's growing isolation in the Latin American community, the difficulties in their social and economic system, and the general failure of the guerrilla armed struggle movement in various parts of Latin America. The Soviets by no means dominated Cuba during this era, and in the end Castro altered his foreign policy tactics to fit the changing conditions, in the long run pursuit of his own constant foreign policy goals and indigenous sense of national communism. By the beginning of the decade of the 1970s, Cuba and the Soviet Union brought their foreign policies back into a shared alignment of mutual interests, having tested the outer parameters of compatible priorities.

NOTES

1. *Twenty-third Congress of the Communist Party of the Soviet Union* (Moscow: 1966); I, p. 222.

2. See *The New York Times,* May 3, 1965, for the text of Johnson's speech.

3. See Walter LaFeber's insightful analysis of this period in his book, *Inevitable Revolutions: The United States in Central America* (New York: W.W. Norton, 1983), pp. 158-59.

4. Ibid.

5. Ibid.

6. See Leo Tansky, "Soviet Foreign Aid to the Less Developed Countries," in *New Directions in the Soviet Economy.* Studies Prepared for the Subcommittee on Foreign Economic Policy of the Joint Economic Committee, Congress of the U.S., 89th Congress, Part IV, *The World Outside* (1960), pp. 947-74; Roger E. Kanet, ed., *The Soviet Union and the Developing Countries* (Baltimore: Johns Hopkins University Press, 1974), chap. 2; and W. Raymond Duncan, *Soviet Policy in Developing Countries* (Walthan, Mass.: Ginn-Blaisdell, 1970).

7. R. A. Yellon, "Shifts in Soviet Policy Toward Developing Areas 1964-1968," in Duncan, *Soviet Policy in Developing Countries,* pp. 225-86; Kanet, *Soviet Union; and The Soviet Union and the Third World: A Watershed in Great Power Policy?* Report to the Committee on International Relations, House of Representatives, by the Senior Specialists Division, Congressional Research Service, Library of Congress (May 8, 1977) Washington, D.C.: (U.S. Government Printing Office, 1977) pp. 17-19.

8. R. A. Yellon, "The Winds of Change," *Mizan,* 9 (1967): 158-59.

9. Adam B. Ulam, *Expansion and Coexistence: Soviet Foreign Policy, 1917-73. 2nd ed.* (New York: Praeger, 1974) chap. 12.

10. Yellon, "Shifts in Soviet Policy" in Duncan, *Soviet Policy.*

11. Ibid., pp. 237-38.

12. See *The Soviet Union and the Third World: A Watershed in Great Power Policy?* p. 29.

13. See Kanet, *Soviet Union,* selected chapters; and Duncan, *Soviet Policy,* selected chapters.

14. Yellon, "Shifts in Soviet Policy" in Duncan, *Soviet Policy,* pp. 282-84.

15. See Vernon V. Aspaturian, "Soviet Foreign Policy at the Crossroads: Conflict and/or Collaboration?," *International Organization,* 23, no. 3 (Summer 1969): 589-620; and Alvin Z. Rubinstein, "Soviet Policy Toward the Third World in the 1970s," *Orbis,* 25, no. 1 (Spring 1971): 104-17.

16. Yellon, "Shifts in Soviet Policy," in Duncan, *Soviet Policy,* p. 275.

17. Ibid., p. 278.

18. W. Raymond Duncan, "Soviet Policy in Latin America Since Khrushchev," *Orbis,* 15, no. 2 (Summer 1971): 643-69.

19. See Mark N. Katz, *The Third World in Soviet Military Thought* (London and Canberra: Croom Helm, 1982).

20. See Wolfgang Berner, "Castro and Moscow's Latin America Strategy," *Aussenpolitik,* (June 1968), pp. 357-67; and Herbert Dinerstein, "Soviet Policy in Latin America," *American Political Science Review* (March 1967), pp. 80-90.

21. Another indication of Soviet interest was the decision to publish a new scientific and political journal, *Latin America,* every other month, edited by the Latin American Institute of the Academy of Sciences. The first issue appeared on February 4, 1970.

22. Jacques Levesque, *The USSR and the Cuban Revolution: Soviet Ideological and Strategic Perspectives, 1959-77* (New York: Praeger, 1978); D. Bruce Jackson, *Castro, the Kremlin, and Communism in Latin America* (Baltimore: Johns Hopkins Press, 1969); Stephen Clissold, *Soviet Relations with Latin America, 1918-1968; A Documentary Survey* (London: Oxford University Press, 1970); J. Gregory Oswald and Anthony J. Strover, eds., *The Soviet Union and Latin America* (New York: Praeger, 1970); J. Gregory Oswald, *Soviet Image of Contemporary Latin America: A Documentary History, 1960-1968* (Austin: The University of Texas Press, 1970).

23. See Levesque, *USSR and Cuban Revolution,* pp. 103-04.

24. See Jackson, *Castro, Kremlin, and Communism,* p. 19.

25. Cited in *Le Monde,* March 22 and 23, in Castro's interview with the French journalist, Claude Julien, as republished in Jackson, *Castro, Kremlin, and Communism,* p. 21.

26. "Declaracion conunta sovietico-cubana," *Cuba Socialista,* (June 1963), pp. 17-18.

27. *Pravda,* May 24, 1963.

28. Andrés Suárez, *Cuba: Castroism and Communism, 1959-1966* (Cambridge, Mass.: M.I.T. Press, 1967), pp. 178-79.

29. Ibid., p. 179.

30. See Castro's speech of September 10, 1964, in *Obra Revolucionaria,* 20 (1964): 24.

31. *Pravda,* January 19, 1965. The precise date of the conference is unknown, *Pravda's* communiqué mentions that the conference occurred "in late 1964."

32. Levesque, *USSR and Cuban Revolution,* p. 109.

33. Speech by Fidel Castro, March 13, 1965, in *Pravda,* March 18, 1965.

34. Twenty-third Congress of the Communist Party of the Soviet Union (Moscow: 1966), I., p. 222.

35. See Jackson, *Castro, Kremlin, and Communism,* p. 35.

36. See the August 1965 issue of *World Marxist Review.*

37. G. Starushenko, "The Struggle Against Neocolonialism is the Business of Every People," *Kommunist* 3 (February 1966): 109-17.

38. A similar situation exists in Soviet–Vietnamese relations, where the relationship is shaped by the Soviet need of Vietnam in its rift with the Chinese. See Douglas Pike, "The USSR and Vietnam," in Robert H. Donaldson, ed., *The Soviet Union in the Third World: Successes and Failures* (Boulder: Westview Press, 1981), chap. 13.

39. See Jackson, *Castro, Kremlin, and Communism,* chap. 6; Levesque, *USSR and Cuban Revolution,* chap. 4.

40. Levesque, *USSR and Cuban Revolution,* pp. 115-16.

41. Ibid., p. 118.

42. See Edward Gonzalez, *Cuba Under Castro: The Limits of Charisma.* (Boston: Houghton Mifflin, 1974), pp. 134-35, for further discussion of these points.

43. Ibid., pp. 136-37.

44. Levesque, *USSR and Cuban Revolution*, p. 118.

45. Ibid., p. 119; Jackson, *Castro, Kremlin, and Communism*, pp. 74-75.

46. Jackson, *Castro, Kremlin, and Communism*, p. 84.

47. Council of the OAS Report, Vol. II, pp. 47-63, also cited in Jackson, *Castro, Kremlin, and Communism*, p. 83.

48. See *Granma*, March 24, 1967; *Cuba Socialista* (August 1966), cited in Clissold, *Soviet Relations*, p. 83.

49. Speech by Fidel Castro at Havana University, marking the tenth anniversary of the assault on the presidential palace, March 13, 1967, Havana television and radio broadcast, March 14, 1967.

50. Proclamation of the general declaration of the conference of the *Organizacion Latino Americana de Solidaridad.* August 10, 1967, published in *Tricontinental* (English edition), 1 (July-August 1967): 33-34.

51. Levesque, *USSR and Cuban Revolution*, pp. 120-31.

52. Ibid.

53. Ibid.

54. An incisive analysis of the "microfaction" affair is provided by Kevin Devlin, "The Soviet–Cuban Confrontation: Economic Reality and Political Judo," *Radio Free Europe Report*, April 1, 1968; for direct Cuban reporting on the microfaction, see Havana Radio Broadcast, February 2, 1968; and *Granma*, February 2, 1968.

55. *Granma*, February 2, 1968; Havana Radio Broadcast, February 2, 1968.

56. See Kevin Devlin, "Castro Strikes at Communist Microfaction," *Radio Free Europe*, February 6, 1968; and Kevin Devlin, "Making the Most of a Microfaction," *Radio Free Europe Report*, February 23, 1968.

57. Paris Radio Broadcast, June 30, 1967; also *The New York Times*, June 27, 1967, p. 1.

58. Havana Radio Broadcast, July 26, 1967.

59. Havana Radio Broadcast, July 28, 1967.

60. *Pravda* also stressed the overwhelming volume of Soviet trade with Cuba, indicating that Castro had little to complain about. *The Miami Herald*, January 17, 1968.

61. *The New York Times*, March 24, 1968.

68. *The New York Times*, May 31, 1968.

63. Levesque, *USSR and Cuban Revolution*, p. 135.

64. *Le Monde*, weekly edition in English (May 21, 1969), p. 1.

65. "Soviet Economic Performance: 1966-1967," Materials Prepared for the Subcommittee on Foreign Economic Policy of the Joint Economic Committee, U.S. Congress (Washington, D.C.: Government Printing Office, 1968), pp. 124-28.

66. *Granma*, August 3, 1969.

67. In his speech of January 2, marking the tenth anniversary of the Cuban revolution, Castro praised Soviet aid to Cuba and said: "On certain occasions we have had differences of opinion on certain matters, and we have expressed them with all honesty. But at the same time this honesty obliges us to point out that this aid was decisive for our country throughout the difficult years." *Granma*, January 5, 1969.

68. On the Cuban defector, see James Nelson Goodsell, "Cuba More Sovietized," *Christian Science Monitor*, July 16, 1969. On party reorganization and citing the Soviet experience as a model, see speech by Armando Hart Davalos, Organizing Secretary and member of the Political Bureau of the Cuban Communist Party (PCC), at the graduating

ceremony for the 1963-69 Department of Political Science course at the University of Havana's School of Humanities, *Granma,* October 5, 1969.

69. *The New York Times,* October 12, 1969.

70. *Granma,* "Report on Internal Order," May 11, 1969. The author's own interviews with newly arriving exiles from Cuba to the United States, in November 1969, suggested that crime had increased in Cuba because of the difficulty in obtaining sufficient food, clothing, and modest consumer goods. Most people interviewed complained of insufficient food and clothing; they indicated the necessity of using *la bolsa negra* (black market) in order to survive. Castro spoke about crime problems in September 1968 at a rally in Havana's Plaza de la Revolucion, commemorating the eighth anniversary of the founding of the Committees for the Defense of the Revolution. Havana Radio Broadcast, September 29, 1968.

71. *Granma,* June 15, 1969, emphasis added.

72. Rodriquez, speech to the Moscow Conference, *Granma,* June 15, 1969.

73. *Granma,* May 3, 1970.

74. See Gonzalez, *Cuba Under Castro,* pp. 155-56.

4

ENTERING THE 1970s: IN PURSUIT OF CONVERGED INTERESTS

Given Cuba's dramatic shifts in domestic and foreign policies following the Soviet invasion of Czechoslovakia in August 1968, it is tempting to characterize the 1970s as a period of Cuba's growing satellite status under Soviet dominance. By this is meant that a number of observers perceive the Soviet Union gaining increased control over Cuba's internal and foreign policies. The implicit assumption in this argument is that as Cuba came under increasing Soviet economic and military dependence, Moscow in turn gained greatly expanded, perhaps even near total control over the vast array of issues involved in Cuban domestic and external policy decision making. A strong case is frequently made along these lines by some scholars and policymakers.[1]

It is true, of course, that Cuba's economic and military systems became increasingly dependent upon and integrated into the Soviet Bloc, first through the establishment of the Inter-Governmental Soviet-Cuban Commission for Economic, Scientific and Technological Cooperation in December 1970 and later in July 1972 through Cuba's admission to the Soviet-directed Council for Mutual Economic Assistance (CMEA). The island's political system underwent a substantial reorganization through the growth of the Cuban Communist Party (PCC)—a process of institutionalization of the Revolution in Leninist terms to give the PCC increased political legitimacy as Cuba's governing institution.[2] And although the Soviets did not sign a formal bilateral defense treaty with Cuba, Soviet military aid and activities with regard to Cuba escalated sharply. Do not these and other features of the close Soviet-Cuban embrace during the 1970s add up to satellite status and consequent assertive power flowing one-way from Moscow to Havana?

A closer examination of this period, with careful attention to the illusions and realities of influence and power suggest a more complex interaction between Moscow and Havana. The record indicates less a case of Cuba under direct Soviet power over all domestic and foreign policy issues, that is, Cuba modifying its behavior to suit Soviet priorities as a result of Soviet pressure, than one of both the Soviets and the Cubans adapting their policies in pursuit of perceived mutually beneficial outcomes. Again, the question of each country's leadership perceptions of the other country's utility in furthering their foreign policy objectives is an important part of the analysis.

This chapter probes several questions about the evolving Soviet-Cuban relationship in terms of who influenced whom in the early 1970s. What aspects of Soviet and Cuban vital interests were pursued by overlapping and mutually supportive policies? How did Cuba further Soviet foreign policy goals during the 1970s and what value did the Soviets attach to their continued and high-cost support of the Castro regime? Within this context, how, and in what ways, did Castro adapt his behavior to encourage Soviet support in an effort to pursue his own long-range objectives? What benefits and costs can be identified as each country began to interact within a range of cooperative issues as the 1970s unfolded? Where, and under what circumstances, did cooperative influence occur between the two countries?

In approaching these questions, a number of preliminary observations merit brief attention. First, the Soviets undoubtedly learned one major lesson from the events of the 1960s: Fidel Castro was a consummate, strong-willed, and tenacious political tactician. He rose to power through enormous will power, charisma and a canny ability to maintain his political control despite heavy odds in a constantly shifting political setting at home, within the Latin American region, and elsewhere in the international arena. Given his tenacity and capacity to hang on to power and his determination to pursue Cuban foreign policy objectives, he was not likely to be pushed around easily by anyone, including the Soviets, as demonstrated time and again during the 1960s.

Second, Castro proved quite capable of changing foreign policy strategies when it suited his purpose.[3] From his perspective, the late 1960s had produced a number of costly conditions relative to Cuba's physical security, pursuit of armed struggle and consequent confrontation with the Soviets and their pro-Soviet Latin American communist parties. Cuba's available resources simply were inadequate to guarantee territorial defense and to carry on this combative foreign posture.[4] Cuba's national economy lay in disrepair, the Cuban-backed guerrilla forces faced declining fortunes, and the Latin American community of states had isolated Havana in the Western hemisphere. Cuba's economy created special problems: the lack of a model of efficiency and inspiration for other socialist-oriented leaders in Latin America; and inability to support international proletarianism and activities to achieve greater international prestige.

Third, this situation led Castro to make a pragmatic decision: alter Cuban strategy to place it more in line with the Soviet Union. In this sense, one sees a rational decision-making process at Work in Havana, rather than a subservient regime caving in to massive pressure from Moscow. To state it differently, while the Soviets had learned that Castro was no pushover in foreign policy during the 1960s, Castro learned the limits of his patron's willingness to endure Cuba's maverick behavior. He knew that by 1968 the Soviets were capable of reducing material aid. He had learned much more about the acceptable parameters within which Cuba could assert its independence in foreign policy that would still allow substantial aid to flow from Moscow.

Fourth, in terms of the influence relationship itself, many cases of influence at the micro level in Soviet-Cuban relations are simply impossible to document. As Soviet-Cuban relations became closer during the decade of the 1970s, with Soviet technicians, economists, military personnel, and other specialists increasing in numbers side by side with their Cuban counterparts, daily cases of interpersonal influence seeking undoubtedly occurred. The larger the number of contacts between Soviets and Cubans, that is, logically created a richer and more complex social setting for influence relationships. So we must restrict ourselves to those macro situations, evidence of clear examples of influence based upon evident patterns of behavior.

Fifth, the distinction between macro and micro level influence situations is made more complex by the likely nature of influence pressures that began to occur during the 1970s. In sharp contrast with the off-and-on adversarial relations between Moscow and Havana during the 1960s, the 1970s were essentially cooperative. A thesis worth examining is whether or not examples of cooperative influence are more difficult to identify than those of assertive and coercive. One is tempted to answer in the affirmative, because assertive and coercive forms of influence are more dramatic, attract substantial press attention and publicity, and hence are more readily identifiable. We must look closely for evidence of cooperative influence and its specific forms during the decade of the 1970s.

Sixth, discussion of Soviet-Cuban relations must be probed with constant attention to each country's policies toward the United States. The early 1970s, for example, produced a period of *detente* in superpower relations between the Soviet Union and the United States, as made evident by the Strategic Arms Limitation Talks agreements of 1972 and 1974. Soviet pursuit of its Cuban client occurred within this context, one of peaceful coexistence with the United States, which placed a premium on Cuba's adopting policies less threatening to the United States and established Latin American states. It was precisely this kind of policy that proved beneficial to the Cubans. For it produced greater acceptance back into the community of Latin American states, signs of reduced threat from the United States, and opportunities for expanded regional and worldwide trade ties. In this sense, Soviet and Cuban interests overlapped through mutually beneficial policies.

In an effort to probe how and why Cuban policies moved toward closer alignment with the Soviets, we can explore a number of aspects of the evolving 1970s: (1) Soviet guarded optimism about Latin American trends in the 1970s; (2) widening Soviet contacts in Latin America; (3) Cuban motivations for a shift toward Soviet accord; (4) Soviet-Cuban cooperation in the 1970s; and (5) Cuba's accommodative foreign policy.

SOVIET GUARDED OPTIMISM ABOUT LATIN AMERICAN TRENDS IN THE 1970s

From the Soviet perspective, Castro's transition toward a more cooperative stance *vis à vis* the Soviet Union came at a time of increased Soviet optimism about the major trends at work in the Third World. Chinese competition with the Soviet Union for leadership of Third World movements had become less strident, although the Sino-Soviet conflict by no means had disappeared. Withdrawal of U.S. troops from Vietnam in the early 1970s after the long drawn out period of support produced a major victory for the communists and obvious defeat for the United States. Following the Vietnam defeat the United States demonstrated waning interest to become involved in other Third World conflicts, thus producing an image to the Soviets of a greatly reduced U.S. power in Third World arenas and a green light for an expanded Soviet presence. In Soviet terminology, the correlation of forces between socialism/communism and capitalism/imperialism distinctly favored the former during the immediate post-Vietnam period. The Soviets could be optimistic about their nuclear weapons capability in light of the SALT I and SALT II agreements, which reduced the likelihood of nuclear war between the Soviets and the United States, although no specific agreements between the two superpowers were formulated as codes of conduct in the Third World. And the Soviets increasingly saw themselves as the natural ally of the Third World, a case frequently made by Fidel Castro during the 1970s.

The Soviets, to be certain, suffered setbacks during the early 1970s. Egypt expelled Soviet advisers in 1972, followed by greatly deteriorating relations with Cairo. Chile's Salvador Allende, who came to power by the electoral route in 1970 and who seemed to legitimize Moscow's emphasis on the peaceful road to socialism as the best route to be followed in the Third World, was violently overthrown in a military coup in September 1973. But these were offset by other events, such as the victories of Soviet and Cuban-supported Marxist groups in Angola and Ethiopia in 1975-77. Other events in Latin America, such as the coming to power of a radical nationalist army group in Peru in 1968, helped to offset Soviet setbacks with continued optimistic momentum about favorable trends at work in the Third World.

Soviet optimism about the Third World is reflected in its perceptions of Latin America during the early 1970s. The Soviets had begun to see in this region major progressive forces which provided new opportunities to project their power while weakening the United States. To the extent the Soviets could ride with the tides at work, essentially radically nationalist in form, they could hope to strengthen the world correlation of forces between socialism/communism and capitalism/imperialism in favor of the former, generally expand Soviet power *vis à vis* the United States, and thereby play a more effective game of power politics on a level of growing equality with the United States. The Soviets, reflecting the pragmatic realism characteristic of the Brezhnev era, were by no means sanguine about an easy and eminent transition to socialism and communism through expanded state sector development, as in the early days of the Cuban Revolution and Nikita Khrushchev's optimism about the road to socialism. But they did foresee long-run forces favoring the correlation of forces running in favor of socialism and, meanwhile, opportunities to project Soviet power into the U.S. backyard in pursuit of Soviet national interests.

The problem for the Soviets in trying to project power into Latin America between 1966-68 lay in balancing its support for a "revolutionary" state (Cuba), with "nonrevolutionary" states in the rest of Latin America. Cuba's aggressive activities undermined Moscow's attempts to project a "peaceful" profile in Latin America as long as Havana—Moscow's chief client—was seeking to overthrow established governments through armed guerrilla warfare. For this reason, Cuba's turn to a more moderate posture, strongly encouraged by Soviet economic pressure, came at a favorable time for the Soviets, who now looked upon the changing Latin American scene with growing, yet guarded, optimism.

In what ways did Soviet perceptions of Latin America reflect caution mixed with hope? On the negative side, the Soviets recognized that Latin America occupied a prime place in U.S. strategic concerns and as the location of enormous U.S. direct private investment channeled through the powerful U.S.-based multinational corporations. Numerous Soviet writers depicted Latin America as a region of continued U.S. neocolonialism, an arena of U.S. enrichment and Pentagon power.[5] As the decade of the 1970s began, the Soviets depicted the Latin American countries as "unequal junior partners" of the imperialist powers, exploited by imperialist monopolies and international banks, where the national bourgeoisie was closely allied with foreign capital.[6] The Soviets also argued that the struggle for national liberation in Latin America was hindered by continued rivalry and struggle among individual large states for spheres of influence in the region. This trend, as in the case of Brazil's great power interests, undermined Latin American unity—a chief goal for the Soviets insofar as it weakened the U.S. position south of the Rio Grande.[7]

Against these negative perceptions the Soviets clearly entertained optimistic assessments of Latin America during the early 1970s. First, they envisioned a major transformation at work in the inter-American system, underscored by the failure of the Alliance for Progress, launched by President John Kennedy in 1961. The failure of the Alliance meant for the Soviets that the United States was unable to contain the anti-imperialist struggle and breakup of the U.S.-dominated inter-American system which began with the socialist transformation of Cuba.[8] The "failure" of the Alliance illustrated for the Soviets the weakness of the United States in solving any Latin American social and economic problems, which they perceived was growing into "crisis" proportions, with vast "anti-American feelings" and a deepening of the structural problems in the inter-American system."[9]

Drawing hope from the failure of the Alliance for Progress, the Soviets saw other signs of eroding U.S. power in the inter-American system. In May 1969 the Andean Pact (the Agreement of Cartagena) was signed, which entered into force in October. It included Bolivia, Chile, Colombia, Ecuador, and Peru. Its goals—reducing trade barriers among the member states; a common external trade barrier; creating an internal market for industrial production with industries assigned to different countries; and to limit the power of competing multinational corporations—were looked upon favorably by the Soviets.[10] In November 1969 The Lima Declaration was signed in the Peruvian capital by the Foreign Ministers of Colombia, Peru, Ecuador, Chile, and Bolivia. It stressed the right and responsibility of the Latin American states to press for their economic development and social progress, the importance of regional corporation and exclusive control over their natural resources against any form of external economic and social pressure. This emphasis on regional cooperation and obvious dissatisfaction with U.S. economic policy added to the Soviet perceptions of growing anti-Americanism in Latin America.

Latin American dissatisfaction with U.S. policy, which set up the motivations for an expanded Soviet presence, lay not only in the collapse of the Alliance for Progress. Consider that President Richard Nixon (1969-74) paid scant attention to Latin America, relying upon Nelson Rockefeller, Governor of New York and probably the most knowledgeable Republican political leader concerning Latin America at the time, to provide policy guidelines. Rockefeller's four trips to Latin America in 1969 were shaky at best, with his inability to enter Peru where leftist-leaning military leaders had assumed power in 1968, anti-American riots in Honduras, and his cancellation of trips to Chile and Venezuela. Rockefeller recommended increased military aid to Latin America, a policy that fit well with the earlier publicized Nixon Doctrine of 1969 that called for a "low profile" by the United States in the post-Vietnam era and more pressure on U.S. allies to provide for their own defense. The Soviets responded to this "new approach" to Latin America as one of continued domination through support of right-wing governments against which the forces of anti-imperialism and anti-Americanism were on the move.[11] The connection between Washington's turn toward a Nixon Doctrine variant for Latin America, on the one hand, and on the other, Latin America's growing sense of solidarity and responsibility for their own destiny was not lost on Soviet observers.[12]

Change in the inter-American system occupied considerable Soviet attention as the 1970s evolved. Moscow was greatly interested in Latin America's emergent nationalism, evident in economic and political forms. Economic nationalism exploded not only in the Cartegena and Lima documents identified above, but also in Peru's expropriation of the International Petroleum Corporation in October 1968, Bolivia's nationalization of the U.S. Gulf Oil Corporation in October 1969, and Chile's takeover of U.S. copper companies during 1970-73 under the leadership of Marxist president, Salvador Allende.[13] Soviet emphasis on the Latin American drive to control their natural resources continued to be stressed in the middle 1970s.[14]

As to political nationalism, Moscow was attracted to the new radical nationalist governments in Bolivia, Chile, Panama, and Peru, as well as in Jamaica out in the Caribbean Basin from the mid-1970s onward. Jamaica's Michael Manley (1972-80), moving into his democratic socialist variant of change, especially attracted Moscow and Havana. Grass roots elements taking up the struggle against local oppressors and foreign imperialists encouraged added Soviet attention. These groups included workers, peasants, and even priests, as in the case of Camilo Torres.[15] Although killed in 1966 after he had joined the guerrillas, this Colombian priest served as a model of representative changes at work in the Latin American clergy. These and other groups strengthened the traditional Soviet claim that broad united fronts, with the communist parties playing leading roles, were on the move in Latin America.[16]

The early 1970s produced another source of optimism for the Soviet Union: the positive role that could be played by radical Third World armies. Leftist military coups had occurred in Iraq, the Congo (Brazzaville), and Peru in the latter part of 1968, followed by Somalia in 1969, Dahomey (Benin) in 1972 and Ethiopia in 1974. These events encouraged the Soviets to emphasize the avant-garde role that progressive military regimes might exercise in the national liberation struggle.[17] As one Soviet writer observed in August 1971, major changes were at work in the social structure of several Latin American armies, transforming them from the old force used by U.S. imperialism to guard the interests of the ruling classes and U.S. multinational corporations.[18] New progressive members of the middle classes and petit bourgeoisie were entering the officer's corps, while many more workers and peasants had become noncommissioned officers. "Today," a Soviet writer observed, "it would be wrong to regard all Latin American armies as units of imperialist mercenaries."[19]

To summarize, Soviet perceptions at the outset of the 1970s were optimistic, though recognizing continued U.S. economic, military and political strength in this part of the Third World. Progressive tides were flowing, anti-American and radical nationalist in form, which the Soviets should encourage through the formation of peaceful broad united fronts. The election of Salvador Allende, Latin America's first elected Marxist president, confirmed Soviet beliefs about the peaceful road to change, thus downgrading the viability of the Cuban model of violent struggle. Grass roots forces of change, working toward a weakening of the U.S privileged position in Latin America, included nationalist-oriented peasants, workers, members of the intelligentsia, the military, the clergy and the petit bourgeoise. These optimistic assessments of Latin America naturally led to expanded contacts in the region.

WIDENING SOVIET CONTACTS IN LATIN AMERICA

Soviet policy toward Latin America during the 1970s centered on the pursuit of several key objectives tied to Moscow's second and third level vital interests as discussed in Chapter two. These objectives set the context in which Moscow sought to align Cuba after the Soviet invasion of Czechoslovakia in 1968. In probing the depths of the Soviet-Cuban influence relationship in the 1970s, Sovet objectives in Latin America merit attention, for they help explain Moscow's continuing commitments to Cuba.

Soviet objectives in Latin America clustered in the following goals: (1) to reduce U.S. influence through support of radical nationalist united fronts in individual countries and Latin American international organizations, such as the Andean Pact; (2) to project Soviet power into commercial, diplomatic and trade relations to gain access to Latin American markets and natural resources; (3) to gain port facilities for Moscow's expanding civilian and military blue water navy; (4) to widen Moscow's presence in Latin American life through increased scholarships and cultural relations; and (5) to cooperate with those governments engaged in processes of change potentially leading to socialist societies.

In translating these goals into specific policies, the Soviet Union widened its contacts in Latin America from the early 1970s onward. As the Latin American states moved to break away from the old U.S.-dominated Pan Americanism, the pattern of expanding diplomatic contacts took shape: Colombia (1968); Peru, Ecuador, and Bolivia (1969); Venezuela and Guyana (1970); Costa Rica, Trinidad and Tobago, Guatemala, Nicaragua, and Jamaica (early 1970s).[20] The end of the 1970s produced Soviet diplomatic relations with 19 Latin American countries, a fact which led Soviet commentators to boast that the wall that had kept Latin America from the socialist world had now broken.[21] Beyond the Soviet Union, Latin America as a whole greatly expanded its relations with communist countries during 1971-76, with a total of 53 new communist country diplomatic missions established between 1971 and 1976.[22] In the Caribbean and Central America, communist resident missions grew from zero in 1971 to a total of 15 in 6 countries by 1976.[23] Leading in the establishment of new missions were the People's Republic of China, East Germany, and Cuba. Cuba's expanded diplomatic ties thus paralleled the Soviet Union's growing presence.

In their economic relations with Latin America, the Soviets pursued an active trade program, perhaps too active insofar as it produced a billion dollar trade deficit and $1.5 billion of previous communist credits unspent by the middle 1970s. That the Soviets were willing to assume this scale of deficit trade relations suggests the extent to which they were prepared in the early 1970s to utilize economic policies to pursue political objectives and propaganda leverage at a time of clear decline in U.S.-Latin American relations. As the 1970s progressed, the Soviets and East Europeans were actively trading with ten Latin American countries, including Argentina, Bolivia, Brazil and Colombia, the bulk of which was focused in Argentina and Brazil, which absorbed 60 percent of Soviet exports by 1979. Mexico signed its first economic cooperation agreements with communist countries in 1976 and Venezuela signed its first economic cooperation agreement with the Soviet Union in that year.[24]

The Soviets tried to increase sales of machinery and equipment—tractors, automobiles, trolley, buses, machine tools, hydroelectric and thermal turbines, and military equipment. They purchased raw materials and food—alumina, wheat, soybeans, fish and other natural resources. Overall, Soviet commerce with Latin America increased sharply during the 1970s, from $124 million in 1970 to $4.96 billion in 1981 (excluding Cuba).[25] By 1981, the Soviet Union was exporting $178 million worth of merchandise and importing about $5.2 billion in Latin American products, indicating that the trade imbalance with Latin America remained throughout the 1970s.[26]

Soviet bloc economic credits increased sharply during this period, as might be expected. As a percentage of Soviet bloc credits to the Third World countries, they rose from 0.5 percent of total Soviet bloc credits in 1968 to 30 percent by 1973 and remained at approximately 15 percent by the end of the decade.[27] They amounted to approximately $2 billion by the end of 1974, the year in which Argentina received more bloc credits than any other Third World country.[28]

Despite the substantial increase in Soviet trade with Latin America during the 1970s, it should be noted that Latin America received considerably less Soviet and East European economic credits and grants than other, more geographically proximate, Third World countries. Between 1954 and 1976, Africa received $1.8 billion in Soviet economic credits and grants, the Middle East and South Asia $8.9 billion, and Latin America $655 million from the Soviets and $1.2 billion from Eastern Europe.[29] This "institutionalization of economic relations," as one scholar describes the period, brought frequent Soviet trade delegations, fairs and expositions into Latin America, and a substantially increased role for the Soviet-directed Council for Mutual Economic Assistance (CMEA).[30] Cuba joined CMEA in 1972, while Mexico and Guyana began to participate as observers.

Following the patterns of an expanded Soviet presence elsewhere in the Third World, the Soviets increased their scientific and technical cooperation with the Latin American countries, undertook cooperative technological projects, for example, in the area of fisheries and hydroelectric power projects, and increased the number of scholarships for study in the Soviet Union and Eastern Europe. In 1970, approximately 2,425 students were attending Soviet bloc academic institutions, but this increased to 4,200 by 1976—paralleling the growth of students invited to the Soviet block countries during the early 1970s.[31] The Soviets greatly expanded their merchant marine and fishing fleet activities from the 1970s onward, a pattern reproduced in Soviet-Cuban relations and in Havana's own policies in Latin America. Wherever possible, then, Moscow penetrated the region, widening its presence at every conceivable level.

Soviet military deliveries south of the Rio Grande, excluding Cuba, remained relatively small compared to other Third World clients at the first half of the 1970s. Between 1972 and 1976, Africa received approximately \$2 billion, the Middle East \$7 billion, South Asia \$1 billion and Latin America \$170 million. A Peruvian order for \$250 million for Soviet jet fighters in 1976 established Moscow as Lima's principal arms supplier.[32] Cuba is the big exception to this pattern of generally low Soviet military transfers. The Grenada Revolution in March 1979 and the *Sandinista* victory over the Anastasio Somoza regime in July 1979 led the Soviets, however, to widen their military sales.

The Soviets were attracted to specific countries at this time of warming relations with Cuba, notably Panama, Peru, Bolivia, and Chile. In Panama, a coup brought General Omar Torrijos Herrera to power. General Torrijos was committed to asserting Panama's independence from the United States and to raising Panama's standard of living. Torrijos pressed for the new Panama Canal Treaty, actively pursued a "banana tax" against the multinational corporations, advocated the return of Cuba to the Latin American family against U.S. pressure, and tried to increase Panama's agricultural productivity. Here was a small, but important radical nationalist military regime, advocating policies that would reduce U.S. strategic power in the Central American region, notably by changing control of the Canal. How could the Soviets resist the attraction of Torrijos?

In October 1968, a group of reform-oriented army officers, led by General Juan Velasco Alvarado, came to power in Peru. They launched the country on a road of dramatic social and economic transformations, based upon a radical nationalist and anti-American orientation pleasing to Soviet decision-makers. Shortly following the Velasco coup, the Peruvian government announced the nationalization of the International Petroleum Company, owned by Standard Oil of New Jersey, and in 1974 they nationalized the giant United States mining complex of Cerro De Pasco. The reformist military soon passed a law calling for the participation of workers in ownership and administration of industrial concerns, called the "industrial community" concept, and by 1973 over 3,300 enterprises had begun to put the law into effect. An intensive agrarian reform law was pursued, allowing more than 170,000 families to receive land. The radical nationalist Peruvian reforms by the military were one of the major causes for Soviet optimism in this era, happily supported by the Cubans and thus a powerful factor in the Soviet-Cuban rapprochement established by early 1970. The Peruvian government tolerated the Peruvian Communist Party. Moscow understandably signed a trade accord with Peru in February 1969, opened diplomatic relations with that country and began to tout its accomplishments in Soviet journals as Peru's relations with the United States deteriorated.[33]

In Bolivia, cause for Soviet interest in a radical nationalist was spirited but short lived. General René Barrientos was killed in a helicopter crash in 1969, which brought to power General Alfredo Ovando Candia, who adopted a nationalist reform policy highlighted by the nationalization of the Bolivian Gulf Oil Company, a decision much in tune with Bolivia's Peruvian neighbors. Military in-fighting soon ensued over General Ovando's approach to change, leading ultimately to the seizure of power by General Juan José Torres. He greatly accelerated the reformist moves in Bolivia by nationalizing the American-owned Maltide zinc mines accompanied by other political reforms. These included expelling the U.S. Peace Corps volunteers and the formation of a "Popular Assembly" to plan for more radical reforms. Following the pattern of high incidences of coups in Bolivia, however, General Torres was in turn overthrown in August 1971, when the more conservative-minded Colonel Hugo Bánzer Suárez assumed control of state authority, thus ending the national reform movement which so attracted the Soviets. But during the rule of Torres, the Soviets looked upon Bolivia, where the revolutionary movement had erupted as early as 1952, with great enthusiasm.[34]

Perhaps the most exciting event for the Soviet Union occurred in Chile in 1970, with the election of Marxist president, Salvador Allende, who headed the Popular Unity Bloc. The Soviets were already attracted to Chile by the time of Allende's election, because during the previous administration of Eduardo Frei (1964-70) the Chilean government had initiated nationalization of the foreign-owned copper industry and had put into effect extensive agrarian reforms. Allende pursued this path with vigor, attempting to move Chile from capitalism to socialism as rapidly as possible.

Total nationalization of the copper companies, sweeping agrarian reform, state control of the banks, and income redistribution programs carried Chile much faster on the reform path than any previous administration.[35] This appearance of socialism in Latin America, through the electoral process and backed by nationalization of foreign industries and agrarian reform, greatly enlivened Soviet prospects about declining U.S. influence in Latin America.[36] The role of the Chilean military during Allende's election, one of studied neutrality, confirmed the Soviet thesis that more and more the Latin American military demonstrated its willingness to permit progressive forces and thereby removed the necessity for national liberation movements to resort to armed struggle.[37]

Yet the economic burden of supporting revolutions in Latin America was already beginning to tell on the Soviet Union by the time of the Allende electoral victory. The Cuban experiment previously had cost the Soviets approximately $1 million per day for many years. These investments propelled Cuba into a $4 billion debt to the Soviet Union during the period when Allende came to power. The Soviets were not favorably disposed to underwrite Chile with massive economic aid, but they agreed to make available credits worth $335 million (of which $185 million were to be in sterling or other hard currencies). They did so, however, a full two years after Allende had been in power and long after it was clear that his government sorely needed economic help. This offer was extremely late in coming, only one year before his violent overthrow by the Chilean military.

Soviet relations with Cuba in the 1970s were conducted within the context of its broader Latin American objectives. Through support of Cuba, the Soviets sought to (1) reduce U.S. influence in Latin America and elsewhere in the Third World, (2) widen Moscow's presence in Latin America, especially in the Caribbean Basin, (3) gain new port facilities for Moscow's blue water civilian and military navy, (4) provide an effective and attractive model of socialist economic transformation in the U.S. strategic backyard, and (5) align Cuba's foreign policy in a manner that would completely coincide with Soviet interests. How, and in what ways the Soviets pursued these objectives through specific policies, and what outcomes and consequences were produced more by Soviet influence than by Cuba's pursuit of its own interests, is discussed below. Before turning to these questions, however, Cuba's motivation for adopting a more conciliatory line relative to the Soviets must be probed, because it helps in understanding where and over what issues Soviet and Cuban interests were intertwined. A look at the Cuban perspective suggests that the changes occurring in Cuba under an increased Soviet presence, while stimulated and partly influenced by Soviet pressure, nevertheless had their separate origins based upon Cuban national interest calculations.

CUBAN MOTIVATIONS FOR A SHIFT TOWARD SOVIET ACCORD

A number of reasons for the Cuban shift to rapprochement with the Soviets were cited earlier: defeat of the Cuban-backed Latin American guerrilla movements; the death of Cuba's "Che" Guevara and the fall of his guerrilla forces in Bolivia in October 1967; continued production and investment difficulties at home and the growing need for outside aid; and the nagging concern for Cuba's defense, which seemed magnified by Castro's increased isolation within the Latin American region during 1966-68. In the context of these problems, Soviet assertive power through economic denial had encouraged the Cuban leadership to reassess its foreign policy options.

By the end of the 1960s, Castro faced a situation of erosion in the attainment of Cuba's first level salient vital interests: overcoming economic underdevelopment; maintaining effective political control; and achieving a high level of territorial security—especially against the possibility of a U.S. invasion. Policies adopted in pursuit of these interests were proving counterproductive, for reasons outside the domain of direct Soviet influence on Cuban decision making, but certainly exacerbated by Soviet-Cuban tensions and the economic and political forms of Soviet assertive power during 1967-68.

Cuba's deep economic difficulties greatly continued the momentum toward a revised posture with the Soviets between 1968 and 1970. Economic goals centered on increased sugar production, and Castro determined to produce a ten million ton sugar harvest, the largest ever, in 1970 as the litmus test of his personalist style in the politics of development. The ten million ton sugar harvest, it was hoped, would eradicate the production and planning woes in Cuba, so visible in the country's waste, apathy, demoralization and mismanagement. Toward the attainment of this ambitious goal the whole country was mobilized.

Castro's brand of economic development, one notably distinct from the prevailing Marxist model in the Soviet Union and a cause of concern for Cuba's Soviet investors, lay in a number of basic guidelines that proved insufficient to meet the ten million ton sugar goal. The Cuban economic model centered on a centralized command planning system with decision making essentially vested in Castro himself or in his personalist followers, rather than in specialists at the middle and lower levels of decision making.[38]

This system generated mismanagement, ineffective participation in decision making and waste stimulated by poor planning. It was a system not based upon monetary calculations or profitability as indicators of progress and stimulators of worker productivity.[39] It substituted moral incentives for material incentives, tried to stimulate a new work ethic based upon an idealized concept of the "new Cuban man" and relied upon other ideological inputs to stimulate worker production, such as trying to develop in the workers a sense of the guerrilla mentality to attack sugar cutting and production quotas.[40] By 1968, many individuals were lining up to leave Cuba because things were not getting better as Fidel had been promising over the years, the black market was thriving, and Cuban stores offered little to buy even if an individual had a pocketful of money.[41]

The ten million ton sugar harvest failed to materialize, which meant that Castro would remain economically dependent upon the Soviet Union whether he wanted to or not. The ten million ton sugar failure poignantly underscored the necessity of major revision in Cuban economic planning and investments, not only to the Cubans but most certainly to their Soviet patrons, and thus the stage was set for a major turn in Cuban economic policies. As Castro acknowledged on July 26, 1970:

> The unquestionable inefficiency of all of us...[meant that] we were incapable of waging what we called the simultaneous battle [on all production fronts]...the heroic effort to increase [sugar] production...resulted in imbalances in the economy, in diminished production in other sectors and, in short, in an increase in our difficulties.[42]

The Soviets commented on this speech through Tass, the official Soviet news agency, by stressing the need to develop administrative reforms in Cuba's economic institutions.[43]

The failure of the ten million ton sugar harvest affected the Cuban political system as well as the country's economic model. It raised questions about the effectiveness of Castro's political leadership, for it strained, as Edward Gonzolez notes, the *Fidelista* personalist model of charismatic rule.[44] In recognizing the sugar harvest as Fidel's most serious personal setback since coming to power, he determined to reorganize the political system as a means to strengthen the economic system and, to some extent, the legitimacy of his own leadership. His speech of July 26, 1970 noted the changes to come: greater worker involvement at the plant level, a restructuring and strengthening of the Cuban Communist Party and government, and the dismissal of unqualified personnel at the top levels of economic decision making. These decisions in turn opened the door to greater Soviet involvement in economic matters and consequently greater leverage for them in Cuba's economic administration and technical matters.[45]

Cuba's deteriorating national security was foremost in the minds of Cuban leaders during the late 1960s, based on major fear of a foreign attack and his clear distrust of the Soviet Union.[46] As Cuba's Armed

Forces Minister, Raúl Castro, pointed out in a speech in July 1967, the country was quite aware of the reported U.S. military contingency plans, CIA covert operations to assassinate Fidel, and other reports that the United States had not promised never to consider an invasion of Cuba as part of the deal struck with the Soviets during the October 1962 missile crisis.[47] The Soviet occupation of Czechoslovakia in August 1968 produced some concern in Cuba that the United States might consider an invasion of Cuba as a response. As to distrust of the Soviet Union's overall military commitment to Cuba, the microfaction affair, the slow down in Soviet oil deliveries to Cuba, and the criticism of Cuba by pro-Soviet Latin American communist parties contributed to substantial uneasiness about the status of Soviet-Cuban relations and what might happen should the United States decide to invade. Raúl therefore made a strong case for self-reliance, costly to be certain, but a better guarantee of Cuban security than exclusive dependence on the geographically distant Soviet Union.[48]

SOVIET-CUBAN COOPERATION IN THE 1970s

From the early 1970s onward, the Soviets and Cubans entered into a cooperative association designed to serve the vital interests of each country. This association entailed costs and benefits for both the Soviets and Cubans, but each party determined that on balance the benefits outweighed the costs. Although it was expensive for the Soviet Union to undertake a vast program of economic and military aid to Cuba, the political and strategic benefits associated with the effort outweighed those costs. From the Cuban perspective, they needed external support in order to strengthen their resource base—that vital ingredient so necessary to pursuit of other goals. Like the Soviets, the Cubans decided that the benefits outweighed the costs of increased dependency on Moscow.

It would be an error to understate the extensiveness of Soviet assistance to Cuba, especially since their cooperative association began after the Czechoslovakian affair of August 1968. In the words of Cole Blaiser, "...there has never been anything quite like it, not in the experience of developing countries in the Third World, nor of the socialist countries, most particularly the USSR."[49] The enormous range of Soviet assistance, well-documented elsewhere, takes many forms—food, oil supplies at below the world market price (which sharply escalated after the OPEC price rises of 1973-74), Soviet purchases of Cuban sugar at over the world market price, free military weapons, technical assistance, and many other needed imports—all of which literally made possible the survival of Castro's Revolution. Castro has recognized the vast significance of Soviet aid on frequent occasions, among which his comments at the first congress of the Cuban Communist Party in December 1975 illustrate the point:

> Without the decisive, steady, and generous aid of the Soviet people, our country could not have survived the confrontation with imperialism. They bought our sugar when our market was brutally suppressed by the United States; they supplied us with raw materials and fuel which we could not have acquired in any other part of the world; they caused to arrive free arms with which we opposed the mercenaries at the Bay of Pigs and equipped our Revolutionary armed forces in order to impose the highest price on any direct aggression by the U.S.; they supported our economy in extraordinary fashion in the critical years of the blockade. Thousands and thousands of military specialists and Soviet technicians helped in the instruction of our Armed Forces or supported almost all branches of our economy.[50]

Soviet-Cuban Military Relations

A brief examination of the range and amount of Soviet assistance indicates both Cuba's increased dependency on the Soviet Union and the costs borne by the Soviets. As to the military costs, which met the needs of Cuba's territorial security and long-range interests in the Third World, the Soviets provided various types of aid. Moscow supplied Cuba with weapons "free of charge" between 1960 and 1975, which amounted to "several thousand million pesos."[51] Soviet weapons deliveries to Cuba increased during the 1970s, especially in terms of expensive equipment for Cuba's Air Force.[52] Soviet weapons transfers to Cuba amounted to approximately $1.5 billion between 1960 and 1970, but the next five years brought an estimated doubling of that figure.[53] In addition, Soviet military technical advice to Cuba increased during the early 1970s; by 1974 over twice as many Cubans were studying in the Soviet Union compared to the pattern of the 1960s. And the number of Soviet specialists, including military technicians, increased in Cuba from approximately 1,000 in the early 1970s to "several thousand" by 1973 and an estimated 6,000 by 1975, half of whom were military specialists.[54] By 1980 the number of Soviet specialists in Cuba had leveled off at approximately 5,000.[55]

As further Soviet military support to Cuba, largely as a consequence of Havana's turn toward a foreign policy more in line with the Soviets, the Soviet Union began military deployments to Cuba. In June 1969, they sent their first naval deployment and between 1969 and 1975, the Soviets sent 14 naval deployments, normally consisting of two major surface combatants, an auxiliary, and at least one submarine.[56] In June 1969, however, the Soviet naval squadron that docked in Cuba consisted of a fleet of eight battleships; in May 1970, another fleet of seven Soviet battleships and a submarine with nuclear capability arrived in Cuba and stayed for nearly one month. Another fleet of nine ships arrived in September 1970 and stayed for four months.

These efforts undoubtedly helped meet Castro's request for a Soviet military commitment as well as meshed neatly with the Soviet objective of projecting a blue water naval presence into outlying Third World areas.[57] Air deployments to Cuba began in April 1970, and while en route these planes frequently conducted reconnaissance of Western ships, such as U.S. aircraft carriers crossing the Atlantic. These activities constituted means of demonstrating the Soviet right to operate close to U.S. shores and to maintain a periodic presence in the Caribbean Basin. They ease deep U.S. concerns about Cuba, perceived as a Soviet proxy, in the U.S. strategic backyard.

Soviet military aid to Cuba entailed more than stepped up arms transfers, training, assistance, and military deployments after 1970. As part of the broader transition inside Cuba toward a Soviet bureaucratic model of decision making, replete with large numbers of Soviet specialists on hand to assist in the process, the Cuban Ministry of the Revolutionary Armed Forces (MINFAR) began transformation into a modern military establishment staffed with professionally trained individuals who attended military academies in Cuba or the Soviet Union.[58] Under the leadership of Raúl Castro, Fidel's brother, the MINFAR soon emerged as Cuba's strongest institutional force and the major repository of specialists trained for Cuba's new organizational life along the lines of a Soviet bureaucratic system. Raúl's talents as an organizer and manager were known to be more effective than his brother's, a fact endowing Raúl with greater acceptability to the Soviets. Led by Raúl, the MINFAR began to supply the personnel that soon occupied high government posts after the 1970 sugar harvest failure, and more and more military men filled the government hierarchy from this period onward.[59]

The central question is whether or not these military developments in Soviet-Cuban relations following 1970 indicate increased Soviet influence in Cuban decision making. Certainly this question merits attention, because in the study of influence it is crucial to try to isolate those instances when influence might have occurred in the relationship.

Three criteria for identifying this kind of situation and for attempting the measurement of influence between the Soviet Union and a host country are: (1) the rapid improvement of the Soviet Union to carry out transactions in the host country, (2) a marked increase in the quantity, quality and variety of resources committed to the host country, and (3) a general improvement in the Soviet strategic position in terms of the host country.[60] These conditions distinctly prevailed from 1969 onward as the Soviet Union stepped up its military aid to the Cubans and as the Cubans modified their external foreign policy in a manner more congenial to the Soviets—another potential situation where Soviet influence might be at work. Did the increased Soviet presence, the Cuban adoption of a Soviet model of professional staffing within the bureaucracy by Soviet-trained military specialists, and the overall role of Raúl's Soviet-supported MIN-FAR in Cuban economic and planning agencies produce evidence of Soviet influence within this specific issue area?

The answer is not easy. On the surface, one must assume that some forms of indirect and cooperative Soviet influence must have occurred in the day-to-day personal interactions between Soviet specialists and their Cuban counterparts. This micro level analysis is difficult to penetrate because of the lack of accurate and balanced information and the closed nature of the Cuban decision-making system. Nor do we have access to the personal diaries of the thousands of actors involved at the micro level, nor can even the most persistent scholar be on the spot to observe these daily interactions—with their complaints, concerns, and probable conflicts and frustrations as two cultural and linguistic groups pursued common tasks. But at the macro level one is reluctant to rush to the conclusion that the Soviet increased presence necessarily translated into automatic influence, certainly of the assertive or coercive type.

This is so for at least four reasons. First, Castro and other Cuban leaders clearly wanted increased Soviet military aid. They were not compelled to make this decision against their will. Second, the MINFAR remained staffed at the highest levels by veterans from the Sierra Maestra, 26th of July individuals who were loyal to either Raúl or Fidel, whose roots went back not to communism but to the radical nationalist origins of the Cuban Revolution. Third, the MINFAR remained under the control of Raúl, himself a 26th of July Movement leader with strong familial and revolutionary ties to Fidel. Fourth, in Cuba's first level salient interest area of Cuban sovereignty and the sacrosanct internal political base of Cuba's ruling elite, it is highly unlikely that the Soviets would have attempted to undermine the *Fidelistas* through influence mounted by way of the military aid issue. They would not likely attempt this method of influence, fearing it would seriously undermine other Soviet goals that motivated the aid in the first place or would strain the outer limits of the relationship to the breaking point and thus produce a total loss of Soviet leverage.[61]

A more professional bureaucratic model of military decision making emerged after 1970, bringing increased professionalism and less personalism into military and government management. But the highest levels of decision making remained in the hands of loyal *Fidelistas*. Cuba's first level salient political interests—maintaining Cuba's destiny in the hands of the revolutionary leadership—had not fallen under Soviet influence. At the highest levels of decision making, the Cubans did not appear to be coerced or otherwise influenced into doing what they did not wish to do in the pursuit of their own interests. What appears on the surface as a likely case turns out rather as a case of the joint interests of the two parties being served. The Soviets were delighted with Cuba's turn to a more moderate foreign policy in Latin America, one dovetailing with the Soviets, while the Cubans were pleased with the increased military aid that heightened their territorial security and which by no means conflicted with the motivations behind their own expanding relations in Latin America from 1969 onward.

Soviet-Cuban Economic Ties

The issue area of increased Soviet economic aid to Cuba from 1970 onward is another ripe arena for potential Soviet influence. Paralleling an increase in Soviet material assistance came the modification of Cuban economic decision making in a manner certainly congenial to the Soviet Union. Opportunities for Soviet advisers to act within the Cuban economy sharply increased. A distinct improvement in the Soviet ability to carry out transactions in Cuba occurred after 1970. The marked increase in the quantity, quality and variety of Soviet economic resources committed to Cuba is implicit in the record of increased military assistance, and the Soviet strategic position—the ability to translate Soviet power into policy flowed into Cuba as the Soviet ships docked in Havana. These aspects of the economic aid issue area are easily enough identified, and they need to be identified before probing the matter of influence itself.

The scope and variety of Soviet aid to Cuba escalated noticeably from 1970 onward. The rise in Soviet aid to Cuba is significant enough as a potential influence arena; it is made more dramatic by comparing Soviet increased aid to Cuba with the rest of the Third World during 1970-74. For the general pattern of Soviet economic assistance during this period is one lagging for the first time behind Soviet Third World military assistance. Soviet aid to Cuba comes in many forms: balance of payments aid (to cover a persistent negative foreign trade balance), sugar and nickel subsidies, petroleum subsidies, the transfer of technology and technicians, and aid in fishing, manufacturing, communications, transport, power, and the sugar industry.[62] By 1976, total Soviet aid to Cuba reached $8.3 billion, in addition to millions of dollars in scientific, educational and cultural assistance, and military assistance worth several billion dollars. Cole Blaiser, a student of Soviet economic aid, estimates that the total package probably reached $11 billion by 1976, not an insignificant figure compared to the estimated $13 billion extended aid agreements by the Soviet Union to all of the Third World countries (excluding Cuba) between 1954 and 1977.[63]

Even more telling as a possible issue area of Soviet influence in Cuba is the manner in which this aid was orchestrated. Soviet-Cuban economic collaboration became coordinated through an Intergovernmental Soviet-Cuban Commission for Economic, Scientific, and Technological Cooperation, established in December 1970. Its first meeting was held in Havana in September 1971, while subsequent annual meetings alternated between Havana and Moscow. The head of the Cuban delegation was Carlos Rafael Rodríguez, a leader of the pre-Castro Communist Party (PSP) and an individual with long and close ties to Moscow. Carlos Rafael is a skilled economist, providing him with the qualifications to head the Cuban delegation. To sweeten further the question of potential Soviet influence in the economic aid issue area, it should be noted that Carlos Rafael was also appointed as a deputy prime minister in charge of international relations, which clearly indicated Castro's quest for closer relations with the Soviet Union.[64] In 1972, Cuba was admitted to COMECON as a full member, which entitled it to "preferential" conditions in economic cooperation.[65] Entry into COMECON meant a close coordination of the Cuban economy with commodity, trade and planning agreements of the other Soviet-directed COMECON states. This goal included keeping Cuba's credit rating strong with the other COMECON members, who held the growing Cuban debt. This economic situation in turn meant that Cuba's export market had to cater to these countries in order to meet Cuba's commitments.[66]

It is all rather remarkable when you think about it. Here was the small island of Cuba, with an economy in obvious bad repair, located only 90 miles off the U.S. shores, thousands of miles distant from the Soviet Union and yet receiving literally millions of dollars in aid weekly from the Soviet Union as the 1970s progressed.

To what extent did these dramatic shifts in the Soviet economic presence inside Cuba contain evidence of influence over Cuban decision making? Here we enter a different domain from that of Soviet relations with other Third World countries like Egypt, Iraq, Libya or Syria, where the relationship was not one of two communist countries, where the client state had entered COMECON, and where joint economic coordination and planning occurred in a large scale and systematic manner. In the Cuban case, it is hard to escape from the conclusion that Soviet indirect and cooperative influence occurred in terms of shaping the structure of centralized planning and administration, the general system of administration of the economy along the lines of the centralized Soviet model, and in decisions relative to commodities, trade and exports within the framework of COMECON.

This conclusion admittedly is attractive. Carmelo Mesa Lago, a respected scholar of the Cuban economy, notes that the "Cuban economy is still heavily determined by outside forces over which national leaders do not have significant control. The USSR has basically the power to set prices, grant subsidies, and extend credit to the island."[67] The island, he notes, "is highly vulnerable to Soviet pivotal economic power and political influence."[68] It can be argued also that the Castro government would undoubtedly prefer to be moving away from dependency on a monocultural economy (sugar), which the COMECON relationship reinforces, as well as from the overwhelming dependency on the Soviet Union to which the Cubans export a few raw materials and from which it buys most of its capital goods.[69] Given this preference, Soviet cooperative influence occurs in a restricted economic sense.

Soviet observers, in turn, appear to perceive that they exert a form of indirect or cooperative influence over the Cubans in the economic issue area. As a Soviet author argued in late 1976:

> ....in 1970 an interrupted process of improvements in all aspects of the revolution began..., the Party grew and was strengthened..., functions of the party and state organs were clearly delineated..., the system of the administration of the economy was completed..., attention to the study of the experience of the USSR and other socialist countries grew.[70]

The Soviets followed a diplomatic style in their economic relations with Cuba highly compatible with cooperative influence seeking. They did not boast of influencing Cuba, as noted in the above statement. And they avoided public airings of any differences they might have had with the Cubans over economic matters—even during the volatile period of 1966-68. Unlike Anwar Sadat, who so vocally criticized the Soviets for their lack in fulfilling military agreements with Egypt, the public airing of which severely undermined Soviet relations with Egypt, the Soviets were successful in exerting cooperative influence in the economic issue area in part because they avoided offending the Cubans in public forums.

But in the joint negotiations with the Cubans, one can infer that cooperative pressure was applied to urge the Cubans to come around to the Soviet model, largely because the Soviets could claim that it would be in the best interests for the Cubans. Not a bad idea in light of the failure of Cuba's previous personalist model, so glaringly demonstrated in the failure of the 1970 ten million ton sugar harvest. That the Soviets exerted indirect or cooperative influence seems all the more likely in view of the position held by pro-Soviet Carlos Rafael Rodríguez in the economic issue arena, not only the key negotiator but one who enjoyed Castro's support. Specific examples of influence can be inferred from joint communiqués during the early 1970s and from the time taken to negotiate agreements. The annual Soviet-Cuban trade pact signed in Moscow on February 22, 1971, followed three months of talks in which a joint commission was set up to study Cuban "economic management and ways to increase the efficiency of the national economy."[71]

These negotiations meant increased movement toward the Soviet centralized model, which the Soviets supported. This does not mean that the Cubans necessarily resisted the trend to centralization, but change in the old system was at work, involving a substantially increased Soviet presence in Cuba. This inference seems valid, because later in September 1971, a comprehensive agreement was signed between the Soviets and Cubans that called for greatly increased Soviet participation in the planning and execution of Cuban economic and technical projects.[72]

That Soviet influence in the economic issue area remained at the indirect and cooperative levels must be stressed. To suggest that the Soviets were asserting their power on Cuba or coercing the Cubans to do something against their will simply does not meet the test of available information and systematic analysis. Although the Cubans became dependent on the Soviets, evidence does not suggest that the Soviets tried to exploit the island economically. Part of Cuba's trade remained with market economies. As the Cubans became increasingly dependent on the Soviets, Carlos Rafael Rodríguez began to negotiate new trade agreements, long-term credits and investment contracts with various nonsocialist countries. He also emerged as a figure advocating closer contacts with the United States. Castro turned toward a close economic relationship with the Soviets, not solely because of Soviet pressure, but as a pragmatic-realist policy designed to further Cuba's long-run vital interests.

On balance the economic issue arena makes one wonder who actually influenced whom? The Cubans bailed themselves out of a disastrous economic situation at the outset of the 1970s, received massive Soviet aid and began to strengthen the economic resource base that helped in the pursuit of Cuban strategies abroad. And given the level of Soviet economic commitment, the Soviets were pulled into the Cuban orbit. The larger and longer-run the duration of Soviet economic assistance, the more likely it would continue as long as the Cubans conducted a foreign policy not diametrically at odds with the Soviet Union. How could previous Soviet investments, ideological fervor, pride and prestige prevent them from trying to make the Cuban economy a going concern in the interest of maintaining a demonstrated example of Marxism-Leninism at work under Washington's nose? Ideology, like sex, has its own forms of seduction.

Soviet-Cuban Political Links

The Soviet-Cuban embrace produced new political transformations in Cuba, which suggest another issue area of possible Soviet influence. During the process of "institutionalizing" Cuba's Revolution following the sugar harvest failure, Castro began reorganizing the state and government structures more in line with the prevailing Soviet model. By 1976 this reorganization produced a new National Assembly of People's Power, a Council of State and Council of Ministers. The institutionalizing process led also to an expanded membership in the Communist Party of Cuba. Between 1970 and 1975 the PCC doubled from 100,000 to 202,807 members, and by 1982 the membership had doubled again to reach 434,143 individuals and candidates for membership.[73] The 1975 PCC Congress also established a new Political Bureau, Secretariat and Central Committee, all of which transformed the Party into a Leninist model as Cuba's ruling institution.[74] In line with these Soviet-oriented changes, the Central Organization of Cuban Trade Unions (CTC) announced ideological shifts which replicated Soviet orthodoxy in Cuba's labor affairs.[75]

At first blush these moves suggest Soviet influence at work, compelling the Cubans to fall into line if they wished to receive continued Soviet aid. A closer look at these changes suggests, to be certain, a greatly modified decision-making system, one providing more qualified individuals access to important levels of administration and management. But as might be expected, the higher levels of decision making remained under Castro's control. The expanded PCC Secretariat, the Executive Committee, the Council of Ministers and the top of key ministries contained nine senior officers from the MINFAR who were loyal to him and to Raúl;[76] Fidel also ensured that party reorganization was conducted by officers loyal to the Castro brothers. By the end of the decade, Fidel remained in multiple leadership positions: first secretary of the PCC, president of both the Council of State and Council of Ministers, and commander in chief. Raúl retained his position of minister of the FAR, in addition to being first vice-president of the Councils of State and Ministers. Other 26th of July loyalists retained high positions in the party and government. The structure of governmental decision making changed along Leninist lines, but the substance of policy making remained in the hands who made the Revolution.

CUBA'S ACCOMMODATIVE FOREIGN POLICY

Castro is not the first Third World leader to change his foreign policy strategy toward the Soviet Union. The late Gamal Abdel Nasser and Anwar Sadat of Egypt, Hafez al-Asad of Syria, and Muammar Qadaffi of Libya traditionally pursued flexible foreign policies toward the Soviet Union, attempting to extract concessions consistent with the pursuit of their foreign policy objectives. Castro was in good Third World company when he reoriented Cuba's foreign relations during the 1970s. To identify these changes—the pursuit of peaceful state-to-state relations with established governments, the turn away from armed struggle, the acceptance of broad united fronts, the forging of diplomatic relations with radical national military regimes, as in Peru, the reduction of conflict with the pro-Soviet Latin American communist parties, and even the moves toward rapprochement with the United States—as accommodative primarily in terms of compatibility with the Soviet Union simply overestimates the role of Soviet power in this issue area.

The changes in foreign policy, as noted above, stemmed from other than purely Soviet-exerted power on Cuba. Their origins lie in Castro's own assessment of the need for a new strategy at the end of the decade of the 1960s. His policies were designed to accommodate not only the Soviet Union, but also the new currents of radical nationalism at work in the Western hemisphere and the new opportunities to expand Cuba's presence in ways other than through guerrilla warfare. Happily for both the Cubans and the Soviets, the decision to adopt a more flexible foreign policy served the joint interests of both countries. That in itself was enough to encourage the huge amounts offered to Cuba by the Soviet Union.

The changes in Cuban foreign policy in effect delivered a new strategy to achieve Cuba's national and international interests, while at the same time guaranteeing the inflows of badly needed Soviet aid. By reducing the "Cuban threat" profile associated with the armed struggle thesis, Cuba began to set up the conditions for its readmittance back into the family of Latin American nations and for a reduced threat emanating from the United States. At the same time, the Cuban leaders were able to pursue their interests in supporting national liberation movements outside the Latin American region. While the Soviets followed their objectives in Latin America and Cuba, the Cubans continued in quest of their own foreign policy goals which remained essentially the same as they were from the beginning: territorial security, survival of the Revolution, overcoming economic underdevelopment, application of Cuba's proletariat internationalism, for example, support for Third World national liberation, and the quest for international status.

Certainly the Castro regime did not perceive its economic dependence as a constraint on Havana's foreign policy. Castro's perception of the situation, one drilled home constantly to students, workers, and the military, was that Cuba was freer and more independent than it had been at any time in its history. As Castro stated in his speech of December 31, 1973, commemorating the fifteenth anniversary of the Cuban Revolution of December 30, 1958:

> . . . . and you, combatants, are the firm guardians, the custodians, the defenders of this opportunity created by our people, because never before in our history have we enjoyed such unity, such strength, such peace; . . . never was the fatherland so much the master of its destiny! And for this sovereign fatherland, for this fatherland that is master of its destiny, for this country where justice prevails, much blood has been shed on this land.[77]

Castro repeated this position during Brezhnev's visit to Cuba during January 28-February 3, 1974. Castro stated that the Soviet Union did not own a single mine, business, or public service in Cuba, nor had it invested a single cent in Cuba expecting profit.[78] And as if to accentuate Cuba's value to the Soviet Union—starkly symbolized by Brezhnev's trip to Cuba, the first made by the General Secretary of the Soviet Union's Communist Party—Castro took the opportunity to point out another fact to Brezhnev. In public ceremonies, with both Castro and Brezhnev on the rostrum, he drove home the point that he had highly touted the Soviet Union, at the September 1973 Nonaligned Conference in Algiers, stressing their role as the central impediment against the military adventurism of the imperialists.[79] The final declaration of these Brezhnev-Castro meetings cited the two country's growing fraternal friendship and complete identity of views on international affairs.[80]

As the Soviet-Cuban relationship became closer throughout the early 1970s, the Cubans consistently emphasized the differences between the character of the Soviet-Cuban relationship compared to the character of the previous Cuban-U.S. relationship before Castro's Revolution. They stressed, among other things, that a major difference between Cuba's dependence on the Soviet Union, compared to the days before the Cuban Revolution under U.S. economic power, is the absence of monopoly capital and multinational corporations. The Cuban leadership argued that the Soviets cannot be labeled "imperialists" because they do not own multinational corporations in Cuba, nor are workers exploited by Soviet capital as under U.S. forms of dependency.[81] The Soviets scrupulously concurred with Castro's emphasis on Cuba's freedom and independence, for as one Soviet observer wrote just a few weeks after Castro's December 1973 speech, "The Cuban people...have taken all the necessary measures to defend their sovereignty and national independence."[82]

What regional and international policies did the Castro regime undertake during this period? Relations began to improve between Cuba and Bolivia, once the radical nationalist military leader, Juan José Torres, assumed power in October 1970, but slowed perceptibly when the rightest regime, headed by Col. Hugo Bánzer Suárez overthrew Torres in August 1971. In June 1970 the Cubans offered their first relief program for a noncommunist country, when Peru suffered a devastating earthquake in May 1970. The election of Chile's first Marxist president, Salvador Allende Gossens, in November 1970, brought the establishment of immediate diplomatic relations, although relations between the two countries were already on a warming trend. In November-December 1971, Castro made a 25-day visit to Chile, and upon his return to Cuba in early December, he stopped over in Peru and Ecuador. Castro hailed this trip, his first to South America since 1959, as a "triumphant success" and "proof that we are not as alone as we once were."[83]

Castro's Chilean trip breached the previously united OAS diplomatic and economic boycott of Cuba launched in 1962. The author witnessed Castro's enthusiastic welcome down the length of the country, where he was cheered by students and workers. The Cuban leader maintained a correct diplomatic style while in Chile, a low-key approach, which ironically alienated many of the more violence-oriented leftists in Chile, such as those associated with the Movement of the Revolutionary Left (MIR).

Throughout this trip, Castro stressed his unity with Latin America, urged the integration of Latin American economies, and praised the military government of Peru and the left-wing Broad Front in Uruguay. In observing Castro's studiously diplomatic performance during these days, one had the distinct impression that Castro had emerged from the foreboding castle of Mordor, not as the previously believed dark threat to the Western hemisphere, but rather as the pragmatic spokesman for progress and development along multiple roads to change. The crowds to whom Castro spoke quite clearly perceived him as a leader in control of his own foreign policy, one with legitimate credentials, not as the spokesman for Soviet interests. They came to see Castro as the leader of the Cuban Revolution rather than as a Soviet dependent.

Cuba's reentry into the Latin American family of nations proceeded at a remarkable rate. Between 1970 and 1976, no less than eleven Caribbean and Latin American countries established diplomatic relations with Cuba (Argentina, Bahamas, Barbados, Chile, Colombia, Guyana, Jamaica, Panama, Peru, Trinidad and Tobago, and Venezuela). In June-July the OAS began to reconsider renewing diplomatic and trade relations with Cuba, which ultimately led to the lifting of diplomatic and commercial sanctions in July 1975. And Cuba played a major role in the formation in 1975 of the new Latin American Economic System (SELA), a regional economic unit that excluded the United States, but included Cuba. This event, and the formation of the joint Caribbean Shipping Company of eight countries (NAMUCAR) was seen by Soviet writers as further evidence of the successful trend leading to the weakening of "imperialism's position."[84] The Soviets welcomed Cuba's growing acceptance in Latin America, for it coincided with other broader trends that strengthened anti-imperialism and anti-Americanism directly in North America's traditional sphere of interest. Soviet writers increasingly highlighted reestablishment of ties with Cuba as a basic issue in inter-American relations, one altering the situation in the Western hemisphere. For Cuba's reentry demonstrated, "even in an area that U.S. imperialists have long regarded as their own backyard they are no longer capable of markedly slowing down the revolutionary process."[85]

As Castro implemented his more flexible policies in the Latin American arena, a new kind of relationship with the United States began to take form. As such it served both Cuban and Soviet interests. By 1974 relations with the United States had begun to reflect a new phase, one of relaxed tensions and hopeful signs of long-run rapprochement. This trend included positive statements emanating from both Havana and Washington, pressure on the United States by a number of Latin American leaders to moderate its position toward Cuba, attention to the matter by then Secretary of State, Henry Kissinger, and visits to Cuba by U.S. businessmen and political figures.[86] This movement toward restored Cuban-U.S. relations, which neatly coincided with Moscow's own detente efforts at the time, was undermined with the onset of Soviet-Cuban military activities in Angola in 1975.

Nevertheless, considerable progress in Cuban-U.S. relations occurred: (1) the signing of an antihijacking pact in February 1973, (2) pressure by the U.S. Congress, beginning in January 1973, for resumption of relations between the two countries, (3) relaxation of the U.S. embargo against Cuba in August 1975, (4) lifting of the U.S. travel ban to Cuba in 1977, (5) establishment of two fishing agreements in 1977, and (6) the opening of U.S. and Cuban "interest sections" in each other's capitals in 1977. The resumption of Cuban support for armed struggle in Latin America in 1978-79 effectively curtailed this major trend. The Soviets, as might be expected, supported these detente-oriented Cuban efforts.

The Castro government expanded its relations outside the Western hemisphere with both the developing and developed countries, Marxist and non-Marxist alike. Havana pursued new economic links with Japan, Canada, Spain, France, Great Britain, and Italy—an equally attractive trend for the Soviets, because it modified Moscow's heavy economic burden in Cuba. For the Cubans, it meant less total dependence on the Soviet Union, as in the case of a $7 million credit line from Great Britain in 1972. Cuba's pace of activities noticeably stepped up in the Third World. In an unprecedented two-month trip during May-July 1972, Castro traveled to Guinea, Sierra Leone and Algeria, with other visits in Bulgaria, Rumania, Hungary, Poland, East Germany, Czechoslovakia, and the Soviet Union. Many of Castro's Third World activities centered in Africa, where the Cuban government began to gain new leverage in negotiating with the Soviets toward the end of the decade of the 1970s—a subject that merits our attention in the next chapter.

NOTES

1. See Leon Gouré and Julian Weinkle. "Cuba's New Dependency," *Problems of Communism* 21 (March–April 1972): 68-72; Carmelo Mesa-Lago, "The Sovietization of the Cuban Revolution," *World Affairs* 136 (Summer 1973): 3-35; James D. Theberge, *Russia in the Caribbean*, Part 2 (Washington, D.C.: Center for Strategic and International Studies, Georgetown University, 1973); Leon Goure and Morris Rothenberg, *Soviet Penetration of Latin America* (Coral Gables: Center for Advanced International Studies, University of Miami. 1975); Lyn D. Bender, *The Politics of Hostility—Castro's Revolution and United States Policy* (San German, Puerto Rico: Inter-American University

Press, 1975), pp. 55-56; George Volsky, "Cuba's Foreign Policies," *Current History* (February 1976): 69-72; also the hearings held regularly over the years by the U.S. Congress, centering on Soviet activities in Cuba, Committee on International Relations, Subcommittee on International Political and Military Affiars.

2. Edward Gonzalez, "Institutionalization, Political Elites, and Foreign Policies," in Cole Blasier and Carmelo Mesa Lago, eds., *Cuba in the World* (Pittsburgh: University of Pittsburgh Press, 1979), pp. 3-36.

3. By strategy is meant the overall blance of ends and means, in realms of military, political, economic, or psychological competition. See John Lewis Gaddis, "The Rise, Fall and Future of Detente," *Foreign Affairs* 62, 2 (Winter 1983/84): 355.

4. On the connections between national security and adequate resources, see Ibid., p. 369.

5. See Y. Yelyutin, "USA–Latin America: Equal Partnership?", *International Affairs* 2 (February-March 1970): 65-71; Y. Yelzutin, "Latin America: Source of U.S. Enrichment," *International Affairs* 9 (September 1970): 36-41; Y. Antonov and V. Komarov, "The Pentagon and Latin America," *International Affairs* 1 (January 1971): 55-59; B. Antonov, "Latin American versus U.S. Domination," *International Affairs* 8 (August 1971): 49-52; and B. Tarasov, "The Pentagon vs. Latin America," *International Affairs* 2 (February 1973): 37-41.

6. See, for example, I. Shreremetyev, "State Capitalism in Latin America," *International Affairs* 11 (November 1970): 49.

7. See S. Mishin, "Latin America: Two Trends of Development," *International Affairs* 6 (June 1976): 54. This negative and cautious aspect of Soviet perspectives about change in Latin America continued into the later 1970s, when debate over the possibilities of change sharpened. Some Soviet observers envisioned Latin America as an arena of "dependent capitalism," with relatively little opportunity for anyone, including the Soviets, to change conditions. As one Soviet analyst wrote in 1979 (before the *Sandinista* victory over Anastasio Somoza in July 1979), "So long as the continent remains within the framework of a world capitalist economy dominated by the giant corporations, independent development becomes absolutely unfeasible, for the stronger capital will always subordinate the weaker." Viktor Volsky, "Relative Maturity, Absolute Dependence," *World Marxist Review* (June 1979): 40-45.

8. Yelyutin, "USA–Latin America: Equal Partnership," p. 66; Sheremetyev, "State Capitalism in Latin America," p. 49.

9. Yelyutin, "USA–Latin America: Equal Partnership" p. 67.

10. See "Readers' Questions Answered," *International Affairs* 5 (May 1970): 44.

11. V. Vasilyev, "The United States' New Approach to Latin America," *International Affairs* 6 (June 1971): 43-49.

12. On the Nixon period and the Rockefeller recommendations, see Walter LaFeber, *Inevitable Revolutions: The United States in Central America* (New York: W.W. Norton, 1983), pp. 197-204.

13. Yelyutin, "USA–Latin America: Equal Partnership?" p. 67.

14. See A. Matlina, "Latin America: Struggle for Natural Resources," *International Affairs* 11 (November 1975): 55-60; A. Glinkin, "Changes in Latin America," *International Affairs* 1 (January 1975): 51-58.

15. Antonov, "Latin America versus U.S. Domination," p. 50. See also S. Gonionsky, "Latin America: the Struggle for Second Liberation," *International Affairs* 11 (November 1972): 38-44.

16. V. Busheyev, "New Horizons in Latin America," *International Affairs* 5 (May 1973): 35-41.

17. See Mark Katz, *The Third World in Soviet Military Thought* (London and Canberra: Croom Helm, 1982), pp. 81-83.

18. Antonov, "Latin America versus U.S. Domination," p. 50.

19. Ibid.

20. See "Soviet Diplomatic Relations and Representation," Bureau of Intelligence and Research, U.S. Department of State (November 8, 1971, 1972); "Communist Diplomatic, Consular, and Trade Representation in Latin America," ibid., January 1977.

21. Vasilyev, "The U.S.'s 'New Approach' to Latin America," p. 48.

22. Bureau of Intelligence and Research, U.S. Department of State, January 11, 1977.

23. Ibid.

24. "Communist Aid to the Less Developed Countries of the Free World," Central Intelligence Agency, August 1977, p. 26.

25. Nikolai Zinoviev, "Dinamaica de las Relaciones Economicas," *America Latina*, 3 (March): 6.

26. Ibid.

27. See Robert S. Leiken, *Soviet Strategy in Latin America* The Washington Papers/93 (New York: Praeger, 1982), p. 19.

28. Ibid.

29. "Communist Aid to the Less Developed Countries of the Free World, 1976," pp. 11ff.

30. Leiken, *Soviet Strategy*, p. 21.

31. Ibid.; "Communist Aid to the Less Developed Countries," p. 11.

32. Ibid., pp. 4, 15.

33. See Yelyutin, "U.S.A.-Latin America," p. 67.

34. See Antonov, "Latin America versus U.S. Domination," p. 49.

35. See W. Raymond Duncan, "Allende's Chile," in Helen Desfosses and Jacques Levesque, eds. *Socialism in the Third World* (New York: Praeger, 1975), pp. 3-31.

36. See V. Mikhailov, "Chile: Copper Industry Nationalized," *International Affairs* 10 (October 1971): 108-09; and E. Kovalyov, "Latin America: Agrarian Problems and the Liberation Struggle," *International Relations* 11 (November 1971): 45-49.

37. See Leiken, *Soviet Strategy*, p. 28.

38. Gonzalez, "Institutionalization and Political Elites," in Blasier and Mesa Lago, *Cuba in the World*, p. 199.

39. Ibid.

40. Ibid.; see also Havana Radio Broadcast, July 26, 1967.

41. Author's interviews with exiles just arriving from Cuba in the United States, Miami, Florida, September–November 1968.

42. *Granma*, August 2, 1970, pp. 3-5.

43. Soviet Radio Broadcast, July 30, 1970.

44. Edward Gonzalez, *Cuba Under Castro: The Limits of Charisma* (Boston: Houghton Mifflin, 1974), p. 222.

45. *Granma*, August 2, 1970, pp. 2-6.

46. Jorge I. Dominguez, "The Armed Forces and Foreign Relations," in Blasier and Mesa Lago, *Cuba in the World*, p. 59.

47. Ibid.

48. Ibid.

49. Cole Blasier, "COMECON in Cuban Development," in Blasier and Mesa Lago, *Cuba in the World*, p. 225.

50. Fidel Castro, *La Primera Revolucion Socialista en America* (Mexico: 1976), pp. 55-56, as cited in Blasier, "COMECON in Cuban Developments," in Blasier and Mesa Lago, *Cuba in the World*, pp. 229-30.

51. Dominguez, "The Armed Forces and Foreign Relations," in Blasier and Mesa Lago, *Cuba in the World*, p. 54.

52. Ibid.

53. Ibid.

54. Ibid.

55. Trevor N. Dupuy et al., *The Almanac of World Military Power* (San Rafael, Calif.: Presidio Press, 1980), p. 118.

56. "Soviet Activities in Cuba—Parts VI and VII: Communist Influence in the Western Hemisphere," Hearings Before the Subcommittee on International Political and Military Affairs of the International Relations Committee, House of Representatives (October, June, and September 1976), Washington, D.C.; Government Printing Office, 1976), p. 2.

57. Jacques Levesque, *The USSR and the Cuban Revolution: Soviet Ideological and Strategic Perspectives, 1959-77* (New York: Praeger, 1978), p. 152.

58. Gonzalez, *Cuba Under Castro*, pp. 228-29.

59. Ibid.

60. On these aspects of influence, see Alvin Z. Rubinstein, *Red Star on the Nile; The Soviet-Egyptian Influence Relationship Since the June War* (Princeton: Princeton University Press, 1977), pp. xv, xvi, xii, and xiii.

61. Ibid., p. xiii.

62. See Blasier, "COMECON in Cuban Development," in Blasier and Mesa Lago, *Cuba in the World*.

63. "Communist Aid to the Less Developed Countries", p. 6.

64. Blasier, "COMECON in Cuban Development," in Blasier and Mesa Lago, *Cuba in the World*, p. 235.

65. Ibid., p. 224.

66. Ibid., p. 250.

67. Carmelo Mesa Lago, *The Economy of Socialist Cuba; A Two Decade Appraisal* (Albuquerque: University of New Mexico Press, 1981), p. 186.

68. Ibid., p. 187.

69. Ibid., p. 186.

70. Blasier, "COMECON in Cuban Development," in Blasier and Mesa Lago, *Cuba in the World*, p. 248.

71. *Facts on File*, p. 33.

72. Ibid., p. 34.

73. *World Marxist Review* (July 1981).

74. Gonzalez, "Institutionalization, Political Elites, and Foreign Policies," in Blasier and Mesa Lago, *Cuba in the World*, pp. 5-6.

75. Ibid., p. 5.

76. Ibid., p. 7.

77. Havana Radio Broadcast in Spanish to the Americas, December 31, 1975.

78. *Pravda*, February 4, 1974; *Izvestia*, February 5, 1974; as carried in the *Current Digest of the Soviet Press*, 26, 5 (February 27, 1974): 1-10.

79. Ibid.

80. Ibid.

81. *Granma Weekly Review*, September 16, 1973.

82. O. Darusenkov, "Cuba – USSR Friendship," *International Affairs*, 2 (February 1974): 16.

83. Facts on File, op. cit., p. 57.

84. See S. Mishin, "Latin America: Two Trends of Development," *International Affairs* 6 (June 1976): 64-71; also A. Shulgovsky, "The Social and Political Development in Latin America," *International Affairs* 11 (November 1979): 52-61.

85. S. Gonionsky, "Latin America: The Struggle for 'Second Liberation,' " *International Affairs* 11 (November 1972): 38.

86. Facts on File, op. cit., pp. 82-83.

5

THE SOVIET-CUBAN INFLUENCE
RELATIONSHIP IN AFRICA

The Soviet-Cuban relationship in Africa, especially from 1975 onward, offers a tantalizing setting to probe how, and in what ways, influence flows between Moscow and Havana. The African setting is appropriate to examine for at least three reasons. First, the Soviets and Cubans began to intervene together in Angola and Ethiopia from 1975 onward. Second, they pursued overlapping parallel military and economic aid programs in a number of other African countries, for example, Algeria, Equatorial Guinea, Guinea, Guinea-Bissau and Mozambique. Third, Cuba had begun to play a number of roles in the socialist community during the 1970s, including Castro's drive for Third World leadership, which placed Cuba in the position of avant-garde and defender of progressive African states. In the context of Soviet-Cuban relations, these events suggest opportunities for influence on the part of both the Cubans and the Soviets.

Two polar interpretations of the Soviet-Cuban relationship can be dispensed with immediately. The first explains Cuba's overseas commitments in Africa as executing Soviet orders.[1] The second envisions Cuba as an autonomous independent actor in Africa.[2] As explanations for the totality of Cuban foreign policy behavior in Africa, neither stands up to close examination, although elements of both polar explanations can be identified in some aspects of Cuban policy. That Cuban policy operated as a Soviet proxy simply avoids the ways in which Cuba exercises influence on Soviet decision making in Africa, especially how Cuban military forces and their willingness to go to Angola and Ethiopia augment Soviet capabilities to engage in direct military intervention.[3] But neither is Cuba an independent actor in Africa; its transformation to a major power in that part of the world has been the product of Soviet military and economic strength, logistical support, and willingness to exploit emerging opportunities to project its presence globally.[4] To these Soviet roles must be added Soviet coordination, especially in Ethiopia, weaponry, military strategic cover, and its huge aid program to the Cuban economy.[5]

The Soviet-Cuban influence relationship in Africa is substantially more complex than these two extreme positions. It is one in which influence of different types flows in both directions at various times over distinct issues. In the joint interventions in Angola and Ethiopia, for example, influence is more of the indirect and cooperative versions as opposed to assertive or coercive power. The evidence does not suggest that the Soviets used sanctions to compel the Cubans to send their troops to Africa. But certainly Soviet supportive capabilities induced the Cubans to go, just as the Cuban willingness to fight induced the Soviets to continue their direct backing of Cuban actions in Angola and to undertake even more direct activities later in Ethiopia.

In Africa, the Soviets and Cubans pursued their second level salient interests as opposed to first level priorities, which meant that cooperative forms of influence were more likely to occur within the Soviet-Cuban alliance (see Chapter 1). Here one must avoid jumping to the conclusion, however, that joint Soviet-Cuban actions automatically mean that the Soviets were constantly influencing the smaller state. In much of the parallel Soviet-Cuban activities in Africa, mutual interests were served. Both sets of leadership elites perceived the benefits to outweigh the costs from their joint actions and, therefore, it cannot be inferred that influence necessarily occurred. In any case, careful attention to the nature of influence, as discussed in Chapter One, illustrates that the Soviets and Cubans in Africa form a more complex affair than may appear at first glance.

In an effort to highlight influence actions in the Soviet-Cuban experiences in Africa, it is useful first to examine Soviet interests there and how the Cuban connection promoted them in ways that undoubtedly affected Soviet decision making. This dimension can be compared to Cuba's intentions in Africa and how the Soviet links made possible their implementation, thereby affecting Cuban actions. We can then turn to the specific cases of Soviet-Cuban relations in Angola and Ethiopia, how Cuba's influence in the relationship increased in Africa following Angola and Ethiopia, and the influence equation associated with Cuba's roles in the socialist community, notably Castro's aspirations for Third World leadership, as they affected African states and the Soviet-Cuban relationship. The latter issue forces us to examine not only the positive aspects of Cuba's influence, but also their limits. Constraints to Cuba's widened African presence following Angola and Ethiopia are, for example, connected to Havana's Soviet ties, as in the case of the Soviet invasion of Afghanistan in 1979, which tarnished Cuba's Third World African diplomacy.

SOVIET POLICY IN AFRICA BEFORE ANGOLA

Following the deposal of Nikita Khrushchev, the USSR's key policy objectives in Africa centered less on Marxist-Leninist ideological prescriptions than on more rational and pragmatic guidelines designed to take advantage of every opportunity to expand the Soviet presence. Ideological considerations appear to have been placed on the back burner, as the Soviets turned increasingly to a more careful and selective support of African leaders heading states geographically situated and politically oriented to advance Soviet interests, or by supporting groups whose policy orientations favored Soviet objectives.[6]

These objectives were to advance Moscow's strategic and political power in ways to demonstrate the Soviet status as a leading global actor in Africa, while at the same time undermining Western power and checking the omnipresent Chinese.[7] The strategic goal turned on establishing logistical facilities for Moscow's growing air and blue water navy capabilities, which required storage and repair operations, intelligence gathering equipment, and staging locations for reconnaissance and other activities.[8] These could be used to offset Western and Chinese power, protect Soviet clients and their anticolonial policies, while generally opening the door to a greater Soviet voice in African affairs.[9] Politically the Soviets pursued various types of opportunities to gain increased leverage, frequently by extending economic and military assistance to those countries who did not receive such aid from the West, and by supporting African liberation movements unable to secure Western support, notably in Portuguese Africa.[10] Soviet policy toward Guinea, Algeria, and Libya (1974 onward) are cases of the former type of opportunity, whereas the MPLA classically illustrates the second type of opportunity.[11]

This backdrop to Soviet-Cuban intervention in Africa on behalf of the MPLA in mid-1975 suggests that from the Soviet perspective, they were following goals already in place. Angola, in this historical setting, was another opportunity to advance Soviet interests—especially if the Cubans were willing to go in. This aspect of Soviet intervention, which highlights the cooperative influence exerted by the Cubans on Soviet decision making, merits closer examination. The fact is that by the time the

MPLA opportunity presented itself in mid-1975, the Soviets had experienced a number of setbacks in Africa and any optimism they may have entertained relative to the international climate for expansionism was offset by the recognized limits and obstacles to previous African experiences.

Admittedly, the international and African regional climate was ripe for the Soviets to jump on the MPLA bandwagon in mid-1975. Chinese competition had subsided in Africa, notwithstanding the ongoing Sino-Soviet dispute.[12] The United States in IndoChina counted as a favorable shift in the world correlation of forces between socialism/communism and capitalism/imperialism. The Soviets had made remarkable progress in nuclear weapons production compared to the United States, arms control agreements had been concluded with the United States, and with the signing of *detente* agreements with the United States, the immediate threat of nuclear war had declined. The Basic Principles Agreement (BPA) on the "rules" of conduct for the regulation of global competition of the two superpowers, signed by President Richard Nixon and Brezhnev at their first summit in Moscow in May 1972, added to these favorable opportunities for Soviet risk taking in Africa.[13] And in Africa, the Portuguese empire had begun to fall.

But Soviet goals in Africa had experienced a number of setbacks, which vividly illuminated Moscow's limited capabilities in this part of the world that Soviet leaders could not fail to observe. The 1960s had produced the painful overthrows of pro-Soviet leaders: Algeria's Ben Bella (1965), Ghana's Kwame Nkrumah (1966) and Mali's Modibo Keita (1968). A military coup in the Congo (Brazzaville) had overthrown the leftist-oriented regime in 1968, leading the new government to reorientation toward France. And in the Sudan, a Soviet-backed government outlawed the local communist party in 1969, which led to additional uncertainty in Moscow about the nature of opportunities for expanded Soviet power in Africa.

The early 1970s brought a host of new frustrations for Soviet policy in Africa. Four influential members of the Soviet Embassy in the Congo (Kinshasa) were expelled for subversive activities in 1970. The Soviets verbally supported an ill-fated coup against the Sudan's President General Ja'far Muhammad Numeiri in July 1971, which led to the execution of a number of high-ranking communists, including the General Secretary of the Sudanese Communist Party—and Numeiri became increasingly convinced that the Soviets were behind the coup, thus straining Soviet-Sudanese relations. In nearby Egypt, Anwar Sadat had become discontent with the Soviets in 1972, in part caused by resentment in the Egyptian bureaucracy over so many Soviet advisers in the country, combined with the activities of the pro-Soviet head of the Arab Socialist Union

(ASU), Ali Sabri, who challenged Sadat on a number of issues. Sadat consequently expelled 15,000 to 21,000 Soviet military and technical experts in July 1972.[14] In Libya, Muammar al Qaddafi came to power in 1969 and until 1974, following the 1973 Middle East War, stressed Islamic fundamentalism and Libyan nationalism, vociferously castigating the atheistic Marxism-Leninism of the Soviet Union.[15] Qaddafi began to change this tune in 1974 when he negotiated his first arms agreement with the Soviet Union, following the 1973 Middle East War.

As the Angolan opportunity presented itself in mid-1975 and as Moscow considered backing a joint Cuban involvement, the Soviets must have been greatly attracted and affected by the Cuban willingness and military strength to go to Angola. For what did the overall Soviet situation entail? As observers stress, by the end of the 1960s the African anticolonialist movement had produced not one Marxist government nor any important Communist parties with the exceptions of the South African, Egyptian and Sudanese.[16] African nationalism was distinctly unreceptive to Soviet political and ideological flirtations, in part because its orientations were toward all foreign governments rather than simply to the former colonial powers.[17] Soviet heavyhanded diplomacy ill fit African sensitivities, as in the Sudan, and did not present the Soviets as interested only in the welfare of their client states. And African nationalism focused on black consciousness, negritude, Pan Africanism, and the "African personality," which in their cultural emphasis did not mesh well with white Soviet cultural traits and apparent lack of sensitivity to the African national consciousness.[18]

In light of this past record of Moscow's African involvements, Cuba's willingness to participate in the Angolan venture augmented Soviet military and political capabilities. In so doing, Cuba cooperatively influenced Soviet decision making regarding its African interests and its perception of the military capabilities required to achieve them—at least as far as Angola and, later, Ethiopia were concerned. The Soviets could not commit their own ground troops in Angola, fearing a direct U.S. confrontation or greater opposition from African leaders already affected by their involvement with the Soviets.[19] And since the Cuban military forces were comprised of a substantial number of blacks and mulattoes, their presence would less likely collide with African cultural and racial perceptions. The Cubans also had considerable experience in Africa, dating possibly as early as 1960, when arms and medical personnel went to the Algerian National Liberation Front, followed by Cuba's first permanent military mission in Ghana in 1961.[20] This experience as a Third World leader helping other African Third World countries could be well adapted to Soviet interests.

CUBA'S PRE-ANGOLAN AFRICAN POLICIES

Although Cuba's military aid to Angola and Ethiopia was the first large scale commitment of ground forces abroad, it was not the first time Cuba had established military aid programs and diplomatic contacts with African states. Cuban foreign policy has always followed a global orientation, stemming from its sense of internationalist solidarity with revolutionary movements experiencing conditions similar to those faced by Cuba before and after its own revolution.[21] This sense of internationalist solidarity does not arise strictly from Marxism-Leninism, but more from Cuba's own national history of struggle against colonialism and imperialism, which predates the Russian Revolution and the birth of Marxism-Leninism on a global scale. Havana's long-standing military operations, military aid and technical assistance to Africa is part of this legacy.

Cuba's attraction to Africa derived from other factors. The range of opportunities to extend its presence in Africa during the 1960s were far greater compared to the Western Hemisphere where the United States circumscribed Cuba's support for revolutionary activities. Cuba's isolation in the Western Hemisphere contrasted with Africa's setting, which offered possibilities to conduct diplomatic relations outside the socialist bloc and where conditions for revolution along the Cuban model seemed possible—without sharp U.S. opposition.[22] Internationally, the Cubans did not have to contend with U.S. opposition before they escalated their operations in Angola, and neither did their relations with the Soviet Union complicate Havana's activities as they did in Latin America.[23] The Soviets were downgrading their African operations in the first place, and in the second place the lack of African Communist parties did not raise the question of armed struggle versus peaceful change, the issue that so divided Moscow and its pro-Soviet Communist parties from Havana's pressing of the violent guerrilla road to change.[24] Havana's export of revolution simply did not face African tensions as it did in Latin America.

Cuba's interest in Africa also stemmed from a natural racial affiliation with Africa, based upon the Afro-Cuban cultural legacy. African culture was deeply rooted in Cuban society—in religion, magic, music, and language among Cuba's black population. And the African heritage was imprinted in Cuban political life: General Antonio Maceo, unquestionably one of the greatest heroes in Cuba's Wars of Independence with Spain, was not white, and Cuban blacks had provided a majority of the Army of Liberation during the Independence struggle.[25] Recognition of the black and mulatto contribution to Cuba's revolutionary struggles against Spain was a key feature of Castro's efforts to fuse a sense of single national consciousness—comprised of white, black and mulatto groups—following the 1959 Revolution.[26] In this sense, Castro's nation-building efforts were closely linked to Cuba's African past.

In pursuing its Third World interests in Africa, the Cubans developed close relations with a number of regimes and movements at the same time the Soviets were following their own interests in Africa. Cuba sent military and medical supplies to the Algerian Liberation Front (FLN) in 1960 and in 1963 forwarded arms and a battalion of combat troops to Algeria to help in the Algerian-Moroccan border dispute.[27] A Cuban military mission remained in Algeria until Ben Bella's overthrow in 1965. The first Cuban military mission was placed in Ghana in 1961 and continued there until Nkrumah's overthrow in 1966.[28]

In addition to these activities, Cuban President Osvaldo Dorticos led a delegation to the Second Conference of Nonaligned Nations, held in Cairo in October 1964, and in 1964-65 Ernesto "Che" Guevara made an extended tour of the continent, where he visited Algeria, Ghana, Congo-Brazzaville, Guinea, Mali, Dahomey, Tanzania, and the United Arab Republic.[29] During the tour, "Che" declared Africa as "one of the most important, if not *the* most important, battlefield against all forms of exploitation in the world."[30] Following the "Che" mission came Cuban aid to Congo-Brazzaville, where the MPLA was based, Guinea, base for the African Party for the Liberation of Portuguese Guinea and the Cape Verde Islands (the PAIGC), and support for the Front for the Liberation of Mozambique (FRELIMO) based in Tanzania.[31] A Cuban military mission was also established in Guinea in 1966.[32]

Cuba's growing military involvement in Africa, at the time of Soviet decline, continued to expand into the early 1970s. After 1971 Cuba sent military missions to Sierra Leone, Equatorial Guinea, Somalia, Algeria, Mozambique, and Angola.[33] In Sierra Leone, a Cuban mission arrived in September 1972 to train a 500 man militia, in Equatorial Guinea over 400 Cuban advisers were in place by November 1974, of which about 80 were military advisers, and the number may have doubled by 1977.[34] In Somalia, the Cubans were advising its military by 1974, a small number of Cuban aircraft technicians were in Algeria by 1975, and Cubans began to arrive in Mozambique by February 1976.[35] And for the first time, Cuban military missions were sent to the Middle East, notably South Yemen, Syria, and Iraq.

Cuba's expanding relations with Africa increased its value to the Soviet Union and undoubtedly provided the Castro government with additional leverage in negotiating economic and military aid agreements with the Soviets. During May-July 1972, for example, Castro made an unprecedented two-month tour of Africa and East Europe, which he ended with a ten day stay in the Soviet Union. Castro's itinerary in Africa included Guinea, Sierra Leone, and Algeria. Castro's frequent public speeches accentuated his support for socialist and revolutionary governments, in addition to constant references about U.S. involvement in the war in Vietnam. The length of the stay in the Soviet Union publicized favorable relations between the two countries. The Castro group undoubtedly argued for increased Soviet assistance during this stay, for the joint communiqué issued at the end of the visit indicated more forthcoming economic and technical aid from the Soviets. The communiqué, significantly, did not mention the problem of Cuban sugar deliveries—irregular and under the planned amounts—and Moscow's principal newspapers also omitted a high-level decree calling for greater Soviet sugar production. The communiqué thereby reflected either direct or indirect Cuban influence.[36]

Castro followed up his June-July 1972 visit to the Soviet Union with another trip in December, to participate in ceremonies commemorating the 50th anniversary of the founding of the Soviet Union. Again, he preceded the Moscow stay with a stopover in a Third World country—this time Morocco, where he praised Soviet aid to Cuba and condemned the United States for its bombing in Vietnam. This time the Soviet visit produced a spectacular new agreement. The communiqué called for five agreements by which the Soviets would extend "extraordinary" new economic aid to Cuba: (1) deferring Cuba's debt to the Soviet Union until 1986 and then to be repaid over a 25 year period, (2) new credits to cover Cuba's 1973-75 trade deficits, (3) agreement on the amount of goods to be traded during 1973-75; (4) up to $390 million in economic and technical aid to Cuba at a new "low" interest rate; and (5) favorable new agreements on Soviet purchases of Cuban sugar and nickel above the world market price.[37] This is not to suggest that Cuba's African posture alone produced these agreements, yet Cuba's expanding presence in the African sector of the Third World increased its credit with the Soviets as a valued ally and thus enhanced Havana's bargaining position on matters of aid and trade.

Four key points about Cuba's activities in Africa attract our attention. First, the Cubans were engaged on the African continent in pursuit of their own interests quite separate from those of the Soviet Union long before the joint Soviet-Cuban operations in Angola and Ethiopia. Yet these interests were compatible with the Soviets, indeed helped in the attainment of Soviet goals. Castro's speeches at the Fourth Conference of Nonaligned Nations, held in Algiers in September 1973, vividly etched Castro's value to the Soviets. For in Algiers, Castro fought against the

Conference's tendency to include the Soviet Union among the imperialist nations who were not friends of the Third World.[38]

Second, Cuba's African presence continued to operate precisely at a time in the late 1960s when the Soviets were downgrading relations with many African regimes, owing to their reasons for pessimism discussed earlier and because the Soviet's faith in African revolutionary potential had declined. This trend further illustrates *sui generis* Cuban interests and intentions in Africa apart from the Soviet Union.

Third, while the Soviet Union was reformulating its African foreign policy less along ideological lines during the mid to late 1960s, the Cuban's ideological adherence to "internationalist solidarity" in support of national revolutionary movements in the African region of the Third World was on the ascendancy.[39] Again, these separate Cuban-Soviet approaches to Africa suggest strongly Cuba's own decision making relative to Africa.

Fourth, Cuba's long-range capabilities to project operations into Africa were limited by Cuba's military and economic resources, not so much military personnel as air and sealift capacities, weapons and supplies, logistical support, and the strength of the Cuban economic base. Here is where Soviet military and economic power would help in cases like Angola and Ethiopia, and that factor in turn cooperatively influenced Cuban decision making to extend large numbers of combat troops to Angola and Ethiopia.

SOVIET-CUBAN INFLUENCE RELATIONS IN ANGOLA AND ETHIOPIA

The Soviet and Cuban leaderships projected their independent African foreign policies in Angola and Ethiopia from 1975 onward, and this factor in turn set up the conditions for two quite distinct influence relationships. In Angola, Soviet-Cuban policies were less coordinated than in Ethiopia, with the Cubans functioning more as an autonomous actor backed by Soviet weapons and logistical support. In Ethiopia, Soviet and Cuban military intervention was closely coordinated from the beginning, and in some ways the Cubans are open to the charge that they acted more as a proxy of the USSR, with influence flowing more from Moscow to Havana than the reverse.

Yet the overall effect of Cuban intervention in Angola and Ethiopia was to have substantially increased Cuban influence over the Soviet Union by demonstrating its usefulness to the Soviets and thereby becoming

what some scholars have identified as a privileged ally from 1976 onward.[40] Following the Cuban interventions in Angola in 1975 and Ethiopia in 1978, the Cubans were able to negotiate favorable economic and
trade accords, and the Soviets provided new arms shipments to build up
Cuba's Revolutionary Armed Forces (FAR) with more sophisticated
weapons.[41]

Angola

In what specific ways were the Soviet-Cuban influence relationships
different in Angola and Ethiopia? In the case of Angola, Cuba began to
develop close ties with the MPLA in 1965, when Che Guevara met with
the MPLA leader, Agostinho Neto. From this early period onward,
Cuban-MPLA ties were solid, and the Cubans provided an uninterrupted
supply of arms and training programs, with MPLA students and guerrilla
recruits coming to Cuba for education and military training.[42] Castro's
attraction to the MPLA lay in its being not only the oldest national liberation movement in Angola, but also its ideological sophistication compared to the rival movements: Holden Roberto's pro-western anti-
Communist National Front for the Liberation of Angola (FNLA) and Jonas
Savimbi's National Union for the Total Liberation of Angola (UNITA).[43]
In addition the Cubans believed Neto's group would be more progressive,
given the nature of the groups who supported it—the socialist bloc, as well
as Nkrumah and Ben Bella with whom Cuba also enjoyed close relations
during the mid-1960s.

The striking feature of Cuban support for the MPLA is its uninterrupted consistency compared to the Soviets, the differences produced by
conflicting policy orientations and underlying assumptions. Cuba's ideo-
logically inspired internationalist solidarity in support of Third World
progressive national liberation movements held firm *vis à vis* the anti-
imperialist MPLA throughout the 1960s and into the 1970s, while the
Soviets were becoming more cautious, pragmatic, and geostrategically-
oriented. In terms of the influence question, this becomes an important
point, illustrating that the Cubans cannot be cast in the role of a surrogate
in the Angolan case. While Cuban support for the MPLA continued right
into the Civil war period of 1974-76, for example, the Soviets ceased their
aid to the MPLA in 1963-64 (before the Cuban connection), slowed down
their military aid in 1972-73 when political frictions began to weaken the
MPLA, and stopped its MPLA aid totally in 1974.[44]

This pattern of distinct Soviet-Cuban policies carried over into the

Angolan civil war period of 1974-76. When the Portuguese dictatorship fell in April 1974, the Angolan civil war was spawned. The Soviets, fearing Chinese influence in the FNLA, resumed their support of the MPLA, but also supported a transitional governmental formula. This agreement was worked out among the three nationalist movements that met in Alvor (a small town in southern Portugal) in January 1975 which called for Angolan independence in November 1975. The Alvor agreement soon fell apart, and the Soviets began to supply the MPLA in March and April to help in their struggle with FNLA and UNITA—by then increasingly backed by the United States, China and South Africa. The MPLA also faced opposition from approximately 1200 regular troops from Zaire, which joined FNLA, another factor that impelled the MPLA to seek additional help, including from the Cubans.

While the Soviets indeed met the MPLA request for additional aid by sending weapons and supplies, they gave Neto a "chilly" reception in June 1975 regarding deeper direct involvement, and they still publicly supported the Alvor understanding. In contrast, while the Soviets had not determined how far they were willing to go in Angola, the Cubans appeared eager to extend their direct combat involvement: a contingent of 230 Cubans had already arrived in May and were fighting with the MPLA by the end of the month while the Soviet Union was still deciding how deep a commitment to make.[45] Again in August—when South African troops crossed the Namibian border and then established training bases for the FNLA and UNITA in Namibia and southern Angola—the MPLA requested more than arms from an unresponsive Soviet Union. The same month found the Cubans agreeing to send several hundred additional troops to Angola in response to an MPLA request, and the first Cuban troop ships began to arrive in Angola in late September and early October, by which time about 1500 Cuban military personnel were in Angola.[46] The Cubans also detached a senior military mission to oversee the Cuban effort and to advise the MPLA military operations.[47]

By this time, Soviet military advisers and technicians had begun to appear in Angola, evidence that the Soviets finally had determined to become more directly involved.[48] Among the reasons for this decision—which include opposition to their U.S. and Chinese rivals and their previous support for the MPLA—Cuban influence probably entered into the equation. The Cubans were in place, they were already fighting, willing to continue to do so and capable of handling the sophisticated Soviet weapons. Not only were these indirect influences operative, but it is conceivable that the Cubans even directly pressured the Soviets to show more vigorous and direct action.[49]

The event that triggered escalated Cuban and Soviet buildups in Angola occurred in October 1975 with the crossing of the Angola-Namibia border by a group of Portuguese mercenaries, South African regular forces, and FNLA troops. Its rapid advancement prompted the Cubans to increase their involvement with four to five Cuban troop ship departures in late October, followed by a troop airlift that began in early November.[50] By January 1976, Cuban arrivals were estimated at 1,000 weekly, and by March 1976 between 18,000 and 24,000 Cuban military personnel had arrived to support the MPLA. As to the Soviets, they substantially increased their air and sealift of arms and ammunition, aided the Cubans in airlifting them to Angola in early 1976 and deployed a small contingency naval force off West Africa.[51] This joint Soviet-Cuban effort led ultimately in February 1976 to South Africa's withdrawal and recognition of the MPLA by the Organization of African Unity and most of the West European countries as the legitimate government of Angola.

The weight of evidence argues that the Cubans did not act as a proxy during the Angolan operations, but rather made most of their decisions to increase their intervention independently of the Soviet Union.[52] Cuban sources confirm this conclusion, as does the semiofficial account by Gabriel Garcia Marquez.[53] Soviet sources similarly attest to the independence of Cuban decision making on its Angolan intervention, which seems all the more likely given the Soviet reluctance to become too deeply involved lest the situation draw them into a direct confrontation with the United States. While the Soviets supplied increased arms—probably under some form of Cuban direct or indirect influence—the Cubans and MPLA commanders planned the campaign and Cuban soldiers fought in direct combat against MPLA opponents. Under these conditions the Cubans and Soviets increasingly coordinated their actions by late 1975, but not in the form of Soviet assertive or coercive power over the Cubans.

The Angolan experience indicates more influence flowing from Cuba to the Soviet Union than the reverse, although it must be said that the Soviets likely had a kind of indirect influence on Cuban intervention. By this is meant that the Cubans may well have anticipated that: first, the Soviets certainly would not oppose their buildup of combat forces in Angola, second, they would support the Cubans to some extent, and third, the Cubans could win rewards from the Soviet Union by acting in a manner that would favor Moscow's interests while at the same time advancing Cuban goals. This indeed is what occurred as made evident by the privileged status among Soviet socialist allies achieved by Cuba through its Angolan actions.

Distinct Soviet-Cuban intentions continued to operate in Angola following the events of early 1976. In May 1977 a *coup* attempt against Neto by Nito Alves, leader of a pro-Soviet MPLA extremist faction, suggested continuing differences in orientation between the Soviets and Cubans. The Soviets reportedly backed the Alves *coup* effort, a likely possibility in view of their previous difficulties with Neto. But the Cubans helped to put down the attempt. In so doing, the Cubans may have indirectly influenced the Soviets, because following the ill-fated and Cuban-opposed *coup* the Soviets determined to sign a treaty of friendship and cooperation with Neto in October in an effort to "broaden and deepen their cooperation."[54]

The MPLA's problems with opposition groups inside Angola, especially from Jonas Savimbi's UNITA and South African forces, did not disappear after the joint Soviet-Cuban military intervention, nor did Angola's massive economic development problems dissolve. Consequently, Cuban military personnel and civilian development technicians were invited to stay on for purposes of guaranteeing MPLA survival and Angolan security, and Soviet economic and technical aid continued. By the early 1980s, the presence of Cuban forces in Angola, while serving the security interests of the MPLA, remained a major source of tension between the United States and Cuba as well as between the United States and the Soviet Union.

Much of the tension centers on the issue of South Africa's administration of South-West Africa (Namibia). While South Africa has stated that the key condition for its granting independence to Namibia is the withdrawal of Cuban troops, this condition is hampered by Pretoria's widely acknowledged support of Savimbi's UNITA. South Africa's call for negotiation between the MPLA and UNITA is not well-received by the MPLA. The Angolan government was equally displeased with South African forces that occupied parts of southern Angola; the MPLA government rather wished to see Pretoria accept the United Nations Plan for Namibian independence and withdrawal of South African forces from Namibia. But this could not be easily arranged, because South Africa faced constant pressure from the Angolan and Cuban-backed South-West Africa People's Organization (SWAPO), which used southern Angola as a base for its own drive to overthrow Pretoria's rule in Nambia.

As negotiations between Angola and South Africa regarding the status of Namibia and withdrawal of Cuban troops proceeded in 1984, the independent role of Cuba *vis à vis* the Soviet Union penetrated the diplomatic process. For these negotiations saw the President of Angola, José Eduardo dos Santos, traveling to Havana for talks with Fidel Castro to discuss the terms of withdrawal regarding the 25,000 troops then in Angola. Together, Angola and Cuba (not the Soviet Union) worked out the conditions for a Cuban military withdrawal: (1) that Pretoria cease supporting UNITA, (2) complete withdrawal of South African forces from Angola, and (3) acceptance of the U.N. plan for Namibian independence and withdrawal of South African forces from Namibia.[55]

These talks were important relative to Soviet-Cuban influence relations. First, they followed an Angolan-South African cease-fire and a nonagression treaty between Soviet-backed Marxist Mozambique and South Africa to bar support for each other's internal enemies.[56] The Soviets made no secret of their irritation with these agreements, for they meant the loss of Soviet leverage in decision making regarding sub-Saharan Africa through its two closest allies and channels to influence.[57] Second, the Angola-Cuban meetings produced additional Soviet irritation because they indicated that Castro could unilaterally withdraw his troops in promoting a Namibian independence settlement—without Soviet participation. The Cuban-Angolan bilateral negotiations and relations with South Africa underline the continuing independent strand in Cuba's policy toward the MPLA and the limited nature of Soviet influence on Cuban decision making in this part of Africa.

Ethiopia

Soviet-Cuban joint military intervention in Ethiopia contrasts significantly with Angola. In Angola, Cuba took the initiative in becoming directly involved with military forces, which the Soviets appear to have followed. In Angola, Cuba used its troops to assert influence when Soviet-Cuban policies diverged, as in the case of the extremist pro-Soviet faction attempted *coup* in May 1977. In Angola, Soviet-Cuban cooperation evolved naturally as their common policies fell into alignment during 1975. But in Ethiopia—a country high on the list of Soviet geostrategic interests centered in the Horn of Africa—the Soviet-Cuban influence relationship reflects sharper Soviet control. Although it can be argued that Cuba came to Ethiopia's assistance on its own volition, when Somalia escalated its military pressure on Ethiopia through the disputed Ogaden region in 1977, Soviet and Cuban policies were more coordinated than in Angola, and the Cubans appear to have been under firmer Soviet guidance than in Angola.[58]

The differences in the Soviet-Cuban influence in Ethiopia compared to Angola stemmed from a number of forces.[59] First, the Horn had long been of Soviet strategic interest, dating back to the days of Peter the Great. As Soviet interests in the Third World developed during the post-World War Two period, Khrushchev invited Haile Selassie to visit Moscow in

1959 in an effort to improve ties, and by the 1960s Soviet geostrategic and political interests in the Horn were rapidly quickening. There the Soviets sought to project their air and naval presence, while weakening the Chinese and U.S. presence. Soviet interests in Somalia began in 1961, first through economic aid and then military assistance, especially from 1971 onward, following Siad Barre's coming to power in 1969. In contrast, the Cuban presence in Somalia did not begin until 1974, then stepped up in 1976 after the Angolan events. Neither was the Cuban presence significant in Ethiopia before 1976, again in direct contrast with the Soviets.

Yet Moscow's state-to-state relations with Ethiopia did not develop favorably under Haile Selassie during the 1960s, given Ethiopia's military dependence on the United States. So the Soviets pursued other outlets on the Horn: disaffection in Eritrea, the Communist Party of the Sudan and the Sudanese government under Siad Barre, who seized power in 1969 and advocated a Sudanese version of socialism—but by no means under Communist Party leadership. Soviet support for the Eritrean national liberation movement was particularly successful, as it contributed to the ultimate fall of Haile Selassie in September 1974. Emperor Haile Selassie's government was replaced by a Provisional Military Government (the Dergue), led by a Provisional Military Council (PMAC). After much internal fighting, a radical faction of the PMAC, headed by Mengistu Haile-Mariam became the head of government in early 1977. These developments led the Dergue increasingly leftward and toward closer ties with the Soviet Union.

In contrast to Soviet interests in the Horn, especially as its blue water navy and global superpower interests projected outward from the late 1960s onward, Cuban involvement was minimal before 1976. It sent several dozen military technicians to Somalia in 1974, a contingent that grew to several hundred by 1976.[60] Cuba did not become directly involved in Ethiopia until 1977, when Castro visited Africa and attempted to mediate a settlement between Ethiopia and Somalia over the Ogaden. Castro's proposal for an anti-imperialist federation comprised of South Yemen, Ethiopia, Somalia, Djibouti, and an autonomous Ogaden did not transpire, as Ethiopia and Somalia could not agree.[61] Similar efforts by Soviet President, Nikolai Podgorny, to mediate the Ogaden conflict during his African visit shortly after Castro's March 1977 discussions, also proved fruitless. That the Soviets and Cubans were coordinating their negotiating is strongly suggested by the similarity of their federated solutions to the Ogaden problem and by Castro's unscheduled trip to Moscow when Podgorny returned from Africa. They remained closely coordinated from this point onward.

The Ethiopian-Somalia negotiations' failure set the scene for increased

Soviet and Cuban aid to Mengistu. For the failure of the federation—strongly backed by Cuba—came at a time of Ethiopia's internal security threats from the Eritrean national liberation movement and externally in the Ogaden region from the Somalia-backed Western Somali Liberation Front (WSLF). The Soviets found themselves incapable of managing Ethiopian-Somalia conflict relations, centering on the Ogaden, a situation that rapidly deteriorated during 1977 when 3,000-6,000 WSLF guerillas entered the Ogaden in May and 40,000 Somali troops invaded the Ogaden in July. Beyond its traditional problems with Ethiopia over the Ogaden, Somalia had become especially discontent with the growing Soviet Ethiopian and Cuban-Ethiopian military embrace.[62] Evidence of these ties soon appeared in the arrival of Cuba's Division General Arnaldo Ochoa in February 1977, the establishment of a Cuban military aid mission in April, and a secret military agreement between Ethiopia and the Soviets in May, soon followed by the arrival of Soviet arms.

Somalia's efforts to resolve its problems with Soviet and Cuban aid to Ethiopia simply did not work out. An August visit to the Soviet Union by Siad Barre failed to reduce the growing Soviet and Cuban aid to Ethiopia, and in September Ethiopia broke off relations with Somalia. In November Somalia abrogated its treaty of friendship with the Soviet Union, withdrew all its military facilities, ordered all Soviet military advisers to depart, and broke off diplomatic relations with Cuba. These events resulted in a dramatic escalation of Soviet and Cuban aid, closely coordinated from the beginning; by early 1978 the Cuban presence had grown from 400 advisors to an estimated 11,000-17,000 regular military personnel who, unlike the Angolan intervention, arrived primarily in Soviet troop transport ships.[63] Cuba's air and ground forces, backed by about 1,000-1,500 Soviet command and staff, led the successful combat against Somalia during February-March 1978. It was headed by Cuba's Division General Arnaldo Ochoa, one of the Cuban commanders in Angola, but now under the overall command of Soviet Lt. General Vasiliy I. Petrov and Grigory Barisov.[64] By March 1978 the Cuban-Ethiopian forces had driven the Somalis back across the border, and another chapter in Soviet-Cuban intervention had been written.

While the Soviet-Cuban influence relationship in Ethiopia indicates closer coordination of activities under Soviet control, it is not completely accurate to suggest the total lack of Cuban influence. As in Angola, the Soviet capability to intervene on behalf of the Mengistu regime depended upon Cuba's willingness to commit its ground forces against the Somalis. The Soviets remained cautious about committing their own combat forces in direct fighting, fearing U.S. reactions and the outside possibility of a direct confrontation should the United States come to Somalia's aid in the Ogaden matter. And Cuba's black and mulatto presence in its combat units would likely be more favorably received than white Soviet forces. The Cubans, as in Angola, were capable of using Soviet sophisticated weapons.

Finally, it would be very helpful to the Soviet Union to be associated with Cuba—a Third World country—in the combat with another progressive Third World country, Somalia. That kind of association could make the entire enterprise more legitimate in the eyes of other Third World states in Africa and elsewhere, than if the Soviets intervened by themselves with strictly their own forces. These factors must have indirectly affected the Soviet decision to commit so much military resources and personnel to Ethiopia's conflict with Somalia in 1977-78.

That Soviet influence over Cuba was by no means of an assertive or coercive type is illustrated by the Eritrean problem, which followed the Ethiopian-Cuban victory in the Ogaden in 1978. The Eritrean independence continued to plague the Mengistu government, which used its Cuban-trained and Soviet-equipped army on the Eritreans. This action brought strong Cuban insistence that its troops would not be used toward this end, because Cuba had supported the Eritreans in their self-determination battles since the time of Haile Selassie—a point stated publicly by Cuban Vice-President Carlos Rafael Rodríguez as early as February 1978.[65] Insofar as the Soviets initially seem to have endorsed Mengistu's use of force to stop the Eritreans, then later switched to stressing a negotiated settlement, it is possible that, again, the Cubans cooperatively influenced the Soviets on this matter.[66]

Since this period, the continued presence of Cuban troops in Ethiopia, long after the Somali threat subsided, coupled with recurring rumors of Cubans actually engaged in the fighting against the Eritreans, undermined Castro's leadership role in the Third World Nonaligned Movement.[67] In addition, the Cubans undoubtedly felt uneasy about having switched their support from both Somalia and Ethiopia to just Ethiopia, and they never reached the high degree of political integration established in Angola. Consequently, Cuba reduced its troops in Ethiopia to 11,000 in 1982 in order to lower its profile relative to the ongoing Eritrean dispute.[68] By March 1984, a phased additional withdrawal of Cuban troops was in progress, their number by then already down to between 2,000-3,000.[69] One suspects this decision was made—as in Angola—independent of the Soviet Union.[70]

As for pronounced Soviet influence in Ethiopia by the early 1980s, that country's evolution toward establishment of communist party rule and plans for formal entry into the Soviet camp illustrate Moscow's pressure.[71] Mengistu previously had resisted this Soviet drive, but he announced in February 1984 the forthcoming birth of Ethiopia's new communist party—the Ethiopian worker's party, "the sole institution to effect the realization of communism."[72] The Soviets and East Europeans were providing several hundred Marxist ideological teachers for planning the new party, and Mengistu stated that he intended Ethiopia to play a leadership role in supporting revolutionary change in Africa.

CUBA'S INCREASED INFLUENCE FOLLOWING ANGOLA AND ETHIOPIA

Because the Soviets were dependent upon Cuban ground troops in Angola and Ethiopia for advancing their objectives, the Cubans emerged from their Angolan and Ethiopian experiences with increased influence in the Soviet relationship.[73] Havana gained its leverage largely by proving its usefulness in projecting Soviet objectives in Angola and Ethiopia and by its new international status toward the end of the 1970s. Cuba's increased influence took several forms, each of which served to increase Havana's capacity to advance not only Soviet goals, but its own vital interests in Africa and other Third World regions.

First, the Cuban military performance in Angola and Ethiopia inclined the Soviets to reward Havana with increased trade, economic and technical assistance, and military weapons. The Soviets, for example, signed an economic cooperation agreement with Cuba in 1976, which called for a doubled level of Soviet-Cuban trade by 1980, increased sugar and nickel subsidies, and a 250 percent increase in economic-technical assistance.[74] On military aid, new inventories and upgraded weapons systems began to flow from Moscow to Havana, including advanced MIG-23 aircraft.[75] This increased materiel well served a number of Cuba's vital interests: economic development, security against the United States, and expanded international solidarity with developing countries.

Second, the Cubans undoubtedly encouraged the Soviets toward a more activist military role in Third World regions. This type of influence is suggested by the effects of Angola on the Soviet intervention in Ethiopia and, conceivably, the effects of both Angola and Ethiopia on increased direct Soviet aid to guerrilla movements and Marxist regimes (Nicaragua) in the Caribbean Basin from 1979 onward (discussed later). The "activist policy" influence for Cuba resulting from Angola and Ethiopia likely occurred through the strengthened positions of Fidel and Raúl Castro in Soviet decision-making circles. The Castro brothers long advocated this orientation in foreign policy, and insofar as Angola and Ethiopia confirmed their arguments about the correctness of direct action, their bargaining position with the Soviets increased. Raúl heads Cuba's Revolutionary Armed Forces (MINFAR), which in their strengthened position following Angola and Ethiopia, further enhanced his voice in joint decision-making circles. Here one sees the connection between direct action in Africa as carried over to Cuba's more geographically proximate neighbors. Unlike the 1960s, Cuba's direct action in Africa and the Caribbean Basin from the mid-1970s onward did not produce sharp friction with the Soviets—an illustration of Cuba's new influence.

Third, Cuba gained new international status in the Third World as a result of its Angolan and Ethiopia efforts. Castro's positive receptions in several African states during his tour of Africa in March-April 1977 was one indication of Cuba's new prestige.[76] During this tour, Castro conferred with the national leaders and civilians stationed in some of the countries; the tour took Castro to Algeria, Libya, South Yemen, Somalia, Ethiopia, Tanzania, Mozambique, Angola, and back to Algeria. And on completing the tour, Castro arrived in Moscow to be hugged at the airport by Soviet Communist Party leader Leonid Brezhnev, Premier Alexei Kosygin, and President Podgorny—their presence and warmth in greetings testifying to the importance they attached to Castro's visit. This new status, furthered by Cuba's expanding presence and economic-technical help to African developing countries from the later 1970s onward, resulted in the designation of Cuba as leader of the Third World Nonaligned Movement during the Sixth Conference of Nonaligned States held in Havana, in August 1979. Cuba's new status as a small state with a global presence enhanced Cuba's value to the Soviet Union, giving it added leverage and freedom of movement—for Cuba's prestige as a perceived independent actor among the African and other Third World states was of more value to the Soviets than a Cuba perceived as a dominated subservient client. Thus it can be assumed that the Soviets were prepared to provide Cuba with maximum leeway to conduct its foreign policy activities in Africa, indeed to make them possible, as long as those goals were compatible with Soviet objectives.[77]

These forms of influence were linked to Cuba's expanded African presence following the Angolan and Ethiopian interventions, which in effect affirmed Havana's new international status and leverage with the Soviets. In pursuing its internationalist solidarity, Cuba vastly increased its civilian economic-technical personnel in Africa and other developing countries during the late 1970s, to match its extraordinarily large numbers of military personnel. Approximately 5,400 civilian Cuban personnel were in Africa in 1977, with another 600 in other Third World regions. The number of Cuban civilians more than doubled during 1978-79, while the number in Asia, the Middle East and Latin America increased by an estimated 5.8 fold.[78] These Cuban civilians performed services in agriculture, sugar cultivation and refining, irrigation, cattle raising, irrigation, construction, education, and medicine, and some estimates place the number of Cuban civilians overseas in 1980 at nearly 20,000.[79] The greatest number in Africa were in Angola, followed by Ethiopia, Libya, and Mozambique. When a country could pay for these services, as in the case of Libya, the Cubans used the receipts to augment their hard currency earnings. The key point, however, is the usefulness of these activities in the advancement of Soviet interests, where Moscow's chief client, Cuba, demonstrated its brand of internationalist solidarity on behalf of Third World African development.

While these Cuban foreign aid programs stemmed from Havana's own ideological predilections and while the Cubans pursued their own independent activities in the context of their Soviet alliance, Soviet economic and military aid to African states overlapped with the Cubans. Where one found Cuban economic and military aid programs from the late 1970s onward, one generally found Soviet and East European military and economic personnel.[80] Within this alliance of foreign aid programs, one witnesses differences of Soviet and Cuban priorities, for example, the Cubans give higher priority to Angola than Ethiopia, while the Soviets are more committed to Algeria and Libya.[81] The essence of this pattern, however, is the compatibility of Soviet and Cuban policies and the ways in which Soviet-Cuban cooperation fostered each country's goals. That mutual dependence is involved challenges the thesis that Havana consistently acted simply as a proxy of the Soviet Union, or that it was a completely independent actor in Africa.

CUBA IN THE SOCIALIST COMMUNITY, AFRICA AND THE SOVIET-CUBAN RELATIONSHIP

Available evidence suggests that by the late 1970s Cuba was playing a number of roles in the socialist community that enhanced its leverage relations with the Soviets in Africa during and after the joint interventions in Angola and Ethiopia. Each of these roles augmented Cuba's prestige in the socialist community and therefore with the Soviets. In so doing, they added to Cuba's psychological power in their cooperative influence relations in Moscow. At the same time, they entailed limits to Cuba's prestige in Africa and the Third World, stemming from questions that could be raised about how independent an actor and how supportive of African development Cuba could be—precisely because it was so closely tied to the Soviet Union. A brief examination of these roles of Cuba as the avant-garde of Third World interests in Africa (and elsewhere in the Third World) suggests both the bases of Cuban influence with the Soviets and the limits to that influence.

The Cubans were playing at least six major roles in the socialist community that positively affected their influence relations with the Soviets during and after the Angolan and Ethiopian interventions insofar as these roles brought prestige to the Soviet-backed Cubans among progressive African leaders. These are: (1) breaking with dependency on Western capitalism, (2) leading in the national aspects of socialism, (3) executing development socialism, (4) creating a new socialist ethic of achievement, struggle and work, (5) assuming a radical leadership position in the Non-aligned Movement and the United Nations, and (6) diplomatic leadership of Third World internationalism.

Breaking with Dependency on Western Capitalism

One key feature of Third World explanations of underdevelopment is the *dependency* thesis, which originated in the writings of Latin American writers and then spread into Africa, Asia and the Middle East.[82] The essential feature of this Third World explanation for underdevelopment is the capitalist-controlled international economic system led by the "core" countries, which in turn dominate the "peripheral" Third World countries. The domination occurs through multinational corporations, foreign technology, international financial systems, foreign embassies, International Monetary Fund (IMF) lending, and other methods of capitalist control.[83] Because Cuba broke with, and continues to defy, U.S. capitalism through its 1959 Revolution, it became an example to other progressive African and Third World states on how to break the "dependency" syndrome. And when accused of replacing one form of dependency (U.S.) with another (Soviet), the Castro government stresses that the Soviets do not own property in Cuba, do not control Cuban economic and political elites, and do not repatriate more capital than they put into the country. The Cubans argue that their goals and interests are not subordinated to the policies of any other socialist state.[84]

Leadership in the National Aspects of Socialism

Nationalism is a potent force in the African countries, as it is through-out the Third World. Cuba's emphasis on its national autonomy and its blending of nationalism with Marxism-Leninism finds a receptive audience in the progressive African states, and Cuba's blending of nationalism and socialism gives it an edge in adapting its foreign policies to diverse African settings—a factor that the Soviets cannot but fail to acknowledge because of their own problems with ethnic nationalism inside the Soviet borders. Working for socialism, the first principle of Cuban foreign policy is highly compatible with Cuba's national revolutionary past—its struggles against Spanish colonialism and U.S. neocolonialism after the Spanish-American-Cuban War of 1898. As Carlos Rafael Rodríguez, a high-ranking member of Cuba's foreign policy decision makers, stated in February 1982, "in order to become a national Cuba, a Cuban Cuba, Cuba had to free itself from the American imperialist yoke."[85]

As the Cuban leadership sees it, nationalism and anti-imperialism/anticolonialism are compatible concepts—not only in Cuba's own past, but in its sensitivity and notion of duty to African and other Third World development struggles. When asked about Cuban policy in Africa during a January 1982 news interview, Rafael Rodríguez responded that, "Here the people feel their African roots most keenly." He went on to state: "... it is the peoples who make revolutions. Revolution cannot be exported and we are not in Africa to make anyone's revolution. We are in Africa quite simply in order to defend the national independence of two countries that asked for our aid for that purpose."[86] A sense of national differences within the African socialist community dominates Cuban foreign relations and helps establish Cuba as an effective avant-garde leader. Attitudes and perceptions like these fall upon welcome ears in the African setting, making Cuba a valuable asset to the Soviets.

Executing Development Socialism

While Cuba's socialist economic development is a subject of major debate, Castro's national socialist Revolution has produced significant advancement in social welfare sectors.[87] These include education, health care and medicine, sports and sports medicine. As one recent report on the Cuban economy notes, Cuba's socialist economic balance sheet includes a number of successes in eliminating almost all malnutrition, particularly among children, establishment of a national health care system that is superior among the developing countries, near complete eradication of illiteracy, and development of a relatively well-disciplined and motivated population with high national identity.[88] Cuba's sports training program also receives high marks in terms of its stress on achievement, inculcating a sense of competition among its participants, and producing a source of national pride.[89] The sports training system became a significant channel to project Cuba into a highly recognized competitor in international events including the Olympic Games—which Cuba determined to boycott in 1984 along with the Soviets.

These activities in socialist development at home provided the structural and ideological bases for Cuba's overseas programs in African and other Third World countries and as a training center for their students. Thus Cuba became not only a model for executing development socialism at home, but it assumed the avant-garde role in making its help available to other socialist and nonsocialist African countries. As the Angolan Minister of Education said in Cuba in May 1982, during the signing ceremonies of a bilateral cultural-educational accord, "Cuba will be a model to be emulated in educational matters."[90] And at the opening of a 10 day poster exhibition in Harare, Zimbabwe, in May 1982, the Zimbabwean Minister of Information, Posts and Telecommunications, stated that "your success will encourage us to repudiate threats and to start to work towards the uplifting of the standards of living of our people."[91] By 1982, Cuba's cooperation extended to approximately 32 countries.[92]

Creating a New Socialist Ethic of Achievement, Struggle, and Work

While the point can be overdrawn, one of the problems of economic development within African countries lies within the domain of attitudes toward achievement and work. This point is recognized by socialist and capitalist countries alike, including the United States and the Soviet Union. As a result of many complicated factors—cultural attitudes and values not conducive to work with the hands, ethnic-racial divisions which subordinate some groups to others, the lack of incentives to strive to get ahead, patron-client relations and corruption, religious fatalism—some cultural settings are less amenable to economic development than others. The problem results in either a divided population not pulling together or the lack of individual motivation to do the basic tasks required if the individual and the whole society are to improve overall living standards.

In this regard, the Cuban Revolution not only introduced socialism as a model of development, but it also utilized Castro's charisma, nationalism, and socialist ideological tenets to forge a new social ethic of achievement, struggle and work—socialized within the Cuban population as a whole. While there is no official reference to a "socialist work ethic," government leaders consistently stress the values of hard work, unity, struggle, self-discipline, and commitment to Cuban development. As Castro said at the ceremony marking the 26th anniversary of the "Granma" landing and founding of the Revolutionary Armed Forces, on December 11, 1982:

> Only a People's Revolution can arm the people. . . . Our main strength does not lie in our weapons; it lies in our morale, our patriotism and our revolutionary consciousness. . . . Let us dedicate ourselves to work, production and the struggle against our economic difficulties as never before. . . [93]

And as any visitor to Cuba will see, the Central Highway is lined with billboards exhorting the population to work, struggle, achievement, and a host of other cultural attitudes and values conducive to a socialist ethic of individual and collective progress.

This socialist ethic undoubtedly rubs off on African and Third World students in Cuba, as well as on other African populations for whom Cuban civilians are working abroad. As a number of Mozambican students remarked in Cuba in August 1982, ". . . we were able to witness that this school has set an example in all areas—in discipline, organization, formal organization, care of social property, productive tasks, cultural activities and sports.[94] And the socialist work ethic is a source of psychological commitment for those Cuban teachers, medical personnel, agronomists, and construction workers going abroad for Cuba's public international service—not an insignificant force for the approximately 25,000 Cuban technicians serving abroad by 1982.[95]

Diplomatic Leadership of African and Third World Internationalism

Because Cuba's foreign policy is rooted in the commitment to contribute to the cause of socialism, the essential feature of its diplomacy is international cooperation.[96] Cuba, in the words of Rafael Rodríguez, is duty-bound "to practice and will always practice revolutionary proletariat internationalism."[97]

As a small socialist state, Cuba is remarkable in the avant-garde in terms of putting into practice the international cooperative aspects of socialism, which indirectly benefited the Soviet Union and gave the Cubans considerable influence with the Soviets. Within the broad range services extended to other African socialist and even nonsocialist countries, the Cubans: (1) provided a climate of importance to other small states' socialist goals, (2) extended dignity to them and their leaders, (3) reinforced their national identity and sense of uniqueness within the international political system, and (4) brought prestige to Cuba's own government, people and revolutionary heritage—backed by the Soviet Union.

Cuba was performing these international and socialist roles in a variety of ways. Among them were the ceremonial functions associated with sending and receiving of representatives covering a number of types of functions, hosting high level meetings in Havana, participating in international sports competition, and utilizing Cuba's radio and television networks for widespread communication of Third World activities. Cuba's emphasis on the use of its human resources on behalf of African socialist development, with a stress on self-help, nonpayment for services rendered (unless, of course, the country can pay, e.g., Libya), and generally advancing the small state's labor-intensive model of development as opposed to a capital-intensive model illustrate additional approaches to the promotion of socialist change through Cuba's leadership in socialist "internationalism."

Radical Leadership within the Nonaligned Movement and the United Nations

Cuba's radical position in the Nonaligned Movement formed a positive attribute of its leverage with the Soviets throughout the 1970s and into the 1980s, not only in its African context but also in terms of its broader impact on the Third World countries. As the 1970s progressed, the Cubans placed considerably more stress on the necessity to confront imperialism, colonialism, and neocolonialism led by the United States than it did the "neutralist" position between the United States and the Soviet Union originally intended by the Nonalignment Movement.[98] The Nonalignment Movement admittedly shifted to the left during the 1970s, as indicated at the 1973 Fourth Summit Meeting in Algiers, which identified "imperialism" as the greatest obstacle toward progress in the developing countries. This shift occurred as a result of the Third World's rising militance on economic matters, underscored by its parallel stress on a New International Economic Order (NIEO) called for in the 1974 and 1975 Special Sessions of the U.N. General Assembly.[99] But within this leftward shift, Cuba persistently pressed its view that the Third World's interests were constrained by the West, led by the United States, rather than by the socialist camp, led by the Soviet Union.

Cuba's influence with the Soviets was aided by another fact. Cuba went well beyond the notion of western imperialism as the enemy of the Third World states by contending that the Soviet Union and the Communist camp represented the "natural ally" of the African and other nonaligned states.[100] This position produced a number of divisions within the Nonaligned Movement following the Soviet invasion of Afghanistan in late 1979. On the General Assembly Resolution to deplore Soviet intervention in Afghanistan, for example, out of the 15 African recipients of Cuban aid, only Angola, Ethiopia and Mozambique voted with Cuba against it. Tanzania voted yes, and all the rest abstained. Earlier, at the Sixth Nonaligned Summit in Havana in August 1979, Cuban support for the Soviet-backed Vietnamese occupation of Cambodia seriously damaged their support in the movement. And at the Seventh Summit Meetings in New Delhi in March 1983, a number of delegations, including Singapore, condemned the Soviets for their Afghanistan occupation and warned that the Soviet Union was trying to capture the Movement—an indirect comment on Cuba's pro-Soviet stance. But on the whole the Soviets had to appreciate Cuba's efforts in attempting to pull more and more African and Third World states toward the Soviet orbit through the "natural ally"— despite the problems caused for this argument by Moscow's direct intervention in Afghanistan.

LIMITS TO CUBAN INFLUENCE IN AFRICA AND THE SOVIET-CUBAN RELATIONSHIP

Because Havana's increased leverage on the Soviets stemmed from their ability to advance Moscow's goals in Africa, as in Angola and Ethiopia, Cuba's future leverage must be assessed in terms of two criteria: (1) the extent to which Cuba can compensate for weaknesses in Soviet military and economic aid programs in Africa and (2) other limits to Cuba's capacity to influence the progressive African states, despite the positive roles discussed above. In looking to the character of the future Soviet-Cuban influence relationship in Africa, the key issue of limits to both Soviet and Cuban military and economic aid programs comes into direct focus.

Concerning the first criterion, the Soviets suffer from numerous constraints to their own direct influence over their African clients. First, Soviet aid to African countries is preponderantly military, to the extent that a number of African leaders argue that the Soviets have not developed relevant economic and political criteria for their development problems. Although military aid is critical in consolidating an African regime's internal and external security, it does not address the central financial development issues facing most of the African states. The problem is compounded when the Soviets demand repayment for its weapons at a time when a small client is impoverished.

Ethiopia is a case in point, where the USSR has supplied over $3 billion in military aid since 1976, largely to help the Mengistu regime continue to seek a military solution to its internal difficulties.[101] By 1984 the Soviets were pressing the Ethiopian government to repay the $1.5 billion owed for weapons supplied since 1979, thus greatly burdening Ethiopia's hard currency problem. And in Angola, the arms deliveries worth $250 million in 1981 and $300 million in 1982 are expected to be repaid in hard currency and trade, largely in fishing.

Second, the Soviet capacity to help the developing African countries economically is notoriously less than the Western world. The Soviet economy is in serious trouble, its foreign technicians infrequently mix well with African counterparts, and many of its extended economic credits go undrawn. This situation is complicated for the Soviets, because they have little to offer Africa financially, they do not participate in Western international economic organizations, such as the World Bank or the IMF, and their ruble is not convertible. It is also complicated because of the poor quality of most Soviet goods—both civilian and military. The latter can be a major problem, as in Ethiopia in late 1981, when it was reported that the Soviets were insisting that if major repairs were needed on heavy technical equipment, it should be transported back to the Soviet Union with Ethiopia paying for the transport costs.

Concerning the impact of this situation on the Soviet-Cuban relationship, in some respects the Cuban position is improved relative to the Soviets. The Cuban experience in human resources development, its own record of labor-intensive development projects at home, and its willingness to send thousands of trained individuals to outlying African countries are distinctly Cuban assets in its Soviet influence relationship. Cubans know what it is to be a lesser developed Third World country, and their understanding of the African dilemmas cannot be denied. But on the negative side, the Cubans can do only so much on the economic front to stimulate development. Beyond human resources, there is the grinding need for financial and developmental capital, not possessed by either the Soviet Union or Cuba, but more exclusively in control of the western developed countries. Hence the attraction of the West and one reason for the shift in foreign policy orientations toward Western capital by Mozambique and Angola in 1984. The shortfall in Cuban and Soviet economic power will continue into the immediate future, and this problem could contribute to a somewhat lessened capacity of Cuba to serve Soviet economic policy aid in Africa. This scenario is not implausible, especially should the Soviets find it necessary to cut back on their direct economic aid to Cuba, a problem discussed later. In any case, the Soviets will likely weigh Cuba's economic development capacities abroad in determining future benefits they derive in supporting the Castro government.

The second criterion involves other limits to Cuba's influence in Africa, which provides Havana with leverage in its Soviet relationship. Evidence suggests that a number of limits to Cuban influence are discernible in Africa: (1) by the early 1980s, the Cubans were being blamed for many problems in the Angolan economic and military sector, (2) they may be playing less of a combat role in Angola against UNITA than imagined and may be less efficient in the bush than the MPLA army, (3) they do not appear to have great influence on their aid recipients, as in the U.N. resolution concerning Afghanistan, and (4) they are not more able to guarantee the political stability or orientation of their aid recipients than any other outside power.[102] As in any other relationship, then, limits to Cuban power in the African setting exist. These in turn limit Cuba's leverage over the Soviets.

CONCLUSION

Soviet-Cuban relations in Africa illustrate the rich complexity of influence in shaping the foreign policies of each country. The patterns of Soviet-Cuban behavior in Africa from the Angolan intervention into the early 1980s indicates not a simple situation of Cuba as a Soviet proxy nor as an autonomous actor. A more intricate relationship is at work—one of different, yet compatible goals, in which each country's cooperation influenced the other's capability to attain its objectives.

Moscow's perception of Cuba as a valued client, following Havana's demonstrated capabilities in Angola and Ethiopia, became a prime force in motivating the Soviets to increase economic and military aid to Cuba. Here we see the importance of *perceptions* in the influence relationship and how a small state's perceived value gives it attributive influence relative to its "more powerful" patron. After the Cubans willingly fought in Angola and Ethiopia, thus reducing the Soviet need to commit a vast number of their own ground forces and risking a direct confrontation with the United States, Moscow began to provide much elevated levels of economic and military assistance to Havana. By 1982 Soviet aid to Cuba totaled $4.9 billion per year or an estimated $13 million per day, much of it attributable to special pricing arrangements for Cuban sugar and Soviet petroleum. And Cuba received free military aid, estimated at over $4 billion in 1981 and 1982. Naturally this assistance greatly aided the pursuit of Cuba's own vital interests.

In terms of the influence equation, Soviet and Cuban *intentions* were less affected than their *capabilities* in the Angolan and Ethiopian cases. Soviet and Cuban policies in Africa were based upon distinct sets of assumptions and intentions before the Angolan and Ethiopian situations changed during 1974-76 (Angola) and 1977-79 (Ethiopia). Once this occurred, each side determined that it could best advance its interests by cooperating to expand the other's capabilities to bring about outcomes favoring their policies. The Cubans provided essentially the human resources, whereas the Soviets supplied weapons and logistical support, and in the case of Ethiopia, overall direction of the combat against Somali forces in Ogaden. The type of mutual influence exerted was *cooperative*, as opposed to assertive or coercive power, and Soviet interests affected by the African issues were essentially of the second level saliency type, if we use the analysis of Chapter One. The affected Cuban interests, by contrast, were of first and second level saliency.

Other conclusions can be drawn from the African experience. Both the Soviets and Cubans benefited from the relationship. The Soviets were able to project their geostrategic and political presence into Angola, the Horn, and elsewhere, thanks to Cuba's cooperation. The Cubans upgraded their leadership position in the Third World Nonaligned Movement by assuming its leadership in August 1979, and they especially improved their first level vital interests by engaging in the Angolan and Ethiopian operations. The massive increases in Soviet economic and military aid helped promote Cuba's vital economic survival interests and simultaneously augmented its physical security with respect to the United States. In deciding to cooperate in Africa, and especially the Soviet decision to join Cuba in direct action of the type over which the Soviets and Cubans had split during the 1960s, both countries calculated that the benefits outweighed the costs of the engagement.

The African experience illustrates how important it is to examine the small state's foreign policy in a patron-client relationship like that between the Soviets and the Cubans. What first may appear as a "surrogate" frequently entails more complex dynamics between patron and client. Cuba possesses resources of high value to the Soviets: radical nationalism, its own revolutionary past and popular desire to help other similar Third World countries in Africa, Castro's charismatic personality, the training and sophistication of Cuba's armed forces, and its diplomatic leverage with developing countries in Africa and the Third World. These became factors of leverage in extracting increased Soviet aid.

Yet Cuba is by no means an autonomous actor in Africa. It continues to depend upon Soviet economic and military aid that makes possible its African presence. As long as these are forthcoming, the Cubans retain the capability to project their own presence and pursue their Third World-oriented goals. Should Soviet economic and military support significantly decrease for a variety of possible reasons in the future, Cuban capabilities would be undermined. From the Cuban perspective then, its perceived role as a Soviet resource power will continue to affect Havana's foreign policy—essentially keeping it within the realm of Soviet acceptability, for example, not publicly challenging the Soviets on their Eritrean posture and not acting in other ways against Soviet interests.

Still, what remains to be seen in the future is the extent to which Soviet and Cuban policies may diverge in southern Africa. Once the Soviets and Cubans intervened to aid the MPLA in Angola and the Mengistu regime in Ethiopia, they then faced the problem of countering insurgency movements against those regimes they had helped bring to power. The MPLA faced UNITA in Angola, and the Mengistu government encountered an ongoing struggle with the Eritrean and Tigrean national liberation movements. How Soviet and Cuban interests might diverge over addressing the question of counterinsurgency against authentic national liberation movements—which both the Soviets and Cubans were on record as supporting in their ideological pronouncements—were emerging questions for the latter half of the 1980s.

The effectiveness of direct action in Angola and Ethiopia undoubtedly influenced both the Cubans and Soviets to step up direct aid to insurgency movements in the Caribbean Basin in the late 1970s. This transition in Soviet foreign policy especially suggests the direct and indirect influence of the lesser partner in the Soviet-Cuban alliance. This is so because it was precisely Cuba's insistence on direct intervention and armed struggle as the path to change that had so divided the Soviets and Cubans during the 1960s. By the early 1980s the Soviets were following the *Cuban* line on armed struggle as the appropriate path to change in the Caribbean Basin—the arena to which we now turn.

NOTES

1. As Daniel Patrick Moynihan described Cuban behavior in Angola, they were "Gurkas of the Russian Empire." See Jiri Valenta, "The Soviet-Cuban Intervention in Angola, 1975," *Studies in Comparative Communism* 11, 1 and 2 (Spring-Summer 1978): 3. On this interpretation, see also Peter Vannemann and Martin James, "The Soviet Union, China and the West in Southern Africa," *Foreign Affairs* 54, 4 (July 1976): p. 745-62.

2. On the view that Cuba is more of an autonomous actor in the African setting, see Nelson P. Valdes, "Revolutionary Solidarity in Angola," in *Cuba in the World*, Cole Blasier and Carmelo Mesa Lago, eds., (Pittsburgh: University of Pittsburgh Press, 1978), pp. 110-13; and Cole Blasier, "The Soviet Union in the Cuban-American Conflict," in ibid., pp. 37-38.

3. It should be noted that intensified Soviet military aid to the Cuban armed forces in the early 1970s helped prepare them for the Angolan and Ethiopian interventions. See Jorge Dominguez, "The Armed Forces and Foreign Relations," in Blasier and Mesa Lago, *Cuba in the World*, pp. 53-86.

4. On growing optimism in Soviet foreign policy during the middle Brezhnev years, 1969-75, see Mark N. Katz, *The Third World in Soviet Military Thought* (London and Canberra: Croom Helm, 1982); Chapter 3; also Roger Kanet, ed., *Soviet Foreign Policy in the 1980s* (New York: Praeger, 1982), chap. 1; and E. J. Feuchtwanger and Peter Nailor, eds., *The Soviet Union and The Third World* (New York: St. Martin's Press, 1981), part 1.

5. Jiri Valenta, "Comment: The Soviet—Cuban Alliance in Africa and Future Prospects in the Third World," in *Cuba in Africa*, Carmelo Mesa Lago and June S. Belkin, eds., Latin American Monograph and Document Series, 3, (Pittsburgh: University Center for International Studies, University of Pittsburgh, 1982), p. 142.

6. These included Algeria, the Congo (Brazzaville), Guinea,, Ghana, Mali, Somalia, the Sudan, and the Marxist-oriented Movement for the Popular Liberation of Angola (MPLA). On the Soviet pursuit of rational guidelines and evolving opportunities to project a global presence, see David E. Albright, ed., *Communism in Africa*. (Bloomington: Indiana University Press, 1980), pp. 50-58; Edward Gonzalez, "Cuba, the Soviet Union, and Africa," in Albright, *ibid.*, pp. 145-67; and Colin Legum, "The USSR and Africa," *Problems of Communism* 27, 1 (Jan.-Feb. 1978): 1-19.

7. Jiri Valenta, "Soviet-Cuban Intervention in the Horn of Africa: Impact and Lessons," *Journal of International Affairs* 34, 2 (Fall/Winter 1980/81): 354-64; also Stephen T. Hosmer and Thomas W. Wolfe, *Soviet Policy and Practice Toward Third World Conflicts* (Lexington, Mass.: Lexington Books, 1983), chap. 7.

8. Valenta, "Soviet-Cuban Intervention in the Horn of Africa," pp. 356-57. See also Charles C. Petersen, "Trends in Soviet Naval Operations," in *Soviet Naval Diplomacy*, Bradford Dismukes and James McConnell, eds. (New York: Pergamon Press, 1979), chap. 2.

9. Albright, *Communism in Africa*, p. 52.

10. See Colin Legum, "African Outlooks Toward the USSR," in Albright, *Communism in Africa*, pp. 24-28.

11. Ibid.

12. See Katz, *Third World,*, p. 65.

13. Unfortunately, the two sides failed to agree on what crisis prevention meant in practice; the operational meaning of the BPA was left ambiguous. See Alexander L. George, ed., *Managing U.S.-Soviet Rivalry: Problems of Crisis Prevention* (Boulder, Colorado: Westview Press, 1983), Introduction and chap. 1; see also Rober Legvold, "The Super Rivals: Conflict in the Third World," *Foreign Affairs* 57, 4 (Spring 1979): 755-78.

14. Mohamed Heikal, *The Sphinx and the Commissar: The Rise and Fall of Soviet Influence in the Middle East* (New York: Harper and Row, 1978), pp. 211-14; Alvin Z. Rubinstein, *Red Star on the Nile: The Soviet-Egyptian Influence Relationship Since the June War* (Princeton: Princeton University Press, 1977), chap. 6.

15. Adeed Dawisha and Karen Dawisha, eds., *The Soviet Union in the Middle East: Policies and Perspectives* (London: Royal Institute of International Affairs, 1982), p. 2; K. R. Singh, "North Africa," in Mohammed Ayoob, ed., *The Politics of Islamic Reassertion* (New York: St. Martin's Press, 1981), pp. 68-71; Claudia Wright, "Libya and the West: Headlong Into Confrontation," *International Affairs* 58, 1 (Winter 1981-82): 13-41; and William Zartman with A. G. Kluge, "The Sources and Goals of Qaddafi's Foreign Policy," *American-Arab Affairs* 6 (Fall 1983): 59-69.

16. Legum, "The USSR and Africa," p. 9.

17. Ibid., pp. 10-11.

18. Ibid., pp. 4-5. Neither did Soviet cultural traits mesh well in the Middle East or Southeast Asia. Syria and Vietnam are cases in point, where the consequence is significant mistrust on both sides. On Syria, see Stanley Reed, "Syria's Assad: His Power and His Plan, " The *New York Times Magazine*, February 19, 1984, pp. 43, 45. On Soviet-Vietnamese dislike, see Douglas Pike, testimony in *The Soviet Role in Asia*, Hearings before the Subcommittee on Europe and the Middle East and on Asia and Pacific Affairs of the Committee on Foreign Affairs, House of Representatives, 98th Congress, July-October, 1983 (Washington D.C.: Government Printing Office, 1983, pp. 211-12.

19. See Valenta, "Soviet-Cuban Intervention in the Horn of Africa," p. 362; and Gonzalez, "Cuba, the Soviet Union, and Africa," in Albright, *Communism in Africa*, pp. 59-60.

20. See William J. Durch's incisive essay that extensively covers previous Cuban activities in Africa, "The Cuban Military in Africa and the Middle East: From Algeria to Angola," *Studies in Comparative Communism*, 11, 1 and 2 (Spring/Summer 1978): 34-74.

21. See Dominguez, "The Armed Forces and Foreign Relations," in Blasier and Mesa Lago, *Cuba in the World*, pp. 53-56.

22. On the evolving opportunities for a Cuban presence in Africa, see Durch, "Cuban Military in Africa;" also Carla Anne Robbins, *The Cuban Threat* (New York: McGraw-Hill, 1983), pp. 61-64.

23. This point is made by Robbins, *Cuban Threat*, pp. 60-61.

24. Ibid.

25. One scholar estimates that 70 percent of the soldiers in Cuba's War of Independence (1895-98) were black, while about 30 percent were white. Rafael Fermoselle-Lopez, *Black Politics in Cuba: the Race War of 1912*, unpublished Ph.D. dissertation, the American University, 1972, p. 1.

26. Castro began to forge a sense of collective national consciousness after 1959 by extolling a past that glorified all Cubans—white, mulatto, and black. This process involved identification with Cuba's past heroes, like Antoneo Maceo, who in the words of the *Fidelistas*, "wielded a sword for Cuba when it needed a soldier, and he was a disciplined

observer of the law of Cuba when Cuba needed a citizen." *Granma Weekly Review*, December 16, 1973; and *Granma Weekly Review*, June 23, 1974.

27. See *The New York Times*, October 15, 27, 28, 30, and 31, 1963.

28. *Manchester Guardian Weekly*, February 22, 1976, as quoted in Durch, "Cuban Military in Africa," p. 43.

29. See William M. LeoGrande, "Cuban-Soviet Relations and Cuban Policy in Africa," in Blasier and Mesa Lago, *Cuba in Africa*, p. 18.

30. As quoted in Durch, "Cuban Military in Africa," p. 46.

31. Ibid., pp. 46–47. By early 1966, the Cuban force in Congo-Brazzaville reached approximately 1,000. LeoGrande, "Cuban-Soviet Relations," in Blasier and Mesa Lago, *Cuba in Africa*, p. 19.

32. LeoGrande, "Cuban-Soviet Relations" in Blasier and Mesa Lago, *Cuba in Africa*, p. 19.

33. Durch, "Cuba Military in Africa," p. 51.

34. See *The New York Times*, November 17, 1977, p. 1; also Durch, "The Cuban Military," p. 52.

35. *Christian Science Monitor*, February 23, 1977, p. 1.

36. *Castro's Cuba in the 1970s* (New York: Facts on Files, 1978), pp. 39-41.

37. Ibid., pp. 40-41.

38. Ibid., pp. 103-104.

39. LeoGrande, "Cuban-Soviet Relations," in Blasier and Mesa Lago, *Cuba in Africa*, p. 39.

40. Gonzalez, "Cuba, Soviet Union, and Africa," in Albright, *Communism in Africa*, pp. 154-57.

41. Ibid., p. 154.

42. LeoGrande, "Cuban-Soviet Relations" in Blasier and Mesa Lago, *Cuba in Africa*, p. 20. And in 1978, Cuba accepted about 1,500 Ethiopian and 1,200 Mozambican school-age children at a new facility on the Isle of Pines. National Foreign Assessment Center, *Communist Aid Activities in Non-Communist Less Developed Countries*, 1978, Central Intelligence Agency (September 1979), p. 16.

43. LeoGrande, "Cuban-Soviet Relations" in Blasier and Mesa Lago, *Cuba in Africa*, pp. 20-21.

44. Ibid., p. 23; also Valenta, "The Soviet-Cuban Intervention in Angola," p. 24.

45. Valenta, "The Soviet-Cuban Intervention in Angola," p. 24.

46. See Gabriel Garcia Marquez, "Cuba en Angola: Operacion Carolota," in *Proceso* (Mexico City), January 8, 1977, translated in the U.S. *Joint Publications Research Service* (JPRS), No. 68687, Translations on Cuba, No. 1613 (February 25, 1977). The Marquez article is considered the semiofficial version of Cuban activities in Angola.

47. See Durch, "The Cuban Military," pp. 66-67.

48. Hosmer and Wolfe, *Soviet Policy and Practice*, p. 82.

49. Valenta, "The Soviet-Cuban Intervention in Angola," p. 49.

50. Durch, "The Cuban Military," p. 68.

51. Hosmer and Wolfe, *Soviet Policy and Practice*, p. 83.

52. See LeoGrande's discussion of this point, "Cuban-Soviet Relations" in Blasier and Mesa Lago, *Cuba in Africa*, p. 25.

53. Garcia Marquez, "Cuba in Angola."

54. Hosmer and Wolfe, *Soviet Policy and Practice*, p. 87.

55. *The New York Times*, March 18, 1984, pp. 1 and 6; *Christian Science Monitor*,

March 22, 1984, p. 9.

56. *The New York Times*, March 17, 1984, p. 1.

57. *The New York Times*, April 8, 1984, p. 11.

58. See Harry Brind, "Soviet Policy in the Horn of Africa," *International Affairs* (London) 60, 1 (Winter 1983–84): p. 78.

59. See Paul B. Henze, "Communism and Ethiopia," *Problems of Communism* 30, 3 (May-June 1981): 55.

60. *The New York Times*, April 5, 1976, p. 1.

61. LeoGrande, *op. cit.*, "Cuban-Soviet Relations," in Blasier and Mesa Lago, *Cuba in Africa* p. 38.

62. See Brind, "Soviet Policy in Horn," pp. 82-86.

63. LeoGrande, "Cuban-Soviet Relations," in Blasier and Mesa Lago, *Cuba in Africa*, p. 39.

64. Hosmer and Wolfe, *Soviet Policy*, p. 92.

65. *Washington Post*, February 27, 1978, p. 1.

66. Gonzalez, "Cuba, Soviet Union, and Africa," in Albright *Communism in Africa*, p. 156.

67. Robbins, *Cuban Threat*, p. 61.

68. *Latin American Weekly Report*, March 30, 1984, p. 3.

69. *Washington Post*, March 13, 1984, p. 1.

70. *Latin American Weekly Report*, March 30, 1984, p. 3.

71. *Christian Science Monitor*, February 15, 1984, p. 27.

72. Ibid.

73. See Sergio Roca, "Economic Aspects of Cuban Involvement in Africa," in Blasier and Mesa Lago, *Cuba in Africa*, p. 166.

74. Ibid.

75. Gonzalez, "Cuba, Soviet Union, and Africa," in Albright, *Communism in Africa*, pp. 158-59.

76. Castro traveled to Algeria, Libya, South Yemen, Somalia, Ethiopia, Tanzania, Mozambique, Angola, and Algeria.

77. Gonzalez, "Cuba, Soviet Union and Africa," in Albright, *Communism in Africa*, p 163.

78. Susan Eckstein, "Structural and Ideological Bases of Cuba's Overseas Programs," *Politics and Society* 11, 1 (1982): 97. Cuba had 5,900 civilian economic technicians in Africa during 1977; the number had risen to 11,420 by 1978: Algeria (50), Libya (400), Angola (8,500), Ethiopia (500), Guinea (35), Guinea-Bissau (85), Mozambique (400), Sao Tome and Principe (140), Tanzania (200), Zambia (20), and other (1,090). National Foreign Assessment Center, *Communist Aid Activities in Non-Communist Less Developed Countries*, 1977 and 1978, Central Intelligence Agency (1977 and 1978).

79. Eckstein, "Structural and Ideological Bases," p. 97.

80. Jorge Dominguez, "The Armed Forces and Foreign Relations," in Blasier and Mesa Lago, *Cuba in the World,* p. 114.

81. Ibid.

82. Tony Smith, "The Underdevelopment of Development Literature: The Case of Dependency Theory," *World Politics* 31, 2 (January 1979): 247-88.

83. Ibid.

84. The Cuban foreign policy leadership emphasizes that the Soviet Union, for example, has "never tried to impose a solution on us or demanded that we assume an atti-

tude that is incompatible with our situation and our interests. They have treated us as equals." Interview with Carlos Rafael Rodriguez, *Revolution*, Paris, France (29 January-4 February 1982), pp. 18-21.

85. Ibid.

86. Ibid.

87. See Carmelo Mesa-Lago, *The Economy of Socialist Cuba: A Two Decade Appraisal* (Albuquerque: University of New Mexico Press, 1981).

88. *Cuba Faces the Economic Realities of the 1980s*, A Study Prepared for the Use of the Joint Economic Committee, Congress of the United States, prepared by Lawrence H. Theriot (Washington, D.C.: Government Printing Office, 1982).

89. See R. J. Pickering, "Cuba," in James Riordan, ed., *Sport Under Communism* (London: C. Hurst, 1978), pp. 141-75; Mark Flannery, "Sports: A Revolutionary Idea," *Philadelphia Daily News*, April 13, 1982.

90. Havana Radio Broadcast, May 7, 1982.

91. Harare, *The Herald*, May 4, 1982, p. 1.

92. Julio A. Diaz Vasquez, "Economic and Scientific Cooperation with the Third World," *Economia y Desarrollo* 68 (May-June 1982): 26-43.

93. *Granma Weekly Review in English*, December 19, 1982.

94. *Granma Weekly Review in English*, August 15, 1982.

95. Julio A. Diaz Vasquez, "Economic and Scientific Cooperation with the Third World," pp. 26-43.

96. Carlos Rafael Rodríguez, "Strategic Principles of Cuban Foreign Policy," *Cuba Socialista*, December 1981, pp. 10-33.

97. Ibid.

98. William LeoGrande, "Evolution of the Nonaligned Movement," *Problems of Communism* 29 (January 1980): 35-52. See also Shaukat Hassan, "Nonalignment and Socialist Foreign Policy," *Asian Affairs* 8 (January-February 1981): 153-65.

99. For the background on development of the Third World position on international economic issues leading to NIEO, see Roger D. Hansen, *Beyond the North-South Stalemate* (New York: McGraw-Hill, 1979), chap. 2.

100. See LeoGrande, "Evolution of the Nonaligned Movement," pp. 35-52.

101. Briefing by Chester Crocker, U.S. Assistant Secretary of State, Presented to United States Information Agency, March 15, 1984.

102. Gerald J. Bender, "Comment: Past, Present, and Future Perspectives of Cuba in Africa," in Blasier and Mesa Lago, *Cuba in Africa*, pp. 149-58.

6

COOPERATIVE STRATEGIES AND CONSTRAINTS IN THE CARIBBEAN BASIN

As anticolonial movements broke the Portuguese empire in Africa and made possible Soviet and Cuban intervention, a new sense of urgency about independence and development caught on in Latin America and the Caribbean Basin. The explosive forces of urbanization, expanded communications, and population growth—measured against deep poverty—created a new political environment in which leaders of all types were pressing for change in the *status quo* to improve the living standards of the masses. The new political accent on development, sovereign control over natural resources, and maximizing options in aid, trade and commerce, among other things led to a distinctly new brand of assertiveness against traditional U.S. power. Latin America and the Caribbean Basin, like the new ex-Portuguese and other excolonial states of Africa in the 1970s, in effect shifted from a U.S.-oriented perception of regional goals and aspirations biased toward security issues to a Third World identity stressing economic development and North versus South interests.

This shift took diverse forms. Among the more prominent must be included Venezuela's leadership in the Organization of Petroleum Exporting Countries (OPEC) oil price rises of 1973-75, whereby Venezuela tried to use oil as an economic and political lever to get more capital, technology, and political clout for Latin America's oil producers. Caribbean Basin and other Latin American states joined the New International Economic Order (NIEO), first proclaimed at the Sixth Special Session of the United Nations General Assembly in 1974, a large Third World group that demanded a restructuring of the international economic system in ways to help the poor developing countries. In the Caribbean Basin—that geopolitical region comprised of the Caribbean Islands, Central America, Mexico, Venezuela and Colombia—the Caribbean Community and Common Market (CARICOM) emerged in 1973, Jamaica and Guyana nationalized the Kaiser Aluminum and Reynolds Guyana Mines in 1974 and 1975, having joined in 1973 with Australia, Guinea, Sierra Leone, Surinam, and Yugoslavia to form the International Bauxite Association (IBA) to gain power in international bauxite operations. And Presidents Jimmy Carter and Omar Torrijos signed new Panama Canal treaties in September 1977—setting up the conditions for Panama to assume full ownership and control of the canal in 1999. It had become clear midway through the decade that the old Western Hemispheric Community Idea, which envisioned the United States and Latin America as two sister areas with a common past and future, had undergone major surgery.

The shift in Caribbean Basin regional politics opened new and exciting opportunities for the Cubans and their Soviet patron. They were especially significant for the Cubans, given their geographic proximity. Castro sensed these trends undermining U.S. power in early 1971 as Chile's experiment in socialism got under way. For Castro saw in Salvador Allende's Marxism the beginning of a new Latin American identity of interests, which led him to hammer home this point during his 1971 Chilean sojourn. Castro stressed the solidarity of Latin American interests, their common struggles for progress, and the concept of a united Latin America. In many of his Chilean speeches, he played upon the themes of "Nuestra America" (Our America) and talked about the return to the will of Bolívar, San Martin, O'Higgins and other patriots who "made possible the independence of Mexico and Central America, and those who fought for Cuban independence."[1] Although the Chilean drama faded by September 1973 under a military coup, Chile nevertheless symbolized the new quest for alternate development models at work in the region.

As the currents of change took on more leftist dimensions during the mid-1970s—in Guyana, Jamaica and Panama—Cuba's interests quickened. For the basin lay close to home where the Cuban leaders could logistically more easily apply their capabilities, help to stimulate socialist development, project their own brand of power, increase their prestige in the region and in the Third World, and augment their flexibility in foreign policy in the context of economic and military dependence on the Soviets. For the Soviets, these were acceptable Cuban aspirations, for they might serve to weaken U.S. power and allow the Soviets to project more dramatically into the U.S. "strategic rear."

The result of the combined changes at work in the Caribbean Basin, notably the impact of leftist radical nationalist and revolutionary forces, significantly affected the Soviet-Cuban influence relationship. As the different brands of leftism caught fire in Grenada, Jamaica, Guyana, Nicaragua, El Salvador, Guatemala, Panama, and elsewhere, Cuban leverage with the Soviets increased. This does not mean that Havana's economic and military dependence decreased, but Castro's government took advantage of the situations close at hand to demonstrate how a privileged ally could advance its own, as well as the Soviets', goals not only in Africa but also directly in the U.S. backyard.

Soviet-Cuban relations changed in at least six ways in the Caribbean basin from the mid-1970s onward. First, the formulas for change in local political systems adopted by the Soviets and Cubans distinctly shifted from Soviet to Cuban interpretations. Soviet and Cuban approaches to Caribbean basin politics since the late 1960s had reflected essentially Soviet preferences. The Soviet line lay in the stress on peaceful state-to-state relations, advocating united fronts against capitalism and imperialism, and leading roles to be played by local pro-Soviet communist parties. These formulas followed the bitter Soviet-Cuban disagreements over peaceful versus violent change during the 1960s. Under Soviet pressure and in recognition of the then unfavorable conditions for armed struggle in Latin America, the Cubans in effect had adopted the Soviet line.

As Caribbean basin politics became radically nationalized and revolutionary, they created opportunities for legitimizing traditional *Cuban* paths to change. By the early 1980s, the Cuban thesis on armed struggle had become prominent in Soviet-Cuban joint actions in the Caribbean basin, certainly in Central America. Following the 1979 Nicaraguan Revolution, the Soviets increasingly adopted the Cuban model of armed struggle and significantly upgraded the Cuban notion of guerrilla warfare as a viable path of change. The guerrilla warfare theories of Cuba's "Che" Guevara were resuscitated by Soviet analysts, and the Latin American pro-Soviet communist parties began to vindicate armed struggle and guerrilla warfare.[2] And in contrast to the former prominence accorded by the Soviets to local communist party leadership, Moscow went so far as to accept the Castroite thesis of political-military fronts as a substitute, under some conditions, for communist parties as the revolutionary vanguard.[3] Soviet and Cuban experience in Africa undoubtedly helped promote these changes in Soviet perceptions, but the effect redounded to Cuba by increasing its value to the Soviet Union in the Caribbean basin.

Second, subtle but distinct differences in Soviet and Cuban policies began to operate in the Caribbean basin setting, as leftist movements and revolutions opened up the opportunities for and expanded joint Soviet-Cuban presence. One basic reason for underlying policy distinctions lay in geography. Where Cuban interests are paramount in the Caribbean basin, the area is of less direct strategic importance to the Soviet Union, although the Soviets continue to try to undermine U.S. power in the arena as long as it does not risk direct confrontation with the United States. The Soviets must be extremely cautious in this part of the world, especially toward the region's revolutionary leaders, for it recognizes the basin as within the U.S. sphere of interest. Another distinction emerged in the way Castro continued to be conditioned by his own revolutionary past, felt close affinity with the revolutionary movements in countries so close to home, became personal friends with their leaders, and demonstrated a more natural support for violent change than the Soviets, who made their decisions from the far-distant and more bureaucratic offices of the Kremlin.

These policy differences by no means meant that Castro was willing to cross the Soviets. Given the island's economic and military dependency on the Soviet Union, the Castro government was more than prepared to work out a joint Soviet-Cuban "anti-imperialist" strategy in dealing with leftist movements in the Basin. In this context, the Soviets appear quite happy to allow Cuba considerable freedom of action to develop effective guidelines for its own actions in the basin, which is not so surprising given the demonstrated privileged ally status achieved by the Cubans through their actions in Africa. Yet, the Soviets and Cubans disagreed on some issues, as in the case of Grenada, where the Cubans sided with Maurice Bishop and the Soviets seemed to support his more hard-line opponent, Bernard Coard.[4]

Third, Soviet-Cuban joint activities in the Caribbean and Central American countries demonstrated increased Soviet willingness to back Cuba in its support for armed struggle. Moscow allowed Cuba to take the lead in supplying weapons, providing political indoctrination and organization, and in the military training of left-wing guerrillas, especially just before and following the success of the July 1979 *Sandinista* Revolution in Nicaragua. Both the Soviets and Cubans became actively involved in supporting the revolutionary regimes in Grenada (March 1979) and Nicaragua after their victories in 1979, and they supported the guerrilla movements in El Salvador at least until the ill-fated guerrilla offensive of January 1981. This support marked a clear difference from Moscow's negative posture regarding Cuba's participation in Latin American guerrilla warfare during the 1960s.

Fourth, Soviet perceptions of Cuba's value in promoting its anti-imperialist struggle against the United States were positively shaped by Cuba's active involvement in the region's leftist activities. Like Africa, but even more sharply pronounced in the Caribbean Basin, Cuba enjoyed a number of capabilities to back regional leftist movements that were unavailable to the Soviet Union. Among these power factors were Cuba's geographic proximity to the major events, its linguistic and cultural ties to local leaders, and a historic legacy that magnified Cuba's understanding of the area's politics as well as its relations with the United States. These power capabilities naturally increased Cuba's value to the Soviets and hence its leverage in negotiating with them over fundamental issues like Soviet economic and military aid to Cuba. As a Soviet writer noted in November 1979, "Cuba has become a guiding star for the Latin American nations in their struggle for social progress and their economic independence."[5]

Fifth, Soviet perceptions of its relations with Cuba turned increasingly on the security threat to Havana posed by U.S. policies. Toward the end of the Carter Administration and into the Ronald Reagan Presidency, Cuba faced mounting pressure from a United States that was highly concerned with its seeming imbalance in military relations with the Soviet Union, the decline of *detente* in U.S.-Soviets relations and with using Cuba to project Soviet power into Third World countries like Angola, Ethiopia, and Mozambique. Given Cuba's geographical location in America's "strategic backyard," Havana automatically became a part of the neo-Cold War between Washington and Moscow, even more dramatically after the Soviet invasion of Afghanistan in December 1979.

As U.S.-Soviet relations deteriorated, the United States increased its pressure on Cuba. President Carter made a major issue of the "Soviet brigade" in Cuba in September 1979, which led to the establishment of a U.S. communications post in Florida, with special forces installed within striking distance of Cuba.[6] From Havana's perspective, the Soviet troop brigade became part of the process leading to an escalation of the U.S. military budget partly directed at Cuba. Throughout the end of 1979 and into 1980, Castro therefore stressed the need to be "ready for action" against the U.S. "imperialist threat" and a new paramilitary organization was established in Cuba, called the Territorial Troop Militia.[7] In terms of Soviet-Cuban relations, the U.S. security threat at least delivered one dividend: increased leverage for the Cubans in negotiating weapons deliveries from Moscow. Increased Soviet economic and military aid in turn provided the Cubans with great capability to advance their own interests in the region.

But it was by no means all sweetness and roses for Soviet-Cuban policies in the Caribbean. A sixth feature of their relationship stemmed from the obstacles they faced in attempting to exert influence over leftist movements. One major obstacle was constant risk of going too far in support of revolutionary movements, leading to a direct conflict with the United

States. In that event, the results could be potential superpower nuclear confrontation or a disaster for Cuba if the Soviets determined that direct defense of the island carried too high a risk. Indeed, as some observers note, Cuba's association with the Soviet Union is in many respects an impediment to Cuban policy in the Caribbean Basin because it carries all the implications of hemispheric penetration by international communism.[8]

Outside of the U.S. threat, other foreign policy limits to Soviet and Cuban influence plagued their foreign policies. These included economic and commercial obstacles, the fragmented and personalist character of internal politics of the Caribbean basin states, and the nature of national communism. Insofar as these obstacles to Soviet-Cuban influence in the area generated compatible policy adjustments, they demonstrated the degree to which the Soviets and Cubans could cooperate in seeking their mutually beneficial interests, as well as differences in the nature of their goals and capabilities. In the case of the latter, their inability to control events, as in Grenada during October 1983, produced undercurrents of discord in the relationship.

In probing economic and political change in the Caribbean basin, dating from the mid-1970s, and its effects on the Soviet-Cuban influence relationship, the following lines of inquiry are natural areas to explore: (1) Soviet-Cuban opportunities in the leftist political transition, (2) Soviet-Cuban policies: convergence and differences, and (3) limits to Soviet-Cuban regional influence and implications for the relationship.

SOVIET-CUBAN OPPORTUNITIES IN THE CARIBBEAN BASIN POLITICAL TRANSITION

The origins of leftism in the Caribbean Basin from the mid-1970s onward developed not from Soviet and Cuban influence, but from internal economic, social, and political forces. Economic stagnation and social pressures gave cause for leftist appeals, growing out of erratic or extremely low economic growth, low food productivity, inequitable income distribution, high rates of inflation and unemployment, unequal land holding patterns, and high rates of population growth and urbanization. Illiteracy plagues the Caribbean basin, which contributes to a swollen unabsorbed labor sector and makes fertile ground for leftist movements. Consider that El Salvador, Guatemala, Haiti, Honduras, and Nicaragua have especially low literacy rates, and these countries, with the exception of Haiti, were scenes of increased leftism during the late 1970s and early 1980s.

Leftist ideas and political movements in the Caribbean basin centered on a broadly shared desire to foster more equitable income distribution and improvements in the social and economic conditions of the "common man."[9] In response to the region's economic and social problems—exacerbated during the 1970s by the worldwide oil price hikes and resulting global recession, inflation and unemployment—Marxist and non-Marxist leaders more persuasively argued for traditional leftist responses: state control of the economy and social mobilization of the masses. They pressed quite naturally for cooperation with other leftist countries, like Cuba and the Soviet Union, in an attempt to widen their economic options in addressing the region's development dilemmas. In the Caribbean islands, cases in point were Jamaica during the leadership of Michael Manley's People's National Party (PNP) during 1972-80, Maurice Bishop's New Jewell Movement in Grenada from 1979-83, and Guyana under the leadership of Forbes Burnham during the 1970s. In Central America, similar, but more revolutionary trends were underway in Nicaragua, El Salvador, and Guatemala. Less revolutionary, but nevertheless leftist, trends could be seen in Honduras and Panama as the decade of the 1970s progressed.

In understanding leftism in the basin, distinctions should be drawn between the Caribbean islands and Central America, because the Cubans clearly understood them in the adaptation of their policies. The political left in the Caribbean island states is typically less prone to violence than the armed revolutionary groups found in Central America. This remains a key difference between the two areas, notwithstanding the unpredicted violence that erupted with the shooting of Grenada's Maurice Bishop in October 1983. The English-speaking Caribbean inherited systems of legitimate self-government, democratic political traditions, British socialist thought, trade union organizations, and a variety of religions from occidental to oriental.

Cuban policy toward Manley's Jamaica developed an appropriate policy for this setting: low-profiled and non-revolutionary, albeit not low enough to escape the scathing attacks of Edward Seaga, who came to power in 1980. Opportunities for the Cubans to extend their presence in Jamaica, as in other Caribbean and Central American countries, hinged on the nature of the leadership. In Jamaica, Manley led the way toward a leftist pro-Cuban orientation under a democratic socialist ideology headed by the People's National Party (PNP). Of added benefit, from the Cuban perspective, was the PNP's emphasis on internal democracy, which meant that Marxists more radical than Manley were given leadership positions over some government ministries. For a time, one minister, D.K. Duncan, headed the new Ministry of National Mobilization that pressed for an adaptation of the Cuban model of combining education and work.[10]

Manley and Castro developed an extemely close relationship, and they exchanged visits between their islands, along with other officials of the Cuban and Jamaican governments. In foreign aid matters, the Cubans extended basically skilled personnel in the relevant fields for economic development: health, education, construction, communications, and transportation. Under Manley, Jamaica hosted the largest economic and technical aid mission in the Caribbean. By 1979, the issue of close Cuban-Jamaican cooperation had become an enormously volatile issue in the presidential campaign between Manley and Seaga.

About the time Cuba's tight relationship with Manley and Jamaica was beginning to come under more intense domestic pressure from Seaga, new revolutionary openings were at work in Grenada. While the 1980 elections in Jamaica brought Seaga to power on his anticommunist and anti-Cuban platform, the New Jewell Movement (NJM) under Bishop was building up a head of steam in the tiny island of Grenada.[11] The NJM, without Soviet or Cuban help, overthrew the corrupt and despotic Prime Minister, Eric Gairy, on March 13, 1979. It was committed to democratization of the political and economic system, and it generally stressed Grenadian nationalism and socialism.[12] It was not long before much of Grenada's political life was patterned after Cuba—a natural outcome of the close ties established between the two countries soon after the NJM came to power. The similarities were not difficult to recognize: a Political Bureau and Central Committee, with the party and government system supported by mass organizations. In Grenada, soon after Bishop came to power, the Cubans began to assist in health, education, agriculture, and fishing. At least fifteen doctors, dentists and technicians served in Grenada for a year during 1980-81.

But unlike Jamaica, the Cubans extended other types of aid that focused U.S. attention on perceived Soviet-Cuban penetration of the basin and contributed to the U.S. tendency to formulate U.S.-Caribbean relations in an East-West model. By 1980 about 100 Cuban military advisers had arrived in Grenada to help train a 2,000 person army, and several hundred Cubans began to arrive in the early 1980s to assist in the construction of Grenada's new international airport. While the Grenadian leaders argued that the purpose of the airport was to stimulate tourism, the United States insisted that it was to be used as a military airbase available to Havana and Moscow.[13]

In terms of the Soviet-Cuban relationship, it was Cuba that assumed a Caribbean "forward" posture through its version of a Marxist Cuban Peace Corps. Yet the Soviets were by no means absent. Manley visited the Soviet Union in April 1979, after relations were established between the two countries, whereupon a number of modest economic agreements were signed. They included arrangements for alumina exports to the Soviet Union, a long-term Soviet loan to Jamaica to finance imports of Soviet goods, and establishment of a joint fishing company.[14] And in Grenada, a visiting Soviet delegation in January 1980 produced agreements for nutmeg exports to the Soviet Union, agricultural aid to Grenada and more limited Soviet aid in fishing.[15]

But in the case of Grenada, discussed below, the Soviets, unlike the Cubans, may have failed to understand the nature of Grenada's Caribbean-based political culture. The Cubans adopted a supportive Caribbean-flavored policy for Grenada under Maurice Bishop, and Castro soon developed an extremely close personal relationship with the NJM leader. The Soviets, in contrast, were impatient with Bishop's less rigid and authoritative Caribbean political style, did not forge a close working relationship with him, and apparently backed the hard-liner, Bernard Coard in his disputes with Bishop. Moscow thereby helped unleash the ill-fated events of October 1983 and subsequent U.S. intervention that set back both Soviet and Cuban aspirations in Grenada.[16]

The Cubans, more than the Soviets, also developed warm relations with Guyana during the 1970s. Once Guyana's leader, Forbes Burnham, declared himself a Marxist and Guyana a "cooperative republic" in the early 1970s, he moved into a closer association with the Cuban government. The two countries enjoyed a compatible approach to Third World problems, and it came as little surprise that Burnham allowed Castro to use Guyana to refuel Cuban transport planes en route to Angola during 1975. Following these events, Cuba provided various types of economic aid to Guyana, notably in sugar production, and Castro sent a small number of Cuban technicians to Guyana.[17]

Central American politics, in contrast to the Caribbean islands, is linked to authoritarian Hispano-Catholic roots. Besides an authoritarian political culture, the region lacks a tradition of legitimate self-government. It is far more prone to violence in political problem solving and much attuned with the tradition that uses bullets rather than ballots for settling political conflict. Central America is an arena of repressive rule, with the exception of Costa Rica, oligarchic privileged elites, vastly unequal income distribution, and little effective sharing in national life by the masses. These conditions help explain why Cuba utilized generally peaceful state-to-state diplomacy in the English-speaking Caribbean islands, but readily adapted a second strategy for Central America along the lines it originally utilized during the 1960s: support for armed revolutionary movements.

In Central America, violence is more the rule than the exception, and leftist revolutionary struggle has a long tradition. With the *Sandinista* overthrow of the Somoza dynasty in July 1979, this tradition produced new openings for an expanded Soviet and Cuban presence because of the Revolution's leftist political orientation and the increasing opposition to it by the United States. Among the more tenacious opposition groups spawned by the Somoza regime, the Sandinista National Liberation Front (FSLN) began its operations in 1961-62. Founded in Havana and Nicaragua during these years, it adopted its name from Nicaragua's most famous nationalist hero, Augusto Sandino, who led a bloody battle against the U.S. marines in 1927, and later led a popular resistance against the United States between 1928 and 1933.[18] As the FSLN continued its guerrilla operations during the late 1960s and into the 1970s, especially in the rural areas of Nicaragua, resistance to Somoza from other groups gained momentum.

Somoza's opposition stemmed from his blatant wealth acquisition through the power of state banks and other state resources to increase his fortunes, backed by the National Guard used to protect the Somoza regime. By 1970, the Somozas owned over half of Nicaragua's agricultural land, industries, agricultural forms, a television network, a steamship line, major stock in an airline, and half interest in the Intercontinental Hotel. By the late 1970s, the total wealth of the Somozas was estimated at $500 million.[19]

Events eventually transpired to undo the Somoza dynasty. First, the Somoza economic group began to isolate itelf from other wealthy interests through exceptionally large scale investments carried out to reconstruct Managua after the 1972 earthquake.[20] And when foreign countries provided aid to Nicaragua after the 1972 earthquake, the Somozas used the aid to enrich themselves, a policy that estranged the powerful Hispano-Catholic church in Managua.[21] Another source of opposition was Pedro Joaquin Chamorro, a businessman and director of the *La Prensa* newspaper in Managua. Chamorro's assasination in January 1978 led to a general strike and further consolidation of the opposition, marking a new stage of open popular action against the Somoza regime.

Following Chamorro's assassination, the Chamorro-inspired Democratic Liberation Union (UDEL) joined with other organizations linked to the *Sandinista* movement to form the Broad Opposition Front (FAO) which first published its democratization program in August 1978. General strikes soon followed, backed by all sectors of the population. Guerrilla warfare continued and eventually the guerrillas formed a unified military command in 1979. Nicaragua erupted into a full-scale civil war in 1979 in which 40,000 to 50,000 people died out of a population of 2,500,000 and another 250,000 fled the country. War damage was estimated at $5,000 million.[22]

The Soviets and Cubans initially were not enthusiastic about the prospects of a *Sandinista* success. Indeed, Cuba sent aid to the Somoza regime, following the 1972 earthquake. The reasons for Soviet and Cuban early pessimism about the *Sandinista* future stemmed in part from their preoccupation with events in Angola and Ethiopia, Soviet attention to Afghanistan, and the memories of the ill-fated Salvador Allende government (1970-73) in Chile. The FSLN did not receive much Soviet attention during 1978, although the Soviets were never reluctant to bestow their verbal support. As the FSLN prospects improved during 1978-79, the Cubans offered training to the FSLN, helped to unify FSLN factions, and arranged for the transfer of weapons to the FSLN from Cuba through Costa Rica and Panama.[23]

The Cubans undertook other actions supportive of the FSLN during 1979. They helped organize, arm and transfer an "internationalist brigade" to fight alongside the FSLN guerrillas—although the Cubans were not involved in command operations. Cuban military advisers from Cuba's Department of Special Operations were with FSLN columns fighting in the final offensive in mid-1979, a number of whom were wounded in combat and evacuated back to Cuba through Panama. As soon as the *Sandinistas* toppled the Somoza government, the top *Sandinista* leaders flew to Havana, where they received a hero's welcome, and the new Nicaraguan government joined the Nonaligned Movement.

Cuba soon sent to Nicaragua approximately 1,200 teachers, about 250 doctors and other health specialists, and around 1,500 military and security advisers.[24] By the end of 1979, it is estimated that nearly 3,000 Cuban teachers and medical personnel were working in the Nicaraguan countryside, with over 100 Cubans attached to the Cuban Embassy in Managua. The Soviets, on the other hand, demonstrated a distinct caution in making commitments to the new *Sandinista* government. Their aid was substantially less than the material assistance provided by the United States, Mexico and Venezuela, although the Soviets subsequently approved a number of economic, technical, and military agreements.

The Soviets elevated their own assistance to the FSLN during 1981, as Nicaragua's relations with the United States deteriorated and the *Sandinistas* came under increased security threats from Washington. During 1981-83, Soviet military hardware arrived in Nicaragua, which only served to convince the United States of Nicaragua's threat to the hemisphere, especially through the U.S. allegations that the FSLN was shipping weapons to Salvadoran leftists. Available evidence suggests that the amount of weapons arriving from the Soviet Union total about 20,000 tons in 1983, or double the amount in 1981 and 1982.[25]

But any assessment of the *Sandinista* rise to power should not overstate the Soviet and Cuban involvement, despite the dramatically increased Soviet and Cuban presence after the *Sandinistas* were installed. The *Sandinistas* procured weapons from Venezuela, Panama, the Middle East, and Mafia sources from the United States—all of whom were either happy to earn hard currency or see the end of Somoza's rule. The *Sandinistas* received economic, political and moral support from a number of organizations in Panama, Mexico, Venezuela, and Costa Rica. The FSLN government in exile used San José, capital of Costa Rica, for its base of operations. These four countries provided more support and political guidance than did Cuba or the Soviets. Both the Cubans and Soviets were extremely cautious lest they trigger conditions for a direct U.S. confrontation.[26] Nicaraguan revolutionary leaders were equally cautious about a too deep Cuban or Soviet involvement for precisely the same reason.[27] The Nicaraguan Revolution was consequently a home-grown affair, not an insurgency movement where the Cubans called the shots.

El Salvador's armed revolutionary movement contrasts vividly with Nicaragua in terms of its internal forces. A Revolution occurred in Nicaragua somewhat along the lines of Cuba's own revolution in 1959. Cuban opposition to Fulgencio Batista parallels Nicaraguan opposition to Somoza; El Salvador is distinct from both these cases. El Salvador's revolutionary process—while a product of poverty, unemployment, and inequitable land holding—is not the result of a single dynasty holding fast to the *status quo*. In El Salvador an oligarchic elite of wealthy families, sharing power with military-based authority and decision-making, is at odds with impoverished peasants. The oligarch and peasants are at odds and have been since 1932. At that time an Indian campesino revolt, ignited by the small Communist Party of El Salvador (PCES) led by Augustín Farabundo Martí, resulted in the military roundup and cold-blooded murder of between 10,000 and 30,000 peasants.[28]

Other major distinctions divide El Salvador's armed struggle from the Nicaraguan Revolution. By 1980, some reforms were underway during the period of rising civil strife between left-wing revolutionaries and the central government. In March 1980, a new land reform helped avert a military takeover by the far right or the far left.[29] Second, the government underwent substantial change during the 1970s and early 1980s, unlike Nicaragua. The Christian Democrats, headed by José Napoleon Duarte, won the election of 1972, but soon were driven into exile because of fraudulent counting of the ballots and subsequent military intervention. This period saw a resurgent left, which argued that only through radical militant change could true reform and economic development occur in El Salvador.

The radical left grew in strength, and eventually the conservative military government of General Humberto Romero was overthrown in October 1979 by progressive young military officers who promised to initiate economic and social reform. Their junta failed in this goal, blocked by their rightest brethren, and the consequences were a rise in insurrectionary violence.[30] The revolutionary left refused to accept the junta, while the army and security forces attacked villagers suspected of supporting radicals. New shifts in the junta followed, with the exiled Christian Democrat, Duarte, eventually emerging as president of El Salvador in January 1981.

As to Soviet and Cuban involvement in supporting the El Salvadoran guerrillas, evidence suggests that the *Sandinista* victory in Nicaragua sparked rising Soviet optimism about the prospects for armed revolutionary struggles elsewhere in Central America and stepped up Cuban aid to the Salvadoran leftists, at least until their ill-fated guerrilla offensive of January 1981. Boris Ponomarev, Candidate Politburo member and secretary of the Central Committee of the CPSU, stated in October 20, 1980, that Nicaragua's revolution was a "major success," comparing it favorably with Angola and Ethiopia.[31] And following the Nicaraguan victory, Soviet analysts selected El Salvador as the next likely country for successful armed struggle, despite the weak communist movement there.[32] Following the Nicaraguan revolution, the Soviet Union advised the small Communist Party of El Salvador (PCES) to change its conservative line on the guerrilla struggle—from nonsupport to a more optimistic appraisal.

This marked a significant change in Soviet thinking, because in early 1979, before the fall of Somoza, the PCES had published a critical assessment of El Salvador's revolutionary groups, like the Maoist-oriented People's Revolutionary Army (ERP) and the Trotskyite Popular Liberation Force (FPL).[33] At the PCES Seventh National Congress in May 1980, the party endorsed violent revolution,[34] and in cooperation with the Cubans, the Soviets began to orchestrate a propaganda campaign backing El Salvador's leftist guerrilla warfare.

As to direct Soviet and Cuban aid to El Salvador's guerrillas prior to the early 1981 offensive, available data do not lead to easy conclusions. The U.S. State Department issued reports in 1981, based on captured documents, that the Soviet Union, Cuba, Vietnam, Ethiopia, and Eastern Bloc countries had for the previous two years provided El Salvador's guerrillas with weapons, military training, political and strategic direction, and propaganda support—drawing a direct analogy with Angola and strongly suggesting that El Salvador's revolution was in effect directed by the Soviets and Cubans.[35] This evidence argued that the Soviets played a major role in arranging for the transport of weapons from Ethiopia and Vietnam to Cuba, and from there to Nicaragua and thence to El Salvador during the fall of 1980. Involved in this alleged weapons transfer operation were the pro-Soviet General Secretary of El Salvador's Communist Party, Schafik Jorge Handal, and Soviet officials connected with Third World affairs, like K. Brutens.[36]

The State Department evidence suggested that the Cubans were playing a more direct and active role in supporting El Salvador's guerrilla operations during 1979-81. It was charged that Castro sought to unify the different Salvadoran guerrilla groups as the basis for large-scale Cuban aid. And the Cubans were depicted as having a substantial degree of political direction over the Salvadoran guerrillas, and were apparently instrumental in encouraging them to launch a general offensive in January 1981.[37] During this period, the Cubans allegedly helped arrange major weapons shipments to the Salvadoran guerrillas and sharply upgraded their guerrilla training program in preparation for the January offensive. The evidence suggested that in effect the Cubans were directing the leftist actors in El Salvador's civil war.

This evidence of El Salvador's civil war as the direct result of Soviet and Cuban intervention was subsequently rebutted. In June 1981 *The Wall Street Journal* and the *Washington Post* published front-page articles stressing the weakness of the State Department's evidence.[38] These reports underscored that the U.S. Administration's interpretation of the evidence overstated what was really a far more limited nature of Soviet and Cuban involvement in El Salvador's leftist guerrilla movements. The rebuttals indicated a major lack of evidence about Soviet-Cuban arranged arms deliveries to El Salvador before the January 1981 offensive, and the far less than central political role played by Cuba in the Salvadoran civil war. As to Handal's trip to the Soviet Union to arrange for weapons transfers, it turns out that the documents *did not* indicate that the Soviets provided air transport for them, rather that Handal was continually "frustrated in Moscow."[39] And Castro stated in November 1981 that the State Department evidence was complete "lies," although Cuban officials admitted that they transported some weapons to El Salvador for the January offensive.[40]

We are left with a picture of less penetrating Soviet and Cuban involvement in the Salvadoran civil war than initially believed. It is by no means inconceivable that the Soviets and Cubans would exercise caution in El Salvador, given the caution they displayed toward the *Sandinista* revolution in Nicaragua. The logic for this conclusion is especially persuasive in view of the intensified campaign against Soviet-Cuban activities in the Caribbean basin undertaken by the Reagan Administration. The Soviets and Cubans could ill-afford a too pronounced intervention—certainly not on the scale of Angola—for fear of the U.S. response.

Although the leftist radical national and revolutionary forces sweeping the Caribbean basin by the late 1970s were internally spawned, they offered opportunities for Soviet and Cuban involvement. The Nicaraguan revolution especially captured the Soviet and Cuban imagination, leading them to believe that the Nicaraguan experiment could be replicated in nearby El Salvador and perhaps, in time, even in Guatemala. The Nicaraguan revolution inspired both the Soviets and Cubans to become more deeply involved in support of armed struggle in their own ways. The shift toward support of armed warfare as part of the "anti-imperialist" struggle marked a dramatic change in Soviet tactics, compared to its previous positions on armed struggle in the Western hemisphere. And it illustrated just how far Cuba had come in its own role as the Soviet Union's privileged ally. For Cuba was now implementing, with the Soviet blessing, precisely what it had argued for in the 1960s. Yet in supporting armed struggle in Central America, combined with economic and technical aid in the Caribbean states, both the Soviets and Cubans approached these new opportunities with marked caution, lest their actions produce undesired confrontation with a highly sensitive and Monroe Doctrine-oriented United States.

SOVIET-CUBAN POLICIES: CONVERGENCE AND DIFFERENCES

Following their cooperative actions in Africa, Soviet and Cuban policies in the Caribbean Basin converged in a number of respects during the early 1980s. What is notable about Soviet-Cuban policy convergence is the common *leitmotiv* of caution, taking advantage of the opportunities to advance political leftism and the revolutionary process without too high a risk of U.S. intervention and without threatening Soviet and Cuban relations with other Caribbean and Latin American governments. Yet the very presence of Soviet and Cuban personnel in the Caribbean basin raised the risks of U.S. intervention, sometimes triggered by events outside the control of Moscow and Havana. Grenada's internal frictions in 1983, and the October 1983 U.S. intervention, illustrated the risks the Soviets and Cubans were taking despite their efforts to minimize them.

Beyond policy convergence, Soviet and Cuban activities in the basin from 1981 onward display a number of differences in approaches to and capabilities for dealing with the evolving opportunities. These differences developed out of the region's less geostrategic priority for Moscow, outside of its relations with Cuba, Moscow's unwillingness and inability to become economically burdened with a costly experiment like Cuba, and the Soviet's more conservative approach to armed struggle compared to the Cubans—despite Moscow's obvious enthusiasm with Nicaragua. Within both the converged and different policy actions lie elements of cooperative influence, the nature of Cuba's own policy formation compared to their Soviet patron, and the limits to potential influence for each country in the region.

Converged Policies

Convergence in Soviet and Cuban policies ranges from defense of Cuba itself to common approaches to opportunity seeking in the basin from 1981 onward. Underlying these arenas of cooperation is a major aspect of the nature of the Soviet-Cuban relationship: how compatibility of interests indirectly supports, and therefore *influences*, each country to continue to cooperate with the other in a given line of action. On the question of physical protection for Cuba, now facing threatening shadows from the north, the Soviets stepped up their military assistance to the island. Soviet arms deliveries to Cuba in 1981 equalled 63,000 tons, the largest single figure since the Cuban missile crisis of 1962. In early 1982, a second squadron of MIG-23 (fighter planes) arrived in Havana, giving Cuba the highest inventory of air, land, and sea capacity in the region. While this Soviet effort to enhance Cuba's ability to defend itself may be interpreted as a method to *avoid* a direct Soviet involvement in Cuba should a military showdown with the United States erupt, rather than providing a comprehensive security pact for the Cubans as the Soviets did for Vietnam, it nevertheless underlined extensive Soviet backing for its key Third World client.[41]

Second, the Soviets and Cubans joined efforts in voicing their great concern over potential U.S. military action against Grenada and Nicaragua. And as tensions increased between the United States, Grenada, El Salvador, and Nicaragua during the early 1980s, the Soviets and Cubans vigorously protested U.S. efforts to detabilize Grenada and Nicaragua and to support antiguerrilla actions in El Salvador. Castro stressed in his message to the Ministerial Meeting of the Nonaligned Countries in New Delhi, India, in February 1981, "open threats are being made in this region (Caribbean basin) to intervene and it would be difficult to decide whether the possibility of war was greater in 1961 [the Bay of Pigs invasion against Cuba, my note]...than it is now, 20 years later."[42] Castro continued to allow revolutionary speakers from Grenada, Nicaragua and El Salvador to use its media sources to voice their concerns about the U.S. threat, as did the Soviets.[43]

In a third policy convergence, the Soviets and Cubans vigorously denied U.S. continuing allegations of communist aid to the Salvadoran guerrillas after the January 1981 offensive failed. Moscow challenged U.S. assertions, arguing that the United States was following the same road in El Salvador as pursued in Vietnam; Moscow insisted that it was not the "threat of communism" that posed a danger to the Caribbean basin, but rather the "alliance of local oligarchies and transnational corporations."[44] The Soviets insisted that allegations about communist assistance were blatant lies, a U.S. "myth" about Soviet involvement in El Salvador as a ruse to cover U.S. intervention there.[45] Paralleling these Soviet declarations, the Cubans persistently refuted all charges that it was continuing to transfer weapons through Nicaragua to the Salvadoran guerrillas.[46] And the Cubans contended that its receipt of massive Soviet weapons deliveries was not destined for El Salvador, but rather to defend themselves "...in view of the plans for aggression which have been openly proclaimed by the U.S."[47] In September 1981, for example, the Cubans stated:

> ...Cuba regrets and condemns as a brazen lie which is completely groundless the affirmation that there are Cuban advisers among the Salvadoran patriots. We categorically state that there has never been nor is there at present a single Cuban military or civilian adviser among the revolutionary forces fighting in El Salvador and Haig and the U.S. government have deliberately lied about this.[48]

High ranking Cuban foreign policy spokesmen confirmed this statement to a group of visiting U.S. newsmen and scholars in April 1982.[49] After the failure of the January 1981 offensive, Nicaraguan government officials also denied they had helped the Salvadoran revolutionaries with weapons supplies received from the USSR or Cuba, although they were allowing Salvadoran leftist guerrillas sanctuaries inside Nicaragua.

Soviet and Cuban policies converged, fourth, on the matter of negotiated political settlements of U.S. disputes with Cuba, Nicaragua, and El Salvadoran leftists. Both the Soviets and Cubans endorsed Mexican President José Lopez Portillo's efforts to bring together the contending parties in Central America, as initially announced in Nicaragua in February 1982. With Lopez Portillo's call for negotiated political settlements, Cuba quickly agreed to the proposal if the United States would end its "threats,"[50] and the Soviets joined in. Only two days after Lopez Portillo's Managua address, Moscow radio reported the speech, indicating that Cuba and Nicaragua had both greeted the proposal with positive responses.[51] Following Lopez Portillo's remarks, the Soviets contrasted Mexican efforts at negotiation with the U.S. rejection of this peace initiative, as indicated by the absence of any reference to it in President Reagan's February 24, 1982 address to the Organization of American States (OAS), where he introduced his Caribbean Basin initiative. The Soviets noted that instead of mentioning Mexico's proposal, President Reagan's message carried sharp attacks on Cuba and Nicaragua for alleged arms shipments to the Salvadoran revolutionaries.[52]

While denying their material support for Salvadoran leftists, the Soviets and Cubans, fifth, strongly endorsed the *legitimacy* of Salvador's guerrilla forces. Moscow and Havana used their media and international diplomacy to legitimize the armed struggle process. The Soviets and Cubans depicted the Salvadoran central government as the puppet of military power backed by the United States in opposition to the "growing revolutionary movement" of the "heroic Salvadoran people" struggling for "democracy and national dignity."[53] El Salvador, in the words of one Soviet commentator, represents an "uprising by the entire Salvadoran people against a Washington-backed junta which is trying to annihilate its own people."[54]

Sixth, as might be expected, both the Soviets and Cubans labeled the U.S.-backed March 1982 elections in El Salvador as a farce in a country where "thousands are killed every year and the most elementary human rights are violated," and where "the oligarchy, corrupt military men and the Yankees wage a war of extermination against the people and a state of seige and curfew are in force day and night."[55] Regarding other Central American elections, Havana and Moscow viewed the March 1982 elections as highly unrepresentative, noting that military dictatorships have ruled for years and that an oligarchy controls 75 percent of the agricultural land. In the Soviet view, "repression and terror" in Guatemala were orders of the day, the victims being "workers and peasants, students and the intelligentsia, the clergy, and representatives of the liberal bourgeois circles."[56]

Seventh, it became quite clear by 1982 that both the Soviets and Cubans were prepared to begin a process to end the U.S.-Cuban confrontation that had accompanied the onset of the Reagan Administration. As a high ranking Cuban foreign policy spokesman told the visiting delegation of U.S. newsmen and foreign policy specialists in April, the Soviets would like to see socialism advance in places like El Salvador, but not in ways that would damage the possibility of *détente* with the United States. This official suggested that the United States was "mentally blockading" itself by attributing the turmoil in Central America to Cuban policies and string-pulling.[57] Wayne Smith, former chief of the U.S. interest section in Havana during 1979-82, argues that both the Cubans and Nicaraguans drastically reduced their support to El Salvador's guerrillas after January 1981 and signaled their desire for improved relations with the United States.[58] The Soviets, we may assume, backed the Cuban and Nicaraguan positions.

Soviet and Cuban Policy Differences

An examination of Soviet-Cuban policy differences highlights how distinct goals, interests, and capabilities operate in their relationship. Although most policy differences are compatible, some are potentially less so. In either case, policy differences become clues to the manner in which cooperative influence directly and indirectly flows between the Soviets and Cubans, reinforcing common interests and pressuring for support of less compatible goals. Policy differences illustrate distinct stakes in the game for each country, and how we are dealing with two different actors rather than a proxy situation, despite Cuba's clear economic and military dependence on the Soviets. Equally relevant, policy differences allow us to project potential discord in future Soviet-Cuban relations, based upon their distinct priorities and commitments—and the ways in which they may attempt subtly to influence each other toward attainment of their different goals.

From the Soviet perspective, the Caribbean basin became strategically significant with the birth of the Cuban revolution, and since then it is communist Cuba that continues to command center stage Soviet attention in the broader Caribbean basin context. For this reason, the Soviets were exceptionally pleased with Cuban policies in the basin by the mid-1970s, well before the revolutions in Grenada and Nicaragua, for they were marked by trends highly favorable, in the Soviet view, of strengthening the global "correlation of forces" between socialism/communism and capitalism/imperialism in favor of the former.

The Soviets believed this for a number of reasons. By the mid-1970s, Cuba had been accepted back into the family of Latin American countries, its diplomatic and trade ties with Caribbean island states were expanding (Barbados, Guyana, Jamaica, Trinidad, and Tobago), and the new Latin American Economic System (SELA) had been formed. SELA included Cuba, but excluded the United States, thus weakening U.S. "imperialism" in the inter-American system. In July 1975, the OAS voted to end its formal embargo of Cuba—a condition long supported by the United States and another indication of its weakened status in its own "strategic rear." And with countries like Jamaica and Guyana nationalizing foreign alumina companies, while expanding their links with Cuba, the Soviets envisioned the Caribbean as a region characterized by a "mounting anti-imperialist struggle for democracy and social justice."[59] For the Soviets, Cuba and other Caribbean basin countries were on the move toward a general strengthening of world socialism. Soviet optimism about favorable trends at work in the Caribbean from the mid-1970s onward contrasted with cause for Soviet pessimism about events elsewhere in the Third World. Egypt and Somalia abrogated their friendship treaties with the Soviets, who were also increasingly bogged down in Angola, Ethiopia and Afghanistan. Not surprisingly, Soviet links with Caribbean countries expanded during this period.

In noting the policy differences between the Soviets and Cubans before the revolutions in Grenada and Nicaragua, one point is clear. The favorable trends in the Caribbean associated with Cuban diplomacy, which the Soviets found so attractive, were produced largely by Cuban, not Soviet foreign policy. It was Cuba that acted in ways to widen its trade contracts, gain reacceptance into the Latin American community, end the OAS embargo, and enter SELA. In pursuing these Caribbean policies, the Cubans were able to generate increased leverage and flexibility *vis à vis* the Soviets and to demonstrate an independence in foreign policy not consistently found in Africa, as Soviet-Cuban relations in Ethiopia demonstrated.

Cuba carved out its own Caribbean niche by also adapting its commitment to Third World development to fit the radical nationalist trends then at work in the Caribbean. Cuban relations with Jamaica is the classic case in point. Approximately 400-450 Cubans—doctors, nurses, school-building teams and mini-dam construction workers went to Jamaica during the Manley years.[60] Jamaican youths in turn traveled to Cuba for training in cultural, educational, and athletic activities. Similar, but less substantial, Cuban ties were established with Guyana. Cuban activities were less political and financial than technical and human services-oriented. In contrast, the Soviets signed economic agreements with Manley's Jamaica for trade in alumina, a joint fisheries company, and a long term to finance imports of Soviet goods.[61]

Following the revolutions in Grenada and Nicaragua in 1979, other Soviet-Cuban policies differences emerged. In Grenada, Castro and Bishop established extremely warm personal ties, and Grenada's ties with the Cubans remained strong until the events of October 1983, which led to the overthrow and subsequent death of Bishop.[62] Prior to the U.S. intervention in Grenada in October 1983, Cuban aid followed patterns established elsewhere: technical personnel and help in construction, health care, culture, housing, sports facilities, advisers on planning, agroindustries, the construction of a new radio station, transportation, and maintenance and development of the island's electricity network. By late 1983, approximately 784 Cubans were in Grenada, of whom 43 were in the armed forces.[63] The presence of 636 construction workers, most helping on Grenada's new international airport, was the more prominent feature of Cuban assistance. The Soviets, in contrast, aided Grenada essentially through financial aid and trade agreements, which were upgraded following the Falklands/Malvinas crisis of 1982, which led the Soviets to give higher priority to Latin America.

Events in Grenada in October 1983 underscored substantial policy differences between the Soviets and Cubans over Grenada. As a contest for leadership of the NJM broke out between Prime Minister Bishop and Deputy Prime Minister Bernard Coard, it became clear that Coard's well-known hard line Marxist position was more appealing to the Soviets than Bishop. Although Bishop was considered a "friend" of the Soviet Union, it was known that a majority of Soviet leaders did not have great confidence in him, although they publicly defended his policy. The difference between the Soviets and Cubans over their preferred leader in Grenada emerged quite clearly in the days surrounding Bishop's overthrow by Coard. The Cubans immediately denounced Bishop's overthrow and condemned the U.S. invasion in strong language, while the Soviets made their formal opposition at a relatively low level.[64] Indeed, circumstantial evidence suggests that the Soviets may have known about the coup as much as two or three weeks before it occurred.[65] Castro, in contrast, would be a most unlikely participant in a coup against Bishop, given his close personal ties with the Grenadian leader.

In Nicaragua, the differences between Cuban and Soviet policies turn on the degree of commitment to extend material aid to the country's economic development and the extent of security guarantees. The Soviets, to be certain, moved rapidly to establish relations with the new *Sandinista* government following its July 1979 overthrow of Somoza. They invited a 14 member delegation to Moscow in March 1980, and concluded a number of bilateral accords with Nicaragua in the fields of culture, economics, and science. In March 1981, the Soviets established an air link between the two countries and donated 20,000 tons of wheat after the United States suspended economic assistance to the *Sandinistas*. Additional economic and military aid agreements were concluded in 1981 and 1982.[66] In addition to a $75 million aid extension in 1981 and another $100 million in 1982, the Soviets reportedly pledged an additional $100 million in 1983.[67] Yet it is clear from Soviet statements that Moscow is not prepared to underwrite the Nicaraguan *Sandinistas* in any form resembling "another Cuba."[68]

The Cubans, in contrast, strongly identify with the *Sandinista* Revolution and back their commitment not only with Castro's personal dedication to its success, but with large numbers of Cubans directly involved in Nicaragua's revolutionary economic development processes. An estimated 4,000 Cuban civilian technicians were in Nicaragua by 1982, including teachers, doctors and other workers. The presence of these Cuban workers suggest that Castro is prepared to go beyond the Soviets to help preserve the *Sandinista* regime, as he did in Grenada, because Cuban workers continued to pour into Nicaragua despite Managua's growing tensions with the United States and the threat of direct U.S. intervention.

Cuba's more active and prominent role in Nicaragua is reflected in military affairs. The Soviet Union admittedly has provided Nicaragua with a variety of military equipment: trucks, armored personnel carriers, antimissiles, small arms, and ammunition. And in 1983 the doubling of Soviet deliveries, compared to 1981 and 1982, brought MI-8 helicopters and about 25-30 Armored Personnel Carriers (APCs), which can be used for counterinsurgency tactics.[69] While these increased deliveries were in response to the rising activities of U.S.-supported guerrilla forces seeking to overthrow the *Sandinistas*, the Soviets had not answered Nicaragua's call for advanced fighter aircraft by the fall of 1984. The Soviets remained generally silent about these requests, while the Cubans repeated Nicaragua's statements in Cuba's newspaper.[70] Added to these differences between the Cuban and Soviet interpretations of Nicaragua's security needs, the number of Cuban military personnel in Nicaragua far outnumber Soviet military personnel, as they did in Grenada before the U.S. intervention. An estimated 2,000 Cuban personnel were stationed in Nicaragua by 1982 compared to the 70 Soviet military advisers in place.

The Falklands/Malvinas crisis of 1982 provided another opportunity for the Cubans to advance their own foreign policy goals in Latin America and to gain leverage in their relations with the Soviets. The Cubans, as the Soviets, supported Argentina, despite the tense relations between Cuba and Argentina before the crisis, owing to Argentina's aid to paramilitary exile Nicaraguan races operating against the *Sandinistas*. In supporting Argentina, Cuba placed itself alongside Costa Rica, Mexico, Panama, Venezuela, Peru, and other countries that denounced U.S. support of British military forces against Argentina.[71] As leader of the Third World Nonaligned Movement, Castro called a conference in June 1982 that assailed British actions, and Argentina's Foreign Minister, Nicanor Costa Mendez, spoke at the conference. Costa Mendez expressed his gratitude to Cuba as the "pride of the Caribbean"—a major change in Argentina's perceptions of Cuba before the crisis. Cuba's actions resulted in a $100 million Argentinian trade agreement with Cuba and an Argentine offer to send 7,000 tons of wheat to help Nicaragua overcome food shortages it sustained in May floodings.

LIMITS TO SOVIET-CUBAN INFLUENCE AND IMPLICATIONS FOR THE RELATIONSHIP

Neither the Soviet Union nor Cuba is the prime source of instability in the Caribbean basin, and their expanding presence in the basin should not be equated with automatic influence. The Caribbean and Central America admittedly are loaded with emerging opportunities for the Soviets and Cubans—anti-Americanism, the behavior of oligarchic elites and multinational corporations, widespread poverty, inequal income distribution, growing awareness of class differences, disaffected youth, and the willingness of many to engage in armed struggle as the only perceived alternative to the *status quo*. As these produce Marxist and non-Marxist radical nationalist groups and movements, the Soviets and Cubans are quite capable of adjusting their foreign policies to adapt to the nature of local "progressive" and "anti-imperialist" forces for change. After all, the Soviets and Cubans have learned a great deal about this business since the early 1960s. But at the same time, the Caribbean and Central American cultural, social and political domain is not easily manipulated by outside forces, including Soviet and Cuban varieties.

Economic Restraints

Neither the Soviets nor the Cubans can extend the kind of massive economic assistance required by these countries for economic development. The Soviets and Cubans provide limited forms of aid, some of it quite useful, as in the case of Cuba's doctors, teachers, and construction workers in Nicaragua. But the levels of poverty in the region simply overwhelm Soviet and Cuban economic capabilities. The Soviets understand this fact well, as demonstrated by their reluctance to underwrite "another Cuba" in Nicaragua, a source of dissatisfaction for the *Sandinistas*. In the case of Nicaragua, however, the matter goes beyond poverty. By 1984, the country's economy was in near chaos, with about 25 percent of its budget going to the war effort against outside enemies supported by the United States. Inflation ran at 45 percent, with a great shortage of consumer goods. From the Soviet perspective, Nicaragua was not a good investment, just as Allende's chaotic economy during 1970-73 was not a sound investment—which helps account for low-level Soviet economic support for Chile and Nicaragua. The matter of economic restraints turns not only on the massive needs in the region, measured against Soviet and Cuban capabilities, but on a regime's ability to manage the economy.

The Soviet-Cuban economic relationship is itself a major source of economic limitation operating on Moscow and Havana. This is so because the Soviets are captive to Cuba's underdeveloped and inefficient economic umbilical cord. The socialist model has not transformed Cuba into a dynamic and rich economy capable of extending great aid to other developing states, and the Soviet-dependent Cuban economic model is not attractive to the region's other left-wing nationalists. Here one discerns connections between the nature of economic constraints on Soviet-Cuban power and the character of their bilateral influence relationship.

First, insofar as Cuba's drain on Soviet foreign aid resources make the Soviets unable to afford "another Cuba," Cuba effectively exerts a direct influence on Soviet decision making toward other countries like Nicaragua by restricting Moscow's potential aid levels and by tarnishing the socialist model as something to be emulated by others. The Soviet-Cuban relationship has produced handsome political dividends for the Soviets, but its economic results are distinctly negative in character.

Second, the long years of pumping Soviet economic aid into Cuba, when its economy has not ignited, has influenced Soviet decision making more than in terms of weakening Soviet economic capabilities. It also has contributed to a psychological predisposition toward less optimism relative to the road to socialism. The Soviets are not reluctant to suggest that developing countries expand their trade ties with the West, and to develop a generally more sophisticated view of the world economic system as interdependent, rather than one divided into the socialist/communist and capitalist/imperialist camp.[72] With Soviet aid to Cuba running at $4.9 billion per year by 1982, or $13 million per day if one includes the special pricing arrangements for Cuban sugar and Soviet petroleum, the

Cuban influence on these emerging Soviet views is understandable. Soviet leader Yuri Andropov made clear the Soviet reluctance to support
other Cubas around the world, simply because they espoused socialism,
when he addressed the June 1983 Central Committee plenum on the issue of Soviet aid to Third World countries:

> It is one thing to proclaim socialism as one's goal and another to build
> it. Certain levels of productive forces, culture and social conscious-
> ness are needed for that. Socialist countries express solidarity with these
> progressive forces, render assistance to them in the sphere of politics
> and culture, and promote the strengthening of their defense. We con-
> tribute, to the extent of our ability, to their economic development, just
> as the entire social progress of those countries, can be, of course, only
> the result of their leadership.[73]

Soviet disinclination to extend substantial aid to countries like Nicaragua clouded efforts made by Nicaraguan leaders in June 1984 to ob-
tain increased economic aid and sophisticated military aircraft from the
Soviet Union. Nicaragua's junta leader, Daniel Ortega, traveled to the Soviet Union in June to try to get massive Soviet assistance, which the
Nicaraguans believed necessary for their survival.[74] Unwilling to get involved in "another Cuba," and not eager to become involved in a military confrontation in geographically distant Central America, the
Nicaraguans came away from the trip empty-handed. The Soviets saw
other problems in Nicaragua that must have reminded them in some
respects of Castro's Cuba in the early days, notably *Sandinista* mismanagement of the public sector. The private sector, meanwhile, refused to in-
vest in Nicaragua, fearing confiscation of property and assets, and the U.S.
pressure on the *Sandinistas* visibly reinforced how much the United States
viewed Nicaragua to be within its sphere of interests—a concept well understood by the Soviet Union.

Third, Castro's experience with the Soviet socialist economic model
led him to proclaim less praise for it in the late 1970s and early 1980s
than during earlier phases in the early 1970s. As the Nicaraguan revolution got under way, Castro advised the Nicaraguan leaders and other
leftists in the basin not to move too swiftly in restructuring their economies and not to break their trade ties with Western market economies.[75]
The negative influencing effect of close economic ties with the Soviets
also led the Cubans by early 1982 to try to secure Western foreign cooperation through joint ventures in tourism, shipping, export, and service industries by means of Cuba's new and first foreign investment law.

Fourth, given the cultural, linguistic, organizational, and political dynamics of the region, Cuba has the more pronounced capabilities to win friends and influence people, despite the highly limited nature of its aid. It is the more able of the two countries to work at the grass-roots level and to stimulate change in key development areas like health and education. In terms of which country, the Soviet Union or Cuba, is best able to carry the good will of "international solidarity" and to build common "anti-imperialist" fronts in Central America, and in being able to communicate and get along with other Caribbean and Central American people, the Cubans clearly carry the day.

It is the Cubans, not the Soviets, who possess, by virtue of their culture, language and historic legacy, the interpersonal skills and ability to gain leverage with local leftist leaders and their followers. The Soviets are not especially well-liked in the Caribbean and Central America—nor are they in other Third World countries like Syria and Vietnam—and they tend to be clannish, travel in groups, seldom speak the language, often make fun of the local population, and do not espouse favorable religious attitudes.[76] Indeed, one can see these Soviet traits at work even in contemporary Cuba.[77] These traits give the Cubans more influence in this geographically proximate and common cultural domain, which in turn allows them to take the lead in many Soviet-backed economic and political activities. The result is added influence for the Cubans, at least in the short term, in dealing with the Soviets.

Regional Political Dynamics

Political dynamics in the Caribbean basin also inhibit Soviet-Cuban influence and condition the character of their own relationship. Within the basin, as in all regions of the world, political dynamics flow from the area's underlying political culture—the operative attitudes, values, and perceptions that condition the way people act regarding authority, political rule, and leader-follower relationships. The English-speaking Caribbean states inherited a political culture that is resistant to Marxism-Leninism, a single doctrinaire political party, and total state control of the economy. Its political culture is based upon egalitarian attitudes and values conducive to self-government, democratic politics, and organized party competition.[78]

In Central America, the political culture produces a type of politics not amenable to outside control or influence. Among the key attitudes and values at work must be included personalism—an emphasis on each individual's unique inner worth that is to be respected for its dignity.[79] Personalism leads easily to interpreting words or actions as insults to one's dignity, to verbal or physical violence, and especially to actions that demonstrate one's daring or absolute self-confidence. *Machismo*, the high value attached to zest for action and verbal expression of inner convictions, is a natural offshoot of personalism. Both can produce strong-willed political leaders, revolutionaries, or dominating military figures. And in terms of leader-follower relationships, personalism tends to lead to the sense that only personal relationships are trustworthy and that political actions are to be based upon personalist ties—not organizational principles or party platforms.

Other key cultural aspects of politics in Central America involve the strength of family ties, an emphasis on words, ideals, and elegance of expression as opposed to material accomplishments, and high emotion as fulfillment of self.[80] As can be readily guessed, these attributes of Central American political culture inhibit strong influence from the outside by either the Soviets or the Cubans, although the Cubans are much more conversant with the Central American political culture than the Soviets. The region's political culture tends to divide and fragment political parties and organizations, stimulates personalist animosities between charismatic and volatile leaders, and makes personalities more important than institutionalized behavior or implemented party platforms. The more obvious consequences of these patterns are weakness in the traditional pro-Soviet communist parties (as in other noncommunist parties), lack of a strong organizational base in trade unions and peasant organizations, and little popular attraction to Marxism-Leninism with its emphasis on rigid bureaucratic behavior and identification with party ideologies and structures.

If a charismatic leader is at the head of a communist or socialist movement, as with Castro in Cuba or Bishop in Grenada, some of the natural political culture dynamics most assuredly can be brought to the service of advancing a leftist regime. But on the whole, the political dynamics of the Caribbean basin simply ill fits behavior demanded of dedicated Marxists. Neither the Nicaraguan *Sandinistas* nor El Salvador's leftists have a single personalist and charismatic leader to mobilize popular opinion; Castro as a socialist *caudillo* (strong personalist leader) has not been replicated elsewhere in Central America.

How do these forces affect the Soviet-Cuban relationship beyond the difficulty of their influencing political movements in the region? First, as a charismatic leader in the tradition of Latin American political dynamics, Castro understands and works within the Caribbean and Central

American political setting more effectively than the Soviets. Just as Castro has frequently perplexed the Soviets with his own erratic behavior, the Soviets are ill prepared by political culture or ideological disposition to work easily with, let alone control politics in, a Jamaica, Grenada, Guyana, Nicaragua, or among the leftist guerrillas in El Salvador.

Because Castro is on more firm ground here, the Soviets have allowed him to take the lead in trying to establish broad political-military fronts, military and political training, and in other activities in support of leftist groups. It is not that the Soviets do this simply because it allows them to maintain a low profile. They give Cuba the lead because they acknowledge Havana's greater sophistication and experience in these matters. In terms of the region's political culture, the Cubans can perform their role of privileged ally with greater competence than the Soviets. This Cuban capability in the basin context becomes a natural feature of Havana's short-range influence with the Soviets. Soviet economic and military aid to Cuba since the Nicaraguan revolution underscores the point.

Second, the region's factionalism continues to plague both Soviet and Cuban attempts to unify movements and guarantee common "anti-imperialist" fronts. This problem has both short-term and long-term implications for the Soviet-Cuban influence relationship. Despite Cuban efforts to unify the five different guerrilla groups operating in El Salvador, they retained their different strategic views and separate organizational strategies into the 1980s.[81] And three of the most important of the five groups have distinct anti-Soviet origins, which are not easily overcome, even by the Cubans.[82] In April 1983, the death of Cayetano Carpio, resulting from political infighting in El Salvador, eliminated yet another leader of the pro-Soviet and pro-Cuban guerrilla factions.

Nicaragua's FSLN, albeit avowedly Marxist, developed independently of Nicaragua's pro-Soviet Communist party, the Socialist Party of Nicaragua (PSN), and has experienced various factions and tendencies within it not easily reconciled by the Soviets and Cubans. The government's membership has changed radically over the years, with former members like Arturo José Cruz, Alfonso Robelo Callejas or former *Sandinista* central bank chief, Alfredo Cesar, dropping out to undertake opposition activities. Alfredo Cesar, for example, has set up a "civic movement" of democratic opposition to the *Sandinistas*, based in Costa Rica.[83] And in trying to retain its Marxist identity, while following an economic and politically pluralist orientation, the FSLN program has remained ambiguous and ambivalent.[84] The FSLN clearly had not become dominated by the Soviets or the Cubans, a point made succinctly clear by statements from leading members of the *Sandinista* organization.[85] But then, the divisiveness characteristic of the FSLN also permeated its opposition, the so-called *contras*, backed by the United States. The two largest *contra* groups were unable to unite, and one of those groups, the Democratic Revolutionary Alliance, continued to be internally split. Neither the Soviets, the Cubans, nor the United States seemed able to bring about unity of their supported groups.

Do these division's in Central American leftist movements affect the Soviet-Cuban relationship? As long as factionalism does not break into open political warfare between groups where the Soviets and Cubans could find themselves supporting opposite leaders, as occurred in Grenada in October 1983, political divisions probably have minimal effects on the Soviet-Cuban relationship. This is so because as long as the *Sandinistas* or the leftist Salvadoran guerrillas keep the United States bogged down and preoccupied in its own backyard, whether they are politically unified or not, the Soviets benefit. More U.S. attention to its immediate geographic sphere of interest means a somewhat modified attention to European, Middle Eastern or other world arenas and divided U.S. military forces. Despite Cuba's inability to forge tighter political unity in El Salvador and Nicaragua, its other forms of support help the leftists, which in turn keeps the United States preoccupied. In this way, Cuba's policies accommodate Soviet interests and do not undermine Havana's leverage as a privileged ally.

U.S. pressure on Nicaragua's FSLN and unwillingness to actively support political negotiations between the leftists and the central government in El Salvador helps reinforce the Soviet-Cuban relationship. For it tends to push the FSLN closer to the Soviets and Cubans, especially in terms of needed military weapons for security and leads toward more centralization of government and less pluralism in the face of external threats. Under U.S. pressure in Central America—support of the *contras*, military exercises in Honduras to intimidate the FSLN, earlier threats and eventually military intervention in Grenada—military events became more decisive than diplomacy from 1981 forward. This type of setting favored both the Soviets and Cubans, especially the Soviets, because it is in the military weapons domain that the Soviets are best able to function as patrons to client states. Even in tiny Grenada, the excuse of U.S. military threats to the island led to five secret military cooperation agreements between the Bishop regime with Cuba, North Korea and the Soviet Union. At the time of the U.S. intervention, the Soviets were planning to ship $27 million in military equipment, North Korea $12 million in supplies, and the Cubans would have provided training for the armed forces.[86]

If, in the short run, incipient political factionalism breaks into open violence among the leftist leadership, it can become an immediate source of discord and possible influence seeking by the Soviets or the Cubans. Grenada illustrates this possibility. Some evidence suggests that the Soviets backed Coard in his disputes with Bishop, may have encouraged him in his coup attempt against Bishop, and in so doing attempted to counteract Cuba's open support of Bishop—much like the Neto affair in Angola in 1977.[87] Considerable activity occurred between the Soviet embassy and Bishop's radical opponents in the days before the coup, and a trip to the Soviet Union by Bishop's opponents was canceled three weeks before the coup, indicating that the Soviets may have known what was happening to Bishop.[88] The Cubans were decidedly outraged by the coup attempt, while the Soviets treatment of it was more low-keyed.[89]

This observation by no means suggests that the Soviets or Cubans would break their relationship over an event of this type, but it does indicate differences in policies and underlying frictions that could undermine Cuban leverage, increase Havana's discontent with overdependence on the Soviets, and reduce Soviet long-run economic and military commitments. This scenario would not occur by one event alone, but rather as the slowly evolving outcome of a number of events that conceivably might reduce Cuba's importance to the Soviets over the long run.

In looking at the long term, it should be noted that Cuba's image as a revolutionary model had begun to fade in the Caribbean Basin with the onset of the 1980s. While many Latin American countries were disturbed by Cuba's resumption of the armed struggle thesis—applied first in Angola and Ethiopia and then in reference to Nicaragua—others do not see Cuba as a successful economic model to be emulated. As noted earlier, even Castro encourages this point of view. Castro told one visiting FSLN delegation to Havana that they should "preserve a private sector and not impose rationing."[90] Reduced Cuban acceptance in this part of the world lessens Cuba's benefits to Soviet policy, with the suggestion of lowered Cuban influence in the relationship.

Of more serious implications were Cuba's strained relations with major countries in the region, like Colombia, Mexico, and Venezuela. Frictions developed between Cuba and these regional powers as a result of various issues. When interviewed in March 1983 on Colombian public television, Castro publicly admitted it had trained M-19 insurgents to operate in Colombia, and he described ex-president Julio César Turbay Ayala (1978-82) as a surrogate of the United States—which did not endear Castro to Colombian President Belisario Betancur, who was on the verge of restoring diplomatic relations with Cuba. Strained relations with Mexico resulted from the continuing Central American conflict and the flood of refugees pouring over the Guatemalan border into Mexico's politically sensitive southern provinces not far from its oil fields. And Cuba backed Guyana in the Essequibo controversy, which led Venezuela not to join the Nonaligned Movement. Frictions with countries with whom the Soviets wish to retain cordial relations remind one of the 1960s, and the implications can be made of potential long-run frictions between the Soviets and Cubans—should the Cubans assert too strongly their defense of the armed struggle route in Central America and thereby undermine the coincidence in Soviet-Cuban regional objectives.

National Communism

A major force that limits and conditions the Soviet-Cuban relationship is nationalism communism. The nationalist elements in Central America's Marxist movements, well illustrated by Cuba as well as Nicaragua, does not lend itself to easy outside manipulation although it is adaptable to diverse forms of communism. Nationalism brings with it an identity with homeland, past struggles against outside oppressors, a sense of a unique people with a common past, present and future, and a legacy of historic events and heroes associated with the homeland. Built into nationalism is pride in country, resistance to outside control. Numerous statements coming out of Nicaragua illustrate nationalist intensity. As Tomás Borge Martínez, a founding member of the FSLN writes,

> I can affirm, with full knowledge of the facts that neither the Cuban ambassador nor Fidel Castro, with whom we have frequently conversed, nor the Soviet leader, Yuri Andropov, with whom we have also spoken, has ever told us what we must do. To think the contrary would be to accept that we have no criteria of our own, that we are simply puppets. . . . We Sandinistas never have been, are not and never will be anybody's satellites.[91]

And as one FSLN junta member remarked in 1980, "We didn't go through all this to exchange American domination for Soviet domination."[92] And the *Sandinistas* bitterly resent being identified as undergoing a Cubanization process. They admit that they look naturally to Cuba, but strongly emphasize that they are building their own Nicaraguan revolution.[93] Nationalism in Central American communism thus greatly restricts Cuban and Soviet control, just as it impedes Soviet control elsewhere in Angola, Mozambique, and Vietnam.

Nationalism denotes the nature of limits to outside control and in the long run makes difficult prediction of precisely what direction governments like Nicaragua will take, at home in domestic policies and abroad in dealing with the Soviets and Cubans. As in the case of how other political dynamics affect the Soviet-Cuban relationship, a Nicaraguan version of national communism resistive to Soviet and Cuban economic models suggests some reduction in Cuba's ability to advance Soviet interests in the region. In this regard, the questions remain as to how nationalist versions of communism will affect Cuba's utility to the Soviets in the basin and thereby condition Havana's leverage in negotiating future Soviet economic and military assistance to advance its own vital interests.

NOTES

1. Castro's speech in Concepcion, Chilean Radio Broadcast, November 18, 1971.
2. See comment on the Nicaraguan Revolution's significance for the armed struggle by Sergo Mikoyan, editor of *Latinskaya Amerika*, in "Las Particularidades de la Revolución en Nicaragua y sus Tareas desde el punto de vista de la Teoría y la Práctica de Movimiento Liberador," *América Latina* 3 (1980): 101; also Boris Koval, "La Revolución, Largo Proceso Historico," *América Latina* 3 (1980): 78. These points are addressed in Robert S. Leiken, *Soviet Strategy in Latin America*, Washington Papers/93 (New York: Praeger, 1982), pp. 34-35.
3. Koval, "La Revolución," pp. 76-79; Mikoyan, "Las Particularidades," pp. 79-80; and Leiken, *Soviet Strategy*, pp. 36-37. The Soviets do not apply the relevancy of armed struggle to all countries. The nonviolent road is still recommended in those countries where armed struggle seems unlikely to succeed, for example, Argentina, Brazil, and Mexico. In these and other countries like them, broad united fronts and peaceful change are recommended, policies of less risk, less likely to cause frictions with important host countries, and less likely to produce a direct confrontation with the United States. See Nikolai Leonov, "Nicaragua: Experienca de una Revolución Victoriosa," *América Latina* 3 (1980): 37; also Leiken, *Soviet Strategy*, pp. 40-42.
4. W. Raymond Duncan, "Soviet Interests in Latin America: New Opportunities and Old Constraints," *Journal of Interamerican Studies and World Affairs* 26, 2 (May 1984): 172.
5. A. Shulgovsky, "The Social and Political Development in Latin America," *International Affairs* 11 (November 1979): 60.
6. The crisis in U.S.-Soviet relations over the supposed brigade of Soviet combat troops stationed in Cuba, discovered in the fall of 1979, is examined by Gloria Duffy in "Crisis Mangling and the Cuban Brigade," *International Security* 8, 1 (Summer 1983): 67-87.
7. On Castro's perceived threats from the United States associated with the Soviet troop brigade affair and after, see his main report to the Second Congress of the Cuban Communist Party, December 17, 1980, *Granma Weekly Review*, December 28, 1980,

p. 4. On the Territorial Troop Militia and the U.S. "imperialist threat," see Castro's observations in *Granma Weekly Review*, February 1, 1981, pp. 2-3.

8. William M. LeoGrande. "Foreign Policy: The Limits of Success," in *Cuba: Internal and International Affairs*, ed., Jorge Dominguez (Beverly Hills: Sage Publications, 1982), p. 179.

9. See W. Raymond Duncan, "Caribbean Leftism," *Problems of Communism* 26 (May-June 1979): 38.

10. Ibid., p. 55. On economic conditions in Jamaica, which attracted Manley to Cuban help, see Wendell Bell, "Inequality in Independent Jamaica: A Preliminary Appraisal of Elite Performance," *Revista/Review Interamerica*, (San Juan, Puerto Rico, 1977), pp. 303-304; also Alan Eyre, "Quasi-Urban 'Melange' Settlement and Its Problems," Paper presented to the meeting of the Caribbean Studies Association, Santiago, Dominican Republic, January 1978. Eyre is Professor of Geography at the University of the West Indies, Mona, Jamaica.

11. The NJM was known in Grenada as the "vanguard party," *El Dia*, Mexico City, June 12, 1981. New Jewell Movement stands for Joint Effort for Welfare, Education, and Liberation, and its 1973 manifesto is both socialist and nationalist. See W. Raymond Duncan, "Grenada," in *1982 Yearbook on International Communist Affairs*, ed. by Richard F. Staar and Robert Wesson (Stanford: Hoover Institution Press, 1982), pp. 100-106.

12. On the various economic and social reforms implemented by the NJM during 1982, see W. Raymond Duncan, "Grenada," in the *1982 Yearbook on International Communist Affairs*, pp. 90-94.

13. This argument became a major background factor for the U.S. invasion of Grenada in October 1983. Ibid.

14. *Keesings Contemporary Archives*, July 27, 1979, p. 29748.

15. Duncan, "Grenada" in *1982 Yearbook*, p. 104.

16. See Duncan, "Soviet Interests in Latin America," pp. 170-75.

17. Ronald E. Jones, "Cuba and the English-Speaking Caribbean," in Cole Blasier and Carmelo Mesa Lago, eds., *Cuba in the World* (Pittsburgh: University of Pittsburgh Press, 1979), pp. 131-46.

18. Walter LaFeber, *Inevitable Revolutions: The United States and Central America* (New York: W.W. Norton, 1983), pp. 65-69.

19. Thomas P. Anderson, *Politics in Central America* (New York: Praeger, 1982), pp. 150-51.

20. *Latin America Regional Report*, Central America, June 6, 1980.

21. Ibid.

22. *Keesings Contemporary Archives*, January 4, 1980, p. 30025.

23. *Cuba's Renewed Support for Violence in Latin America*, Special Report no. 90, U.S. Department of State, Bureau of Public Affairs, December 14, 1981, p. 6.

24. Ibid.

25. *The Washington Post*, July 2, 1983, p. 1.

26. *The New York Times*, July 4, 1979, p. 1.

27. One revolutionary leader, Father Erneso Cardenal, stated that his colleagues did not want "any help from Cuba" because they did not wish to "give the pretext" for intervention to the U.S. government. See LaFeber, *Inevitable Revolutions*, p. 235.

28. Leonel Gomez and Bruce Cameron, "El Salvador: The Current Danger," *Foreign Policy* 43 (Summer 1981): 71-78.

29. Roy L. Prosterman, Jeffrey Riedinger, and Mary N. Temple, "Land Reform in El Salvador: The Democratic Alternative," *World Affairs* 144, 1 (Summer 1981): 36-54.

30. Anderson, *Politics in Central America*, chap. 6.

31. *Kommunist*, no. 6, November 1980, pp. 30-34.

32. V. Korionov, "El Salvador: The Struggle Sharpens," *Pravda*, December 30, 1980; and Jiri Valenta, "The USSR, Cuba, and the Crisis in Central America," *Orbis* 25, 3 (Fall 1981): 715-46.

33. See *Cuba's Renewed Support for Violence*, pp. 6-7; Department of State Special Report no. 80, *Communist Interference in El Salvador*, February 23, 1981; and Valenta, "USSR, Cuba," p. 741.

34. Valenta, "USSR, Cuba," p. 739.

35. *Cuba's Renewed Support for Violence in Latin America.*

36. Ibid.; also Valenta, "USSR, Cuba," p. 741.

37. Valenta, "USSR, Cuba," p. 741.

38. Jonathan Kwitney, "Apparent Errors Cloud U.S. 'White Paper' on Reds in El Salvador," *The Wall Street Journal*, June 8, 1981; Robert Kaiser, "White Paper on El Salvador is Faulty," *The Washington Post*, June 9, 1981, p. 1.

39. Kaiser, "White Paper on El Salvador," p. 1.

40. See Castro's letters to *The New York Times* and *The Washington Post* on these points, November 12, 1981, pp. 7 & 9. See also Carla Anne Robbins' treatment of this subject in *The Cuban Threat* (New York: McGraw-Hill, 1983), chap. 7.

41. Robert Rand, *Radio Free Europe Report*, RL 63/82, p. 1.

42. *Granma Weekly Review*, February 22, 1981, p. 2.

43. See *Granma Weekly Review*, Special supplement on Grenada, July 12, 1981, interview with Maurice Bishop, which contains a discussion of U.S. "warlike positions" against Grenada, Cuba, and Nicaragua. Bishop denounced U.S. aggression, saying that "we are not in anybody's 'backyard.'" See also *Granma Weekly Review*, March 22, 1981, p. 11. Also statements by Jaime Wheelock, a member of the *Sandinista* government, regarding U.S. aggression in El Salvador, *Granma Weekly Review*, December 13, 1981, p. 10. And Havana Radio Broadcast, January 21, 1982, for examples of Cuban political and diplomatic support of Grenada, Nicaragua and the Salvadoran leftists. Examples of extensive Soviet media support for leftist Central American and Caribbean governments include Moscow (Radio) *Krasnaya Zvezda*, February 26, 1982; Moscow World Scene (Radio) in English, February 25, 1982; Moscow interview with Miguel Marmol, one of the founders of the Salvadoran Communist Party, Moscow radio broadcast in Spanish, February 4, 1982.

44. *Izvestiya*, February 7, 1982, p. 5.

45. Robert Rand, "The USSR and the Crisis in El Salvador," *Radio Free Europe Report*, RL 85/82, February 17, 1982, p. 1, and Moscow (Radio) *Selskaya Zhizn* in Russian, March 6, 1982.

46. *Granma Weekly Review*, September 13, 1981, p. 1.

47. Ibid.

48. Ibid.

49. Conversation with one of the visiting scholars, Robert Legvold, Senior Research Analyst, Council on Foreign Relations, N.Y., N.Y.

50. *The New York Times*, February 24, 1982, p. 1.

51. Moscow (Radio) *Pravda* in Russian, February 22, 1982; Moscow *TASS* in English, February 24, 1982; Msocow in Spanish to Cuba, February 25, 1982; and Interview

with Jacinto Espinoza, Nicaraguan Ambassador to the USSR, Moscow *Sovietskaya Rossiya*, March 13, 1982.

52. Moscow *Isvestiya* in Russian, March 3, 1982; also *The New York Times*, February 25, 1982. Leonid Brezhnev supported the Mexican proposal for peace talks at a dinner in honor of Finland's President, Mauno Koivisto, in March 1982. Moscow *TASS* in English, March 11, 1982.

53. Moscow in Spanish to Latin America, March 1, 1982.

54. Moscow *Komsomolskaya Pravda*, in Russian, March 7, 1982.

55. *Granma Weekly Review*, March 7, 1982, p. 1.

56. Moscow *Pravda* in Russian, March 4, 1982, p. 1.

57. James Hoge, *Chicago Sun-Times*, April 6, 1982, p. 1.

58. Wayne Smith, "Dateline Havana: Myopic Diplomacy," *Foreign Policy*, 48 (Fall 1982): 157-74.

59. L. Klochkovsky, "The Struggle for Economic Emancipation in Latin America," *International Affairs* (Moscow) (April 1979): 39-47.

60. U.S. Congress, House, Committee on Foreign Affairs, Caribbean Nations: Assessments of Conditions and U.S. Influence. Report of a Special Study Mission to Jamaica, Cuba, the Dominican Republic, and the Guantanamo Naval Base, January 3-12, 1979 (Washington, D.C.: Government Printing Office, 1979), pp. 8-9.

61. *Keesings Contemporary Archives*, July 27, 1979, p. 29748.

62. Duncan, "Soviet Interests in Latin America," pp. 170-75.

63. *The New York Times*, October 31, 1983, p. 10.

64. *The New York Times*, October 26, p. 19, and November 2, 1983, pp. 17-18.

65. *The New York Times*, October 16, p. 3 and 26, p. 19, 1983. See also Duncan, "Soviet Interests in Latin America," p. 174.

66. *El Nuevo Diaro*, June 21, 1983, p. 1.

67. See *The New York Times*, June 19, 1983, p. 1; *The Wall Street Journal*, June 20, 1983, p. 1; and *Barricada*, September 2, 1982.

68. Ibid.

69. *The Wall Street Journal*, August 17, 1983, p. 1; *Christian Science Monitor*, October 28, 1981, p. 1; and *The Washington Post*, July 19, 1981, p. 1.

70. *Barricada*, September 2, 1982, p. 1.

71. *The New York Times*, June 7, 1982, p. 1.

72. Elizabeth Kridl Valkenier, *Soviet Union and the Third World: The Economic Bind* (New York: Praeger, 1983).

73. Yuri Andropov, *Pravda*, June 16, 1983, pp. 1ff.

74. *Christian Science Monitor*, June 29, 1984, p. 1.

75. *The New York Times*, July 9, 1980, p. 1.

76. Howard J. Wiarda, "Soviet Policy in the Caribbean and Central America: Opportunities and Constraints," Paper presented at a conference on Soviet foreign policy, the Kennan Institute for Advanced Russian Studies, Woodrow Wilson International Center for Scholars and the United States Information Agency, Washington, D.C., March 2, 1984, pp. 23-24.

77. My own observations in a visit to Cuba in January 1983.

78. The political culture of democracy is based upon the sense that society is a matter of cooperation, society is not of a permanent or fixed order, authority is delegated, and power is of a representative nature. For more discussion of these matters, see Zevedei Barbu, *Democracy and Dictatorship: Their Psychology and Patterns of Life* (New York:

Grove Press, 1959), Part 1.

79. John P. Gillin, "Some Signposts for Policy," *Social Change in Latin America Today*, ed. by Richard N. Adams et al. (New York: Vintage Books, 1960), pp. 28-47.

80. Ibid.

81. Leiken, *Soviet Strategy in Latin America*, pp. 80-81.

82. Ibid.

83. *The Washington Post*, June 25, 1984, p. 1.

84. See Peter Zwick, *National Communism*, (Boulder, Colorado: Westview Press, 1983), pp. 196-97.

85. Ibid.

86. *The New York Times*, November 6, 1983, pp. 1 & 21.

87. Duncan, "Soviet Interests in Latin America," pp. 170-75.

88. Ibid.

89. Ibid.

90. *The New York Times*, July 9, 1980, p. 1.

91. *Manchester Guardian Weekly*, August 21, 1983, p. 1.

92. *The New York Times*, July 9, 1980, p. 1.

93. *The New York Times*, January 3, 1980, p. 1.

7

BENEFITS, COSTS, AND FUTURE STRAINS

The influence relationship examined in this study illustrates that Cuba is far from a strictly proxy or surrogate of the Soviet Union. The Cubans entered the relationship because Soviet economic and military assistance helped them pursue their vital interests, not out of loyalty to Marxism-Leninism or love of Soviet domestic and foreign policies. Certainly the Cubans were not coerced to join forces with or support Soviet military policies in Angola, Ethiopia, Grenada, or Nicaragua. For the most part, Soviet-Cuban relations are those of two countries pursuing compatible interests, which is distinct from either country exerting power over the other.

Cases of assertive or coercive power by the Soviets over the Cubans are rare. One vivid example occurred in 1967-68, when the Soviets cut back on oil supplies to attempt to force the Cubans to cease their emphasis on armed struggle in Latin America. But even then, what compelled the Cubans to shift to the pro-Soviet line of peaceful change were a number of other domestic and regional forces: among them, problems of productivity and worker morale inside Cuba, the poor showing of Latin American guerrilla movements, and the death of "Che" Guevara in Bolivia. In this key example of Soviet sanctions against Cuba, it is inaccurate to portray Soviet power as the cause of Cuba's policy change. The rich complexity of Soviet-Cuban relations simply defies so easy a description of their interactions.

Cuba is admittedly dependent on Soviet economic and military aid for survival, which appears to justify the case for its performance as a surrogate. Yet as this study demonstrates, the Soviets derive numerous benefits from the Cubans. They arise from Havana's "anti-imperialist" posture toward the United States, commitment to "internationalist duty and solidarity" in the Third World, geographic location in North

America's "strategic rear," and stability of Castro's regime. And as Soviet economic and military investments in Cuba mounted over the years, they tightly locked Moscow into continued commitments lest its most important client go under. Even more did the Cubans demonstrate their usefulness to the Soviets in Angola and Ethiopia, which increased their leverage in negotiating favorable economic and military aid arrangements and elevated the Cubans to the position of a privileged ally. The benefits in the Soviet-Cuban relationship are not one-sided. This is a key feature that conditions the nature and effects of Cuban "dependency" on the Soviets.

BENEFITS THROUGH COOPERATION

A coincidence of benefits, connected with each country's goals and capabilities, more accurately depicts the nature of the Soviet-Cuban relationship. This does not suggest influence or power by one side over the other. Yet Soviet-Cuban policies concatenate in a form of mutual cooperative influence in a number of cases: Angola, Ethiopia, Nicaragua, and El Salvador. By this is meant that Cuba's capabilities to send combat troops into Angola encouraged (influenced) the Soviets to support armed struggle—directly in Ethiopia and indirectly in El Salvador by backing the Cubans. Similarly, Cuba's demonstrated strength in armed struggles in Africa, combined with the success of the *Sandinistas* in Nicaragua influenced the Soviets to modify their position on the armed struggle thesis, which they strongly opposed in the 1960s.

The Cubans, on the other hand, were influenced by continued Soviet cooperation in supporting their activities in Angola, Nicaragua, and El Salvador. They were also influenced by the higher levels of Soviet economic and military aid that accompanied Cuba's actions in Africa and the Caribbean Basin, and by continued Soviet diplomatic support for Cuban foreign policy. Cuban armed struggle activities did not end with Angola, owing to the nature of support they expected from the Soviets. Soviet cooperation thus influenced Cuba's actions. Mutual cooperation does not indicate assertive or coercive power by one country *vis à vis* the other. But it does produce perceived backing of each other's specific actions on a range of issues. The result is a kind of cooperative influence flowing both ways, rather than a one-way model of proxy status by the "weaker" state.

Regional and global international relations affected the evolution of the Soviet-Cuban influence relationship. Opportunities for each country to pursue their separate policy objectives erupted with the collapse of the

Portuguese empire in Africa and the shifting regional politics of the Caribbean Basin during the 1970s. Each country brought different capabilities to bear in these situations, which marked the unique character of their foreign policies, but the ways in which they cooperated illustrated how joint actions made their policies more attainable. At the global level, Soviet and Cuban adversarial relations with the Untied States greatly shaped their relationship with each other, just as Soviet-Chinese conflict relations stimulated support of Cuba, owing to the Soviet wish to gain Cuban backing in the Sino-Soviet dispute. From another perspective, U.S. security threats to Cuba and its allies in the Caribbean Basin, Grenada and Nicaragua, tended to drive all three countries into a closer military-security embrace with the Soviets.

Marxist-Leninist ideology is a factor in the relationship, more so than in any other Soviet ties with a Third World client, excepting Vietnam. Castro's adoption of Marxism-Leninism helped provide a unifying ideology for the Revolution, solidify institutionalization of Castroite leadership within a single-party system, and stimulate continued Soviet economic and military support, especially since Cuba became a member of the Council of Mutual Economic Assistance (CMEA).

Yet Marxism-Leninism is not the crux of the relationship, at least from Cuba's perspective. It is not a factor leading to Soviet use of Cuba as a surrogate. A close examination of the evidence illustrates sharp distinctions between the motivations of Cuban and Soviet foreign policy within the ideological domain. These center on Cuba's brand of national communism, identity with the Third World, and commitment to solving North-South issues. Given his Third World goals and own revolutionary past, Castro is more committed to armed struggle than the white collar Kremlin bureaucrats who focus on global superpower relations in the East-West context. Nor do Soviets go abroad in droves like the Cubans to engage at the grass roots level of work in agriculture, construction, rural education, and health.

COSTS IN THE RELATIONSHIP

Soviet patronage of Cuba entails enormous economic and political costs. Soviet hard currency outlays are high. From about $100 million annually during 1960-73 (because of low world oil prices and reexport of Cuban sugar after refinement in the Soviet Union), they rose annually to $1.2 billion in 1978 and $1.5 billion in 1979.[1] This rise, attributable to the escalation of world oil and grain prices after 1973 and to Soviet hard currency purchases of Cuban sugar, represents about 6 percent of Soviet hard currency exports.[2] The hard currency burden occurs through the subsidized prices Moscow pays for Cuban sugar (when they go above the world market sugar prices), the prices paid for Cuban nickel (when above the world market price), and from the supply of Soviet petroleum at below the world market price.

Cuba's economic costs to the Soviets are no light matter. By 1983 the Soviets were believed to be paying the Cubans three to four times the world market price for sugar, with the Soviet sugar subsidy rising from about $1.4 billion in 1981 to about $2.6 billion in 1982. This situation arose primarily because Soviet purchases of Cuban sugar increased by 40 percent in volume in 1982. Cuba's oil subsidy amounted to approximately $1.5 billion in 1981, but dropped to $950 million in 1982, when the Soviets increased the price of oil to its CMEA clients, including Cuba. By 1983, the Soviets were supplying oil to Cuba at around $24 per barrel, substantially below the world market price. As Soviet oil production levels off or declines during the 1980s, an added economic burden with Cuba will occur, because Moscow must supply oil to its other clients in Eastern Europe and Vietnam. The Soviets also rely on oil exports for approximately one-half of their hard currency earnings.[3] When these economic features of the relationship are added to the other Soviet aid figures cited in this study, Cuban economic cost to the Soviets is extraordinary.

In political terms, the Soviet presence in Cuba has created obvious strains in the U.S.-Soviet relationship. Soviet-Cuban intervention in Angola and Ethiopia sharply undermined *détente* between the two superpowers and a major Soviet goal. And Soviet-Cuban interventions in Africa contributed to the collapse of the Strategic Arms Limitations Talks (SALT II), another goal of Soviet foreign policy, but one given the kiss of death with the Soviet invasion of Afghanistan. Soviet relations with the Cubans in Nicaragua, El Salvador, and Grenada continued the process of erosion in Soviet-U.S. relations. The Soviet-Cuban relationship, raising fears of Cuba as a Soviet proxy and Marxist-Leninist penetration of the Western hemisphere, has not benefited the Soviet concept of peaceful coexistence with the United States, but rather fueled a neo-Cold War, arms race, and higher risk of nuclear confrontation.

Cuba's costs in the Soviet relationship take their own economic and political forms. The economy is in well-known bad health, despite progress in education, health and welfare, and it has remained afloat only because of Soviet help. The reasons for the major problems in the Cuban economy are not strictly a result of Cuba's trade and commercial dependence on and planning integration with the CMEA network. About 25-

30 percent of Cuba's trade is oriented toward the noncommunist West much of which hinges on sugar and its international price. Other non-CMEA factors are the costs of Cuba's military burdens and the much talked about difficulties in production: job absenteeism, mismanagement of economic activities, and lagging morale.[4]

Yet many of Cuba's economic problems continue to stem from the extent and nature of Cuba's CMEA-oriented planning and trade system. Cuba remains essentially a single-export economy (sugar). It suffers opportunity losses regarding hard currency because of CMEA-based trade, logistical costs of CMEA trade, the quality of CMEA goods, and the negative effects of Cuba's planned economy. The latter has lowered Cuban creativity and labor productivity, while contributing to its inefficiency and lack of innovation. As one observer of the Cuban economy sums up the situation, the country is overburdened with an inefficient and ineffective administrative bureaucracy and ever more dependence on the Soviet Union for economic aid and trade:

> In the past, consistent increases in economic aid from Moscow have allowed the Cuban leadership to postpone adjustment to the realities of economic development which Cuba, like all the non-oil-producing countries, now confronts. . . . In theory the Soviet economic model, adapted to Cuba, promised to eliminate the unemployment and inflation that plague market economies. But theory has not matched practice. Cuba faces substantial structural unemployment and its agricultural based economy is incapable of generating sufficient jobs to absorb the growing, relatively well-educated, labor force. On the price side, suppressed inflation has long been evidenced by rationing, queuing for essential products and widespread black market.[5]

Another indirect economic cost to Cuba's Soviet relationship is the U.S. trade embargo. Although different interpretations can be applied to its effects on Cuba's economy, one conclusion is generally stressed by most observers. The embargo forced the Cubans into the dependent economic relationship with the Soviets, as it restructured trade away from the U.S. market.[6] The United States did not intend to help forge a close Soviet-Cuban relationship during the early 1960s, but rather wished to punish Cuba with sanctions for nationalizing U.S. property and for flirting with the Soviets. A similar counterproductive consequence of U.S. pressure appears to have occurred in Nicaragua under the *Sandinistas*. As history seems to have repeated itself, the *Sandinistas* also turned to closer military ties with the Soviets as U.S. economic and security threats mounted.

The one flaw in this analysis is that the *Sandinistas*, more than their early Cuban counterparts in the 1960s, seemed bent upon a pro-Soviet centralized political system during their immediate postrevolutionary victory over Somoza—at a time when the Carter Administration recognized and extended the hand of friendship to them. While the Carter Administration soon changed its posture toward the *Sandinistas*, it is questionable how much, and in what political and economic directions, the *Sandinistas* might have reoriented their domestic political orientations under good neighborly relations with the United States.

The negative political costs to Cuba are easily discerned. The United States opposed the Cuban regime for over two decades through many forms. They range from initial attempts to topple the Cuban government in the Bay of Pigs invasion of April 1961 to its successful efforts to remove the Castro government from the Organization of American States (OAS) in 1962, assassination attempts against Castro, and more lately, talk of direct military intervention as the new United States Administration assumed power in the early 1980s. Largely as a consequence of Cuba's relationship with the Soviets, the United States became a geographically proximate security threat that forced constant Cuban military preoccupation and investments.

Cuba's attention to physical security—combined with its foreign military activities—has placed exceptionally high demands on and legitimized Havana's military defense spending and recruitment of thousands of Cubans into military and paramilitary service. Much of these military expenses, to be certain, are carried by the Soviets. And it is true that the U.S. threat serves to help mobilize Cubans into common actions against the outside threat, such as exhorting them to higher production, more work, and greater effort in education. Much of Cuban life has become a "lucha" (struggle) against the capitalist-imperialist colossus of the north. Nevertheless, it is extremely difficult to undertake the economic development process of capital formation, infrastructure-building and diversifying the economy with such huge investments diverted to the military sector. To the extent that Cuba's ties to the Soviets produced U.S. actions, which in turn led to the militarization of Cuba's society and to its military actions abroad, the Cubans indirectly contributed to their own economic problems.

U.S. opposition to the Cuban-Soviet embrace in the Caribbean basin creates other difficulties for Cuba's governing elites. While the point can be overstated, the U.S. financial, lending and trade power in the basin exerts major influence on regional leaders—to Cuba's disadvantage. In Jamaica, U.S. opposition to Prime Minister Manley's links with Cuba resulted in making a case for the conservative opposition, led by Edward Seaga. Seaga won his bid for presidential power in 1980. Growing U.S. concern with the renewed Soviet-Cuban activities in support of armed revolutions in Central America contributed to the ferment of concern in the region about the effects of Soviet-Cuban activities, although they were not the cause of regional revolutionary movements. The fallout from this situation led to severance of relations between Costa Rica and Colombia with Cuba, warnings from Panama, growing friction between the Cubans and Nicaraguans with Venezuela, and deepening uneasiness in Mexico.

Cuba's close alignment with the Soviets produced other difficulties for Castro in his quest for Third World leadership. It weakens Cuba's credentials as chief spokesperson for the Third World Nonaligned Movement, certainly during 1979-82, when Castro led the movement after the Soviets invaded Afghanistan. As the Soviets dug into Afghanistan, some members of the Nonaligned Movement characterized Cuba as advocating the importance, causes, and policies of the Soviet-led socialist bloc, rather than the true interests of the developing countries. The Cubans are not pleased with Soviet actions in Afghanistan, and they do not go to great lengths to support the Soviets on this issue. But the Cubans do not voice their opposition publicly and this does not help their position with a number of Third World colleagues.

FUTURE STRAINS

Soviet assistance to Cuba in the coming era will be affected by competing demands on Soviet subsidized oil. The necessity to sell oil for hard currency and to supply it to other clients such as the CMEA countries, Vietnam and Ethiopia, comes at a time when Soviet oil production is leveling off. As the Soviet economy faces its own difficulties, it may not be able to maintain the export levels of raw materials and technology it has guaranteed to Cuba. Cuba noticed this problem in late 1979, when the world recession affected the prosperity of both Moscow and Havana. Cuba's energy and technology demands will escalate in the future, at a time when its supply of energy and technology from the Soviets becomes more uncertain. This situation puts pressure on Cuba to expand its non-communist trade and commercial relations, an objective that Cuba is giving increased attention. Havana is seeking joint ventures with foreign Western governments, has made overtures to Canadian investors, and continues to demonstrate a desire for negotiations with the United States.

The future for Cuban sugar is not bright. Soviet demand for sugar will not substantially increase through the mid to late 1980s. The projected world consumption is not expected to grow by more than two percent during this period, and the demand for sugar from Cuba's East European partners is unremarkable. This gloomy scenario is reinforced by the low international sugar prices that affect about 25-30 percent of Cuba's noncommunist trade.

One major source of strain between Moscow and Havana is Cuba's desire to move toward more rapid industrialization rather than continuing to supply agricultural products to other CMEA members. This issue emerged as a cause of friction during the June 1984 CMEA summit meetings in Moscow. When it became clear that this Cuban overture would meet with an unresponsive Soviet Union, Castro decided not to attend the summit meeting, leaving Vice President Carlos Rafael Rodríguez to carry on Cuba's negotiations. More than just an expression of discontent, Castro's absence may have been an attempt to exert influence on the Soviets for greater attention to Cuba's economic needs. If so, it may have worked, because at the October 1984 CMEA meetings in Havana, the Soviets signed a new 15-year economic agreement with Cuba, and Castro lauded the Soviets for their great help.

Still, the Soviets are concerned about Cuba's economic performance and may become disillusioned as the costs to support the Castro regime mount during the 1980s. Since the early 1970s, the Soviets have pressured Cuban managers to adopt "principles of scientific socialism," which is undermined by continuing difficulties in labor productivity, absenteeism, lagging worker incentives, and problems in Cuban economic management. These problems were cited by Castro in his famous December 1979 speech, suggesting the undercurrents of economic pressures in the Soviet-Cuban relationship that are not disappearing. Cuba's debt repayments are due to begin in 1986, which further complicates this picture.

Future political strains are highly possible in the Soviet-Cuban influence relationship. The Cubans insist their bonds with the Soviet Union remain solid, but Soviet intervention in Afghanistan, intimidation of the Polish government, and support for Grenada's Bernard Coard in his running conflict with Maurice Bishop undoubtedly "worry" Cuban government officials. In Afghanistan, they argue that they have "never given support for what happened there" and that they had been "consistently working for a political solution," despite their vote in the U.N. regarding the Afghanistan episode.[7] Cuban foreign policy specialists characterize Poland as a "socialist tragedy," saying that the Polish government "should have the opportunity to solve the problems themselves."[8] The Cubans were clearly at odds with the Soviets in the 1977 coup attempt against Angola's Augustinho Neto and over the Coard-Bishop feud in Grenada. The Cubans insist that their intervention in Africa was a Cuban policy, not a response to pressure from the Soviet Union. Nor are they sanguine about the Ethiopian Central government actions against the Eritreans, a policy with which the Soviets appear more comfortable. [9]

The Soviets and Cubans differ markedly over their Third World economic postures, which leads to another source of political strain. While the Cubans constantly stress North-South development priorities, Soviet foreign policy declarations depict a higher priority to their own economy, security, and cooperation within the Soviet bloc, to East-West tensions, and the limited nature of their economic capabilities to help Third World countries. Given Moscow's growing internal economic problems, declining energy resources, and East-West agenda, Soviet and Cuban tensions over Third World priorities are likely to continue.

Soviet future military aid is another matter of concern in Cuba. Despite substantial Soviet arms shipments to the island over the years, the Soviet military commitment is not as strong as the Cubans would like. Cuba does not have a treaty arrangement as does Vietnam, and it is aware that little direct Soviet military support could be expected in a major crisis with the United States. The Cubans have not forgotten the October 1962 missile crisis.

But an imminent break in Soviet-Cuban relations is unlikely. With Soviet aid running at over $4 billion from 1982, of the population, the Cubans make no secret of their need for continued economic and military support from the Soviets. Yet, Soviet-Cuban strains exist and could be exacerbated by hard-line Soviet policies and blatant Soviet intervention in another country of the type that occurred in Afghanistan. Barring these events, future economic pressures on the Soviets will be reflected in their relations with the Cubans. These may weaken the degree of Soviet commitment measured in terms of material aid. Future trends suggest new opportunities for U.S.-Cuban diplomacy, where a process leading to restored diplomatic relations and Cuban access to U.S. trade might stir the more independent coals of Cuban foreign policy by moderating Cuba's dependence on the Soviets. Castro communicated his continuing interested in a diplomatic opening of this type by releasing a number of American and Cuban prisoners to the Rev. Jesse Jackson in June 1984.[10]

The Soviet-Cuban relationship remains one of two countries pursuing their special interests through cooperation combined with each side attempting to influence the other in mutually beneficial directions. Although Soviet and Cuban foreign policies are based essentially on differing world views—the Soviets being a global power with special East-West concerns and the Cubans pursuing their brand of national communism with its strong Third World orientation—they typically reinforce each other's interests in the Third World. Cuba's activities in Southern Africa and the Caribbean Basin since the mid-1970s, including its military aid, direct combat, educational help and medical assistance, illustrate the point. When either the Soviets or Cubans pursue a line of action that conflicts with the other's interests, however, strains in the relationship occur. Moscow's backing of Bernard Coard in Grenada and Cuba's close relations with Maurice Bishop suggest how divergent policies and consequent discord between the Soviets and Cubans develop.

Despite strains in the Soviet-Cuban relationship, Havana remains high on the list of Moscow's preferred clients. The agreement signed at the October 1984 CEMA conference in Havana illustrates the continued special treatment accorded Fidel Castro's government by the Soviet Union. Castro's role as a special ally is likely to continue for some time, because Cuban foreign policy advances Moscow's interests in the Third World. Periodic discord in the relationship will result from each side seeking to advance its own objectives through different types of leverage, and this effort includes the Cubans as much as the Soviets—for the Cubans are distinctly not without leverage within the relationship. Yet the overall relationshp will remain intact, because Cuba provides the Soviets with a channel to enlarge their presence in the Third World, while Castro remains in great need of Soviet economic and military aid.

The Soviet-Cuban relationship is likely to remain strong for another reason: a high level of projected political instability in the Third World where Moscow will continue to seek new opportunities to compete with the United States for global power status. Third World political turmoil is produced by the growing debt burden, population growth, food shortages, and the constraints on both the Soviets and the U.S. relative to their foreign economic aid capabilities to assist the lesser developed countries in their quest for economic growth. Unresolved ethnic national conflicts add another dimension to Third World turbulence, as in the differences between the MPLA and UNITA in Angola or between the Mengistu government and the Eritrean national liberation movement in Ethiopia.

As an arena for projected Soviet power and competition with the United States, the Third World will continue to fuse Moscow and Havana into a mutually beneficial relationship. Cuba is highly likely to enjoy a future preferred client status, whose own policy objectives and capabilities often advance those of its patron. Within this privileged ally position, Havana will benefit from its leverage *vis-à-vis* the Soviets, which goes with its rank. This means in turn that Cuba should be able to pursue its own interests in foreign policy, largely through a situation of cooperative influence within the Soviet embrace.

NOTES

1. Lawrence H. Theriot, "Cuba Faces the Economic Realities of the 1980s," paper prepared for the Joint Economic Committee, U.S. Congress, by the Office of East-West Planning, International Trade Commission, U.S. Department of Commerce (December 1981), p. 18.

2. Ibid., pp. 18–19.

3. Ibid.

4. See Jorge Dominguez, "Cuba in the 1980s," *Problems of Communism* (March-April 1981), pp. 49–52.

5. Theriot, "Cuba Faces Economic Realities," p. 14. My own travel and observations in Cuba during January 1982 confirms some of these conditions. The black market operates, and there are extremely long queues for newly arriving goods in department stores.

6. Theriot, "Cuba Faces Economic Realities," p. 11.

7. Leslie Gelb, *The New York Times*, April 6, 1982.

8. Ibid. These points were confirmed by Robert Legvold, April 1982, one of the scholars who visited Cuba in 1982 and with whom Cuban leaders made these observations.

9. Ibid.

10. On the Jesse Jackson trip to Cuba in June 1984, which led to Castro's release of U.S. Cuban prisoners, see *The New York Times*, June 28 and 29, 1984.

BIBLIOGRAPHY

BOOKS

Abel, Elie. *The Cuban Missile Crisis.* Philadelphia: Lippincott, 1966.

Albright, David E., ed. *Communism in Africa.* Bloomington: Indiana University Press, 1980.

Allison, Graham T. *Essence of Decision: Explaining the Cuban Missile Crisis.* Boston: Little, Brown & Co., 1971.

Atkins, G. Pope. *Latin America in the International Political System.* New York: The Free Press, 1977.

Bell, V. J. *Power, Influence, and Authority: An Essay in Political Linguistics.* New York: Oxford University Press, 1975.

Bender, Lyn D. *The Politics of Hostility: Castro's Revolution and United States Policy.* San German, Puerto Rico: Inter-American University Press, 1975.

Blasier, Cole. *The Giant's Rival: The USSR in Latin America.* Pittsburgh: University of Pittsburgh Press, 1983.

Blasier, Cole, and Carmelo Mesa Lago, eds. *Cuba in the World.* Pittsburgh: University of Pittsburgh Press, 1979.

Bobrow, Davis. *International Relations.* New York: The Free Press, 1972.

Bonachea, Rolando, and Nelson P. Valdes, eds. *Cuba in Revolution.* Garden City, New York: Anchor Books, Doubleday & Co., Inc., 1972.

Castro, Fidel. *La Primera Revolucion Socialista en America.* Mexico: 1976.

———. *Second Declaration of Havana.* Havana: Imprenta Nacional Unidad, 1962.

Clissold, Stephen, ed. *Soviet Relations with Latin America.* London: Oxford University Press, 1970.

Collingwood, R. G. *The Idea of History.* New York: A Galaxy Book, 1956.

Coplin, William D. *Introduction to International Politics.* 3rd ed. Englewood Cliffs, N.J.: Prentice-Hall, 1980.

Cuba, the U.S., and Russia, 1960-63. New York: Facts on File, Inc., 1964.

Deutsch, Karl W. *The Analysis of International Relations.* 2nd ed. Englewood Cliffs, N.J.: Prentice-Hall, 1978.

Dinerstein, Herbert. *The Making of a Missile Crisis: October 1962.* Baltimore: Johns Hopkins University Press, 1976.

Dominguez, Jorge, ed. *Cuba: Internal and International Affairs.* Beverly Hills: Sage Publications, 1982.

Donaldson, Robert H., ed. *The Soviet Union in the Third World: Successes and Failures.* Boulder, Colorado: Westview Press, 1981.

Duncan, W. Raymond. *Soviet Policy in Developing Countries.* New York: Robert Krieger Publishing Co., 1981.

———. *Soviet Policy in the Third World.* New York: Pergamon Policy Studies, 1980.

Duncan, W. Raymond, and James Nelson Goodsell, eds. *The Quest for Change in Latin America.* New York: Oxford University Press, 1970.

George, Alexander L. *Managing U.S.-Soviet Rivalry.* Boulder, Colorado: Westview Press, 1983.

Gonzalez, Edward. *Cuba Under Castro; The Limits of Charisma.* Boston: Houghton Mifflin, 1975.

Gouré, Leon, and Morris Rothenberg. *Soviet Penetration of Latin America.* Coral Gables, Fla.: Center for Advanced National Studies, 1975.

Guerra y Sanchez, Ramiro. *Sugar and Society in the Caribbean: An Economic History of Cuban Agriculture.* Translated from the Spanish by Marjoy M. Urquidi and with a foreword by Sidney W. Mintz. New Haven and London: Yale University Press, 1964.

Hodgkinson, Christopher. *The Philosophy of Leadership.* New York: St. Martin's Press, 1983.

Holsti, K. J. *International Politics: A Framework for Analysis.* Englewood Cliffs, N.J.: Prentice-Hall, 1967.

Horn, Robert C. *Soviet-Indian Relations: Issues and Influence.* New York: Praeger Special Studies, 1982.

Hosmer, Stephen T., and Thomas W. Wolfe. *Soviet Policy and Practice Toward Third World Conflicts.* Lexington, Mass.: Lexington Books, 1983.

Jackson, D. Bruce. *Castro, the Kremlin, and Communism in Latin America.* Baltimore: Johns Hopkins University Press, 1969.

Jervis, Robert. *Perception and Misperception in International Politics.* Princeton: Princeton University Press, 1976.

Kanet, Roger, ed. *Soviet Foreign Policy in the 1980s.* New York: Praeger, 1982.

———. *The Soviet Union and the Developing Nations.* Baltimore: Johns Hopkins University Press, 1974.

Karol, K. S. *Guerrillas in Power.* New York: Hill and Wang, 1970.

Katz, Mark N. *The Third World in Soviet Military Thought.* London: Croom Helm, 1982.

Knorr, Klaus. *The Power of Nations: the Political Economy of International Relations.* New York: Basic Books, 1975.

LaFeber, Walter. *Inevitable Revolutions: The United States in Central America.* New York: W. W. Norton, 1983.

Lamar Schweyer, Alberto. *La Crisis de Patriotismo.* La Habana: Editorial Marti, 1929.

Lasswell, Harold D., and Abraham Kaplan. *Power and Society: A Framework for Political Inquiry.* New Haven: Yale University Press, 1950.

Leiken, Robert. *Soviet Strategy in Latin America.* Washington: The Washington Papers/93, Praeger Special Studies, 1982.

Levesque, Jacques. *The USSR and the Cuban Revolution: Soviet Ideological and Strategic Perspectives.* New York: Praeger, 1978.

Mansbach, Richard W., and John A. Vasguez. *In Search of Theory: A New Paradigm for Global Politics.* New York: Columbia University Press, 1981.

Mesa-Lago, Carmelo. *The Economy of Socialist Cuba: A Two Decade Appraisal.* Albuquerque: University of New Mexico Press, 1981.

Morgenthau, Hans J. *Politics Among Nations.* 5th ed. New York: Alfred A. Knopf, 1973.

Oswald, J. Gregory, and Anthony J. Strover. *The Soviet Union and Latin America.* New York: Praeger, 1970.

Oswald, J. Gregory. *Soviet Image of Contemporary Latin America: A Documentary History, 1960-1968.* Austin: The University of Texas Press, 1970.

Portell-Villa, Herminio. *Historica de Cuba en sus relaciones con los Estados Unidos y Espana.* Havana, 1938-41, 4 vols.

Ratliff, William E. *Castroism and Communism in Latin America, 1959-1976.* Stanford: Hoover Institution Press, 1976.

Robbins, Carla Ann. *The Cuban Threat.* New York: McGraw-Hill, 1983.

Rosenau, James N., et al., eds. *World Politics: An Introduction.* New York: The Free Press, 1976.

Rubinstein, Alvin Z. *Red Star on the Nile: The Soviet-Egyptian Influence Relationship Since the June War.* Princeton: Princeton University Press, 1977.

———. ed. *Soviet and Chinese Influence in the Third World.* New York: Praeger, 1975.

Ruiz, Ramon Eduardo. *Cuba: the Making of a Revolution.* Amherst: The University of Massachusetts Press, 1968.

Second Congress of the Communist Party of Cuba: Documents and Speeches. Havana: Political Publishers, 1981.

Sobel, Lester A., ed. *Castro's Cuba in the 1970s.* New York: Facts on File, Inc., 1978.

Spanier, John. *Games Nations Play.* 5th ed. New York: Holt, Rinehart and Winston, 1984.

Suarez, Andrez. *Cuba: Castroism and Communism, 1959-1966.* Cambridge: M.I.T. Press, 1967.

Suchlicki, Jaime, ed. *Cuba, Castro and Revolution.* Coral Gables Fla.: University of Miami Press, 1972.

Sullivan, Michael. *International Relations: Theories and Evidence.* Englewood Cliffs, N.J.: Prentice-Hall, 1967.

Theberge, James D. *The Soviet Presence in Latin America.* New York: Crane, Russak, Inc., 1974.

Thomas, Hugh. *Cuba: The Pursuit of Freedom.* New York: Harper and Row, 1971.

Torres Ramirez, Blanca. *Las relaciones cubano-sovieticas (1959-1968).* Mexico: El Colegio de Mexico, 1970.

Valkenier, Elizabeth Kridl. *The Soviet Union and the Third World: An Economic Bind.* New York: Praeger Special Studies, 1983.

ARTICLES

Brind, Harry. "Soviet Policy in the Horn of Africa." *International Affairs* 60 (Winter 1983/84): 75-95.

Durch, William J. "The Cuban Military in Africa and the Middle East: From Algeria to Angola." *Studies in Comparative Communism* 11 (Spring/Summer 1978): 34-74.

Gonzalez, Edward. "Political Succession in Cuba." *Studies in Comparative Communism* 9 (Spring/Summer 1976): 80-107.

Hanson, Philip. "Economic Constraints on Soviet Policies in the 1980s." *International Affairs* 57 (Winter 1980-81): 21-41.

Katz, Mark N. "The Soviet-Cuban Connection." *International Affairs* 8, (Summer 1983): 88-112.

Legvold, Robert. "The USSR and the World Economy: The Political Dimension." In *The Soviet Union and the World Economy*, edited by Robert Legvold. New York: Council on Foreign Relations, 1979.

——. "The Super Rivals: Conflict in the Third World." *Foreign Affairs* 57 (Spring 1979): 755-78.

LeoGrande, William. "Evolution of the Nonaligned Movement." *Problems of Communism* 29 (January 1980): 35-52.

Rothenberg, Morris. "Latin America in Soviet Eyes." *Problems of Communism* 32 (Sept.-Oct. 1983): 1-18.

Sanchez, Nestor. "The Communist Threat." *Foreign Policy* 52 (Fall 1983): 43-50.

Valenta, Jiri. "Soviet and Cuban Reponses to New Opportunities in Central America." In ed., *The International Aspects of the Crisis in Central America*, edited by Richard Feinberg. New York: Holmes & Meyer, 1982.

——. "The USSR and Cuba in Africa," In *Cuba in Africa*, edited by Carmelo Mesa-Lago. Pittsburgh: University of Pittsburgh Press, 1982.

——. "The USSR, Cuba and the Crisis in Central America." *Orbis* 25 (Fall 1981): 715-46.

——. "Soviet-Cuban Intervention in Ethiopia." *Journal of International Affairs* 34 (Fall/Winter 1980/81: 353-67.

——. "Soviet Decision-Making on the Intervention in Angola, 1975." In *Communism in Africa*, edited by David Albright. Bloomington: University of Indiana press, 1980.

——. "Soviet-Cuban Intervention in Angola, 1975." In *Studies in Comparative Communism* 11 (Spring/Summer 1978): 1-33.

Varas, Augusto. "Ideology and Politics in Latin American-USSR Relations." *Problems of Communism* 33 (Jan.-Feb. 1984): 35-47.

GOVERNMENT DOCUMENTS

Communist Aid Activities in Non-Communist Less Developed Countries, 1979 and 1954-79. Washington, D. C.: Central Intelligence Community, October 1980.

Cuban Armed Forces and the Soviet Military Presence. Washington, D.C.: Department of State, Special Report No. 103 August 1982.

Cuba's Renewed Support for Violence in Latin America. Washington, D.C.: Department of State, Special Report No. 90 December 14, 1981.

Federal Broadcast Information Service (FBIS), Washington, D.C., Selected Years.

Impact of Cuban-Soviet Ties in the Western Hemisphere, Spring 1980. Hearings before the Subcommittee on Inter-American Affairs, Committee on Foreign Affairs, House of Representatives, Washington, D.C.: Government Printing Office, 1980.

Joint Publications Research Service (JPRS), Washington, D.C. *Soviet Policy and United States Response in the Third World.* Report for the Committee on Foreign Affairs, House of Representatives, by the Congressional Research Service, Library of Congress, Washington, D.C.: Government Printing Office, 1981.

Theriot, Lawrence H. *Cuba Faces the Economic Realities of the 1980s.* A Study Prepared for the Joint Economic Committee, Congress of the United States, Washington, D.C.: Government Printing Office, 1982.

The Soviet Union and the Third World: A Watershed in Great Power Policy?'' Report to the Committee on International Relations, House of Representatives, Congressional Research Service, Washington, D.C.: Government Printing Office, 1977.

INDEX

ABOUT THE AUTHOR

W. Raymond Duncan is Distinguished Teaching Professor of Political Science, State University of New York (S.U.N.Y.). College at Brockport. He has published five previous books on Soviet policy in the Third World and on Latin American politics. His published journal articles on Soviet and Cuban foreign policies in the lesser developed countries have appeared in the *Journal of Inter-American Studies and World Affairs, Orbis,* and *Problems of Communism.* He has contributed numerous chapters to other books dealing with Soviet–Third World relations, Cuban foreign policy, and Latin American politics.

Dr. Duncan received his Ph.D in 1964 from the Fletcher School of Law and Diplomacy, having completed his earlier training at the University of California at Riverside. He has travelled extensively in many Third World countries in Latin America and Southeast Asia, and he made a trip to Cuba in January 1983. In addition, he met with several key Cuban foreign policy advisers at a major international meeting in Bonn, West Germany, in April 1983.

STUDIES OF INFLUENCE IN INTERNATIONAL RELATIONS

Alvin Z. Rubinstein, *General Editor*

SOUTH AFRICA AND THE UNITED STATES
The Erosion of an Influence Relationship
Richard E. Bissell

SOVIET-INDIAN RELATIONS
Issues and Influence
Robert C. Horn

SOVIET INFLUENCE IN EASTERN EUROPE
Political Autonomy and the Warsaw Pact
Christopher D. Jones

U.S. POLICY TOWARD JAPAN AND KOREA
A Changing Influence
Chae-Jin Lee and Hideo Sato

SOVIET AND AMERICAN INFLUENCE IN THE HORN OF AFRICA
Marina S. Ottaway

THE UNITED STATES AND IRAN
The Patterns of Influence
R. K. Ramazani

SOVIET POLICY TOWARD TURKEY, IRAN AND AFGHANISTAN
The Dynamics of Influence
Alvin Z. Rubinstein

THE UNITED STATES AND PAKISTAN
The Evolution of an Influence Relationship
Shirin Tahir-Kheli

THE UNITED STATES AND BRAZIL
Limits of Influence
Robert Wesson

THE UNITED STATES, GREECE AND TURKEY
The Troubled Triangle
Theodore A. Couloumbis

THE UNITED STATES AND MEXICO
Patterns of Influence
George W. Grayson

THE SOVIET UNION AND THE YEMENS
Influence in Asymmetrical Relationships
Stephen Page